The Rising Global Cancer Pandemic:
Health, Ethics,
and
Social Justice

Edited *by*

Andrea Vicini, SJ, Philip J. Landrigan,
and Kurt Straif

PICKWICK *Publications* · Eugene, Oregon

THE RISING GLOBAL CANCER PANDEMIC
Health, Ethics, and Social Justice

Global Theological Ethics

Pickwick Publications
An Imprint of Wipf and Stock Publishers
199 W. 8th Ave., Suite 3
Eugene, OR 97401

www.wipfandstock.com

SOFTCOVER ISBN: 978-1-6667-533506
HARDCOVER ISBN: 978-1-6667-5336-3
EBOOK ISBN: 978-1-6667-5337-0

Cataloguing-in-Publication data:

Names: Vicini, Andrea, editor | Landrigan, Philip J., editor | Straif, Kurt, editor

Title: The rising global cancer pandemic : health, ethics, and social justice / Andrea Vicini, SJ, Philip J. Landrigan, and Kurt Straif.

Description: Eugene, OR: Pickwick Publications, 2022 | Series: Global Theological Ethics | Includes bibliographical references.

Identifiers: ISBN 978-1-6667-533506 (paperback) | ISBN 978-1-6667-5336-3 (hardcover) | ISBN 978-1-6667-5337-0 (ebook)

Subjects: LCSH: Pandemics -- Religious aspects — Christianity | Epidemics -- Moral and ethical aspects | Public health -- Moral and ethical aspects | Bioethics. Medical ethics.

Classification: QH332.R57 2022 (print) | QH332.R57 (ebook)

To cancer patients, researchers, and caregivers accompanying them in their struggles, ordeals, and hopes.

Global Theological Ethics — Book Series

Series Editors

Jason King, St. Vincent College
M. Therese Lysaught, Loyola University Chicago

The Global Theological Ethics book series focuses on works that feature authors from around the world, draw on resources from the traditions of Catholic theological ethics, and attend to concrete issues facing the world today. It advances the *Journal of Moral Theology*'s mission of fostering scholarship deeply rooted in traditions of inquiry about the moral life, engaged with contemporary issues, and exploring the interface of Catholic moral theology philosophy, economics, political philosophy, psychology, and more.

This series is sponsored in conjunction with the Catholic Theological Ethics and the World Church. The CTEWC recognizes the need to dialogue from and beyond local cultures and to interconnect within a world church. Its global network of scholars, practitioners, and activists fosters cross-cultural, interdisciplinary conversations—via conferences, symposia, and colloquia, both in-person and virtually—about critical issues in theological ethics, shaped by shared visions of hope.

Online versions of the volumes in the *Global Theological Ethics* series are available for free download as chapters at jmt.scholasticahq.com. Paper copies may be purchased from Wipf & Stock. This dual approach reflects the *Journal of Moral Theology*'s commitment to the common good as it seeks to make the scholarship of Catholic theological ethicists broadly available, especially across borders.

Series Titles

Ethical Challenges in Global Public Health: Climate Change, Pollution, and the Health of the Poor, edited by Philip J. Landrigan and Andrea Vicini, SJ (2021)

The Rising Global Cancer Pandemic: Health, Ethics, and Social Justice, edited by Andrea Vicini, SJ, Philip J. Landrigan, and Kurt Straif (2022)

Table of Contents

Part 3: Ethical Issues and Practical Approaches

Part 4: International Perspectives: Major Cancer Problems and Prospects for Prevention

Part 5: Surviving Cancer

Conclusions: Looking at the Future

Acknowledgments

We express our deep gratitude to our many colleagues—at Boston College, across the U.S.A., and internationally—who generously shared their passion and expertise in reflecting on the ethical challenges that confront the rising global cancer pandemic and how it affects local and global efforts to promote health. We are grateful that some of their contributions are gathered in this book.

The Boston College community—with its dedicated faculty, students, administrators, and staff, its commitment to science and the humanities, and its longing for social justice—continues to be an inspiring formative context for ethically-inspired education, research, and practice in global public health. As a university, Boston College has enabled us to engage in examining urgent issues in global public health, identifying and addressing social inequities, striving to promote the common good, advancing justice, and caring for the Earth—our common home. These are complex times, while the whole world continues to struggle because of the COVID-19 global pandemic, added to the many pre-existing and enduring challenges that affect the health of individuals, populations, and of the whole planet. For all these reasons, we are very thankful.

This volume continues to rely on and joins diverse academic entities and initiatives at Boston College that foster this ethos and that aim at training students and citizens attentive to address ethically and with competence the multiple issues affecting global public health across the planet. In particular, we mention the Schiller Institute for Integrated Science and Society; the program in Global Public Health and the Common Good, with its minor and forthcoming major; the William F. Connell School of Nursing; and, within the Morrissey College of Arts and Sciences, the Biology Department, the Environmental Studies program, the Engineering Department with its recently launched major in Human-Centered Engineering, and the minor in Medical Humanities, Health, and Culture.

Andrea Vicini, SJ, Philip J. Landrigan, and Kurt Straif

Introduction

Introduction: The Challenging Global Cancer Pandemic

Andrea Vicini, SJ

To introduce the volume, Andrea Vicini, SJ, stresses the need to address the global cancer pandemic, while the world struggles with the ongoing pandemic caused by COVID-19. Cancer affects millions of people. It is the first or second cause of death in 134 countries, the leading cause of death in most high-income countries (i.e., 10 million deaths in 2020), and the leading cause of death by disease in American children. Cancer is also unjust. Striking inequities can be traced within and between countries in cancer incidence and survival by race, ethnicity, and socio-economic-status. Survival is much higher among the wealthy than among the poor. An overview of the volume introduces the following chapters.

While the world is experiencing the tragically disruptive consequences of the global pandemic caused by the virus called COVID-19, it might appear surprising to invite readers to point their attention to what we consider another pandemic: the pervasive presence of cancers across the planet. One might wonder whether it could be wiser to focus on one pandemic at a time, at least to avoid being emotionally overwhelmed. Prudence is certainly an essential virtue, even when one reflects on global health. However, what challenges the health of populations requires attention, without delay. Human ingenuity and the commitment to promote what is good and just, strengthened by specific systemic and structural arrangements and reinforced by technological developments, testify to the human ability of facing health challenges as they come, even when they are represented by two pandemics.

Hence, this volume presupposes that health can be promoted in ethically just ways with great benefit for individuals, populations across continents, and the whole planet. Health is a comprehensive and inclusive good. What threatens health could be, at the same time, what stimulates in renewed ways the human capacities to rise to the occasion and protect, promote, and restore health. While this volume focuses on the cancer pandemic, the authors' contributions point to a holistic ethical framework. Everything concerning the health of individuals and populations is inseparably interconnected, as the stress on the social and political determinants of health exemplifies.

Cancer

Cancer is the first or second cause of death in 134 countries, the leading cause of death in most high-income countries (i.e., 10 million deaths in 2020), and the leading cause of death by disease in American children.[1] An estimated 19.3 million new cases of cancer are diagnosed across the world each year, and this number is expected to rise to 29 million by 2040. Most of the increase will occur in low- and middle-income countries, the countries least capable of confronting the cancer pandemic or affording expensive therapies.[2]

Cancer is unjust. Striking inequities can be traced within and between countries in cancer incidence and survival by race, ethnicity, and socio- economic-status. Survival is much higher among the wealthy than among the poor. In the U.S., outcomes are much more favorable among Whites than among Blacks and Latinos. Moreover, scientific contributions and ethical inquiry should help civil society in identifying and naming these inequities and, at the same time, recognizing successful strategies to promote health and articulate further constructive proposals.

---

[1] For a history of cancer, see Siddhartha Mukherjee, *The Emperor of All Maladies: A Biography of Cancer* (New York: Scribner, 2010).

[2] See The Cancer Atlas, "The Burden of Cancer," *canceratlas.cancer.org,* 2019, canceratlas.cancer.org/the-burden/the-burden-of-cancer/; World Health Organization, "The Top 10 Causes of Death," December 9, 2020, www.who.int/news-room/fact-sheets/detail/the-top-10-causes-of- death; World Health Organization, "Cancer," September 21, 2021, www.who.int/news-room/fact-sheets/detail/cancer.

The Volume

To examine the cancer pandemic and its inequities, this book gathers a selection of contributions presented, in an initial form, at the international conference hosted at Boston College, on October 2, 2021, by the Program for Global Public Health and the Common Good in partnership with the Schiller Institute for Integrated Science and Society and the Theology Department of the Morrissey College of Arts and Sciences. Both the conference and this book mark the third year of the increasingly popular minor in Global Public Health and the Common Good while the university is considering approving a major in Global Public Health and the Common Good. Moreover, both the conference and the volume build on the success of the 2019 conference on *Ethical Challenges in Global Public Health: Climate Change, Pollution and the Health of the Poor*, followed by the publication of selected contributions in a special issue of the *Journal of Moral Theology* and the edited book with the same title launching the Global Theological Ethics series published by the *Journal of Moral Theology*,[3] in conjunction with the global network Catholic Theological Ethics in the World Church,[4] and with Pickwick Publications of the publisher Wipf and Stock. Both the conference and this volume also aim to celebrate the 50-year anniversary of the National Cancer Act signed into law by the U.S. President Richard M. Nixon on December 23, 1971.[5]

The following pages feature the contributions of a distinguished group of scholars—from Boston College, across the United States, and internationally—in cancer prevention, global public health,

---

[3] See Philip J. Landrigan and Andrea Vicini, SJ, "Ethical Challenges in Global Public Health," *Journal of Moral Theology*, 2021, jmt.scholasticahq.com/issue/3180. See also Philip J. Landrigan and Andrea Vicini, SJ, eds., *Ethics Challenges in Global Public Health: Climate Change, Pollution, and the Health of the Poor*, (Eugene, OR: Pickwick Publications by Wipf & Stock, 2021).

[4] See Catholic Theological Ethics in the World Church, "A Global Ethics Network Fostering Connections within the World Church," 2022, catholicethics.com.

[5] See National Cancer Institute, "National Cancer Act of 1971," February 2, 2021, www.cancer.gov/about-nci/overview/history/national-cancer-act-1971.

economics, public policy, and ethics to the examination of the scientific and ethical challenges facing global cancer control in the 21st century. In such a way, the volume aims to fill an important gap in the debates and literature on the cancer pandemic. Despite the clear connections between global public health and social justice, there has been surprisingly little scholarly exploration of the ethical challenges that confront global cancer control, which could further strengthen the emerging field of global health ethics.

Overview

The various chapters accompany the readers in engaging the rising global cancer pandemic by focusing on some of its significant components and, at the same time, exploring which responses and strategies of interventions are needed. While the book aims at comprehensiveness, not every necessary aspect is addressed. Hence, these pages become an opportunity for further developments in engaging the pandemic scientifically and ethically, by considering legal and economic aspects, by delving further in local contexts while continuing to consider its global dimensions and repercussions.

With its five parts the book examines the essential elements that characterize a critical assessment of the cancer pandemic globally, both scientifically informed and ethically inspired. In Part 1, first, Kurt Straif provides a historical and global overview on trends in cancer incidence, disparities, and social inequalities, with a particular attention given to cancer in children and adolescents. Second, by stressing that the majority of cancers can be prevented, Philip J. Landrigan focuses on the troubling consequences of pollution on individual, social, and planetary health, which are inequitably distributed, with the most significant increases in cancer incidence and mortality occurring in low- and middle-income countries—i.e., the countries least capable of confronting the disease and least well able to afford costly therapies. Third, Arvind Kumar and Raja M. Flores discuss the economic aspects that accompany cancer spending for prevention, screening, and treatment in the U.S. and examine health hazards in low- and moderate-income housing in New York City. Finally, the ethical imperative voiced by colleagues from the Universidad Católica de Chile (Lilian Ferrer, Rodrigo López, Francisca López, and María Isabel Catoni) stresses the urgency of providing universal access to healthcare services on a global scale because health is a social good and a social right.

Part 2 articulates critical approaches to healthcare within social contexts (Richard J. Jackson), including policy making and the contributions of non-profit organizations (Nsedu Obot Witherspoon). In reflecting on cancers, Richard Jackson stresses the serious social harms caused by inadequate prevention and, within the social fabric, he examines what he calls the "cancer accelerants": water, power, money, and greed. They are specific factors that require ethical attention. Water powerfully influences past and future health and well-being, for human beings and for the planet. Water conflicts and powers at play within the medical/industrial complex lead to further power imbalances in the social fabric, which are increased and worsened by structural racism and systemic impoverishment. Money further complicates any attempt to promote greater social justice whether one considers, on the one hand, financial interests and, on the other hand, lack of financial resources and poverty. Finally, greed poisons human and social interactions by inhibiting virtuous behaviors and choices, both at the personal and social level.

While the role of governments in promoting health policies and regulations to protect and support all its citizens, particularly those who are more vulnerable, needs to be reaffirmed, the work of non-profit organizations should be highlighted. As an example, Nsedu Obot Witherspoon discusses the mission, contributions, and actions of a national non-profit organization—the Children's Environmental Health Network—that strives to foster equity, protect all children— and their health—from environmental hazards, and promote safe and healthy environments for children to thrive in. This commitment is challenged by the traditional approach to environmental health laws and regulations that is based on proving harm from environmental hazards, such as carcinogens, before measures are taken to protect all, especially the most vulnerable and, among them, children. The goal of fostering a cancer free society is a collective and shared endeavor, which requires acknowledging and addressing the troubling effects of systemic discrimination and racism on low wealth, Black, Indigenous, and People of Color communities.

In Part 3, focused on discussing ethical issues and practical approaches, Elizabeth A. Williams articulates a womanist approach that, while it denounces the racial disparities and inequities in access to preventive, diagnostic, and therapeutic services for Black women, shows how grass-roots organizations empower women and allow them to take back their health—for example by controlling and preventing breast cancer.

Conor M. Kelly further examines social inequities and, by strongly advocating for social justice, frames ethical priorities. In particular, he invites us to focus not only on what we do not know about cancer (e.g., in terms of scientific understanding and medical know-how), but also on what we already know about cancer's toll on human beings and societies, as well the continuing and even increasing inequities in cancer care across the planet.

Finally, in light of his experience as a clinical bioethicist in a healthcare institution in the U.S.A. (i.e., Anne Arundel Medical Center in Annapolis, MD), Christian Cintron reflects on concrete challenges— from the COVID-19 pandemic to the increasing costs of cancer care for individuals and families—that test the ability of providing care to cancer patients and that demand policy reforms aimed at transforming practices in prevention and in providing care, while avoiding what he calls "financial toxicity."

Moving from North America to other continents, Part 4 enlarges the horizon of reflection by turning to international perspectives. Rengswamy Sankaranarayanan discusses major cancer problems and prospects for prevention in Asia by showing, on the one hand, the diverse cancer incidence in various countries and, on the other hand, strategies to prevent, screen, diagnose, and treat that are implemented in these countries. To address, reduce, and eliminate the glaring inequities in cancer prevention and care between countries, political commitments should allocate adequate resources, implement targeted programs, improve health infrastructures, strengthen human resources, provide universal healthcare, promote efficient and socially conscious public- private partnerships, and develop efficient monitoring systems.

Similarly, Walter Ricciardi discusses challenges and strategies to address the cancer pandemic within the European context, by featuring initiatives across Europe—like the Mission on Cancer—aimed at supporting and strengthening national commitments to foster prevention, diagnostics and treatment of cancer, and the quality of life of cancer patients, survivors, and their families and caregivers, while continuing to support research efforts.

Finally, Michail K. Shafir examines the very different scenarios that can be encountered in Latin American countries by pointing to challenges in prevention, monitoring the incidence of specific cancers (i.e., breast, gastric, and cervical), tracing the uneven presence of cancer registries, providing healthcare services, and addressing social and national inequities in access to healthcare.

This international overview, while incomplete, confirms the urgency of further engagement in examining not only national data, healthcare systems and structures, and the quality of care that is provided but in expanding the critical assessment of the cancer pandemic at the regional and continental levels. Such an approach could highlight trends and devise shared strategies with beneficial impacts in providing a better picture of the cancer pandemic and in joining forces to address the multiple challenges of the cancer pandemic.[6]

---

[6] For examples of literature regarding cancers in the African continent, see Nina Arhin, Paddy Ssentongo, Morris Taylor, Elizabeth Josephine Olecki, Colette Pameijer, Chan Shen, John Oh, and Cathy Eng, "Age-Standardised Incidence Rate and Epidemiology of Colorectal Cancer in Africa: A Systematic Review and Meta-Analysis," *BMJ Open* 12, no. 1 (2022): e052376, 10.1136/bmjopen-2021-052376; Walburga Yvonne Joko-Fru, Mirko Griesel, Nikolaus Christian Simon Mezger, Lucia Hammerl, Tobias Paul Seraphin, Jana Feuchtner,

Introduction: The Challenging Global Cancer Pandemic

Personal narratives further expand our understanding of what cancer's diagnosis and treatment imply and what it means to become a cancer survivor. In Part 5, with their diversity, four contributions bring to light some shared experiential, emotional, and relational traits by pointing to commonalities that go beyond the age differences and the professional locations. A Boston College alumna, Bridgette Merriman, now medical student, and a Boston College alumnus, Woody Hubbell—currently employed in an investment bank and financial services company focusing on healthcare—describe their journey with cancer. While experiencing cancer in early childhood (Merriman) or during college (Hubbell), both their stories stress the outstanding care

---

Henry Wabinga, Guy N'da, Assefa Mathewos, Bakarou Kamate, Judith Nsonde Malanda, Freddy Houehanou Rodrigue Gnangnon, Gladys Chebet Chesumbai, Anne Korir, Cesaltina Lorenzoni, Annelle Zietsman, Margaret Ziona Borok, Biying Liu, Christoph Thomssen, Paul McGale, Ahmedin Jemal, Donald Maxwell Parkin, and Eva Johanna Kantelhardt, "Breast Cancer Diagnostics, Therapy, and Outcomes in Sub-Saharan Africa: A Population-Based Registry Study," *Journal of the National Comprehensive Cancer Network* (2021): 1–11, 10.6004/jnccn.2021.7011; Zafar Ahmed Khan, Muhammed Uzayr Khan, and Martin Brand, "Gallbladder Cancer in Africa: A Higher Than Expected Rate in a 'Low-Risk' Population," *Surgery* (2022), 10.1016/j.surg.2021.09.016; Doreen Ramogola-Masire, Rebecca Luckett, and Greta Dreyer, "Progress and Challenges in Human Papillomavirus and Cervical Cancer in Southern Africa," *Current Opinion in Infectious Diseases* 35, no. 1 (2022): 49– 54; Anel Van Zyl, Paul C. Rogers, and Mariana Kruger, "Improving the Follow up of Childhood Cancer Survivors in South Africa," *South African Medical Journal* 111, no. 12 (2021): 1170–1171; Luchuo Engelbert Bain, "Are We Doing Enough for Our Patients with Terminal Cancer? A Moral Imperative to Step up Palliative Care Practice in Sub-Saharan Africa," *BMJ Supportive & Palliative Care* 5, no. 5 (2015): 467–468; Fiona McKenzie, Annelle Zietsman, Moses Galukande, Angelica Anele, Charles Adisa, Herbert Cubasch, Groesbeck Parham, Benjamin O. Anderson, Behnoush Abedi-Ardekani, Joachim Schuz, Isabel Dos Santos Silva, and Valerie McCormack, "African Breast Cancer-Disparities in Outcomes (ABC-DO): Protocol of a Multicountry Mobile Health Prospective Study of Breast Cancer Survival in Sub-Saharan Africa," *BMJ Open* 6, no. 8 (2016): e011390, 10.1136/bmjopen-2016-011390; Saskia Mostert, Festus Njuguna, Gilbert Olbara, Solomon Sindano, Mei Neni Sitaresmi, Eddy Supriyadi, and Gertjan Kaspers, "Corruption in Health-Care Systems and Its Effect on Cancer Care in Africa," *Lancet Oncology* 16, no. 8 (2015): e394–e404; M. Okeke, O. Oderinde, L. Liu, and D. Kabula, "Oncology and COVID-19: Perspectives on Cancer Patients and Oncologists in Africa," *Ethics, Medicine, and Public Health* 14 (2020): 100550, 10.1016/j.jemep.2020.100550.

9

that they received and the remarkable support and accompaniment that they enjoyed. Care is more that diagnostic prowess, an up-to-date pharmacological arsenal, and targeted therapies. Care is also shaped by caregivers, families, and friends.

As a Boston College staff member, Laura Campbell vividly describes how cancer disrupted her life and, in very similar ways, the lives of any worker. It makes a great difference if the employer's healthcare plan and the working environment support patients in their ordeals and in the process of recovery. Hence, while personal narratives teach us about individual experiences,[7] they further highlight the ethical urgency of critically examining workplaces and healthcare systems with the services that they provide and by paying attention to those who are left out.

Finally, as a cancer survivor and a Boston College faculty member, James F. Keenan, SJ, stresses how considering cancer as a global health emergency is urgent and implies a necessary and beneficial change of perspective. In fact, cancer is usually experienced as a personal ordeal, centered on who is affected. As Keenan's indicates, shared accompaniment and advocacy—as presented by Elizabeth Williams in her chapter describing women's organizations of breast cancer survivors—further exemplify how new forms of collective support, social action, and lived solidarity contribute to change the patterns of cancers' stories by giving voice and agency to the patients and survivors who are voiceless and disempowered.

The volume ends by looking at what could be possible concrete ways to articulate strategies to address the ongoing cancer pandemic. What the future will reserve to us depends in large part by how civil society will deal with the cancer pandemic today and by which approaches are set in place now and in the years to come.

Striving to be focused and concrete, Silvia de Sanjosé offers a specific example to inform our present and future commitments by articulating a global strategy for eliminating cervical cancer, while highlighting ongoing challenges and stressing the existing opportunities for

---

[7] See also Meghan O'Rourke, *The Long Goodbye* (New York: Riverhead Books, 2011).

prevention, screening, and vaccination. In the closing chapter, I indicate how the ethical reflection stresses that addressing the cancer pandemic is hampered by the existing inequities and disparities in providing healthcare to citizens across the planet, which are further exacerbated by the global pandemic caused by COVID-19. Thinking about the future requires us to consider the social, cultural, political, and religious contexts where inequities limit efforts aimed at preventing, diagnosing, and providing care. Ethically, a multilayered approach that strives to promote research, prevention, and therapies, and that engages individuals, institutions, and populations in collaborative efforts seems to be promising and able to generate realistic hopes.

At Boston College, **Andrea Vicini**, SJ, is Chairperson, Michael P. Walsh Professor of Bioethics, and Professor of Theological Ethics in the Theology Department and an affiliate member of the Ecclesiastical Faculty at the School of Theology and Ministry. MD and pediatrician (University of Bologna), he is an alumnus of Boston College (STL and PhD) and holds an STD from the Pontifical Faculty of Theology of Southern Italy (Naples). He taught in Italy, Albania, Mexico, Chad, and France. He is co-chair of the international network Catholic Theological Ethics in the World Church. His research and publications include theological bioethics, sustainability, public health, new biotechnologies, and fundamental theological ethics.

Part 1
The Changing Context

Chapter 1: The Global Cancer Pandemic: Trends and Disparities

Kurt Straif

Kurt Straif provides a historical and global overview on global trends in cancer incidence, disparities, and social inequalities among countries and within countries, with a particular attention given to cancer in children and adolescents. To reduce social inequalities, the author proposes to reexamine research priorities: first, to generate knowledge and monitor progress; second, to expand research focused on prevention; and, third, to focus on equality when implementing and assessing cancer control measures.

Fifty years ago, on December 23, 1971, President Richard M. Nixon signed the National Cancer Act into law.[8] The campaign that was launched was also called "The War on Cancer" and Fort Detrick, the United States Army Futures Command installation for biological warfare facility, located in Frederick, Maryland, was converted into a cancer research center to serve as the headquarter as the Frederick Cancer Research and Development Center. Later, in 2016, President Barack H. Obama launched the Cancer Moonshot Initiative and asked Vice President Joseph R. Biden to lead the initiative to increase research funding and accelerate cancer discoveries.[9] From the start, and reasserted with the Moonshot Initiative, there was a disproportionate focus on finding a cure for cancer. But why had cancer has become such a prominent topic in the 1960s?

Between 1346 and 1352, 25–33 percent of the European population died of the Bubonic plague, also called the "Black Death," which was believed to be caused by "Miasmas" (from the Greek word for

---

[8] See National Cancer Institute, "National Cancer Act of 1971," February 2, 2021, www.cancer.gov/about-nci/overview/history/nationalcancer-act-1971.

[9] See The White House, "Cancer Moonshot," 2016, obamawhitehouse.archives.gov/cancer moonshot.

"pollution" from noxious vapors and gases from decaying matter and characterized by its foul smell).

Later, in the 18th century, cholera swept into Europe with major epidemics in big cities like London and Paris. Four hundred years after the Black Death, miasmas were still believed to be the cause of the devastating and deadly cholera epidemics. However, with his investigation of the cholera outbreak of 1854 in London, Dr. John Snow (1813–1858) showed that cholera was transmitted by fecal contamination of drinking water. Followed by the identification of Vibrio cholera as a bacterium by the Italian anatomist Filippo Pacini (1812–1883), and the discovery of the German physician and microbiologist Robert Koch (1843–1910) that this bacterium is the cause of cholera, the miasma paradigm was supplanted by the germ theory. In 1882, Koch also discovered the tubercle bacillus that caused tuberculosis, and in 1900 tuberculosis was, together with pneumonia and influenza, one of the two leading causes of death, followed by gastrointestinal infections as the third ranking cause of death in the U.S. Only ranking fourth, heart disease was the first chronic non-communicable disease among the top causes of deaths in 1900. The death rate of cancer—ranking 8th—was only about one fourth that of cardiovascular deaths (Table 1).

With the demographic transition and the epidemiological transition, starting first in high-income countries, this pattern changed radically. The demographic transition is characterized by population-level shifts from a pattern of high birth rates and high death rates to one of low birth rates and low death rates. Changes in mortality rates and causes of death that reflect underlying changes in exposure to risk factors define the epidemiological transition. Specifically, during the past century mortality from infectious diseases declined and led to the dominance of non-communicable diseases (NCD). Among NCD, more recently, and particularly in medium or high-income countries, greater reductions in mortality rates for cardiovascular diseases than for cancer resulted in cancer now figuring as first or second leading cause of premature death (i.e., among adults 30–69 years old) in 134 of 185 countries.

Table 1. Top causes of death in the U.S. in 1900 and 2019 (per 100,000 population)

Cause of death	1900	2019
Pneumonia or influenza	202.2	12.3
Tuberculosis	194.4	-
Gastrointestinal infections	142.7	-
Heart disease	137.4	161.5
Cerebrovascular disease	106.9	-
Nephropathies	88.6	12.7
Accidents	72.3	49.3
Cancer	64	146.2

The Table 1 is based on data from Statista, "Top 10 Causes of Death in the U.S. in 1900 and 2020 (per 100,000 Population)," 2022, www.statista.com/statistics/235703/major-causes-of-death-in-the-us/.

However, cancer is not one disease, but refers to a large, heterogeneous group of diseases that have a common underlying pathology defined by uncontrolled cellular growth. From a global perspective, some cancer types are significantly more frequent than others, but the cancer-specific pattern also varies considerably if we employ the different classic epidemiological measures of disease frequency, incidence (i.e., newly diagnosed cases), mortality, and prevalence. For cancer, the latter is typically (but arbitrarily) estimated based on the five-year survival after the initial diagnosis.

For each measure, and for both sexes combined, somewhat different top five cancers constituted about half of all cancers among middle-aged adults in 2018. Total cancer incidence was 18.1 million, and the leading causes were lung and breast cancer, followed by colorectal cancer and prostate cancer. In contrast, for cancer mortality, lung cancer was by far the leading cancer, breast cancer was only fifth, and prostate cancer did not make it into the top five. Instead, liver cancer showed and ranked fourth, closely after stomach cancer. Total cancer mortality was about half of the incidence, i.e., 9.6 million deaths.[10]

The percentage distribution differs for the estimated 43.8 million prevalent 5-year cancer survivors. Here (see Figure 2), breast cancer leads and lung cancer barely shows up among the top 5 cancer survivors. Prostate cancer is back and ranked third, and thyroid cancer emerges as one of the top

---

[10] Jemal, Torre, Soerjomataram, and Bray, *The Cancer Atlas*.

five cancers among 5-year survivors. Only colorectal cancer has a similar percentage of about 10 percent across all three frequency measures.

There are important differences by sex for the ranking of most frequent cancers, and these differences vary further by region. For cancer incidence among women, globally breast cancer is the number one ranking cancer in most countries. However, cancer of the cervix uteri is most common in several low and medium-income countries (LMIC), particularly in Africa. In terms of mortality, cancer of the cervix ranks first in even more countries and in all Sub-Saharan Africa. In many high-income countries (HIC) and in China, lung cancer leads the mortality rates. In Mongolia, liver cancer is the most frequent cancer in terms of incidence and mortality.

Among men, liver cancer is also the most frequent cancer in Mongolia. Moreover, this is true in several countries in South-East Asia and Africa. In terms of incidence, prostate cancer ranks number one in the Americas, Australia, European and African countries, while lung cancer leads in many Asian countries. For mortality, lung cancer takes the lead before prostate cancer, with notable exceptions in several countries of Africa and Central and South America. Only in the Indian sub-continent, cancers of the lip and oral cavity are the most frequent cancers, for both incidence and mortality.[11]

On a finer grid, there is even more important variation across cancer registries. Even when restricted to the variation between the 10th and 90th percentile, the relative magnitude of cancer incidence varies more than fifty times for melanoma of the skin with lowest rates among Qataris and highest in Georgia, USA. The incidence of cancers of the prostate and testis varies by about 15 times globally, with lowest rates in Maanshan, China, and Chennai, India, and highest rates in Limousin, France, and Wales, respectively. The age-standardized rates depict the absolute variations. Closer to the highest rate of prostate cancer, lung cancer incidence in Chelyabinsk, Russia, and colorectal cancer in Trento, Italy,

---

[11] Jemal, Torre, Soerjomataram, and Bray, *The Cancer Atlas.*

stand out. The smallest relative variation among the depicted 22 cancer types is leukemia and is still more than twofold.[12]

There have been substantial trends over time as illustrated with sex-specific cancer mortality rates in the United States from 1930 to 2011. Lung cancer—today's top-leading cause of cancer death—was only one of the less frequent cancers in the 1930, before age-standardized lung cancer death rates among men increased by more than ten times and peaked around 1990. However, lung cancer was still by far the leading cause of cancer death in 2011. A similar trend, but later and less pronounced, was observed among women, starting to increase in the late 1960s, and its decline is showing only recently. In contrast, stomach cancer was the leading cause of cancer deaths in the early twentieth century, but monotonically decreased in both sexes over the last century.[13]

Trends over time may differ noticeably even over shorter times, between neighboring countries and in different age groups among adults. Trends of colorectal cancer incidence in Canada from 1980 to 2010 among adults 50 years and older are relatively stable, while in the United States, after a peak in the mid-1980s, an almost monotonic decline has now resulted in incidence rates that are lower than those in Canada. In contrast, in both countries, among adults less than 50 years old the incidence of cancers of the colorectum (and the uterine corpus) started to increase in the early 1990s.[14]

Cancers in Childhood and Adolescence

Cancers occurring in childhood and adolescence differ markedly from the cancer patterns in adults. Globally, the most common cancers in children are leukemia and lymphoma, while major cancers that are

---

[12] Jemal, Torre, Soerjomataram, and Bray, *The Cancer Atlas*. See Freddie Bray, Murielle Colombet, Les Mery, Marion Pineros, Ariana Znaor, Roberto Zanetti, and Jacques Ferlay, eds., *Cancer Incidence in Five Continents Volume XI* (Lyon: International Agency for Research on Cancer, 2021).

[13] Based on data from Max Roser and Hannah Ritchie, "Cancer," *Our World in Data*, 2019, ourworldindata.org/cancer.

[14] Jemal, Torre, Soerjomataram, and Bray, *The Cancer Atlas*.

typical among adults—such as cancers of the lung, breast, or colon—are extremely rare in children. Among the younger children (ages 0–14) leukemia and tumors of the central nervous system are most frequent and lymphoma is third, while in adolescents (ages 15–19), incidence rates of lymphoma surpass those of leukemia and tumors of the central nervous system. Further, epithelial tumors and melanoma emerge in this older age group.[15] Overall, cancer in children is about ten times less frequent than in adults, but, as in adults, important variations are seen across regions and ethnicities.

Social Inequalities in Cancer

Descriptive cancer epidemiology provides numerous illustrations of major structural inequalities, for instance when one considers survival from acute lymphoblastic leukemia, the most frequent cancer in children. Figure 1 depicts the 5-year survival from this cancer based on results of cohort studies. The size of the circles indicates the number of cases from available cohorts that contributed to the region-specific survival data. Therefore, these numbers are not valid for incidence or mortality comparison between regions. However, the survival data by region highlight the poor survival in LMIC. While survival in HIC was 90 percent and higher, survival in Africa was only 43 percent. Particularly in LMIC such survival data likely represent the upper end of survival (e.g., among children who were diagnosed and treated in a major specialized cancer hospital, and later followed-up in a cohort), while in the poorest countries only 10 percent of children can hope to survive.

Inequalities are not only prominent across countries of different income but also within countries. Figure 2 summarizes age-standardized mortality rates per 100,000 by deprivation quintile in England for all cancers combined for the period 2007–2011. While these all-cancer mortality rates are generally higher in men than in women, in both sexes a significant trend with increased mortality by increasing deprivation

---

[15] Reprinted with permission from Jemal, Torre, Soerjomataram, and Bray, *The Cancer Atlas*.

quintile is documented. All-cancer mortality in the most deprived quintile is 50 percent higher than in the least deprived, for both men and women.

Many important disparities by race or ethnicity have been revealed. Female breast and colorectal cancer mortality ratio by race in the U.S. illustrates this structural problem. Cancer mortality rates for female The descriptive illustration of social inequalities in cancer concludes with an example of incidence and mortality of cancer of the cervix uteri—one of the most frequent cancers in women—by country income level. For both incidence and mortality, there is a strong trend across country income levels with highest occurrence in low-income countries. Moreover, the ratio

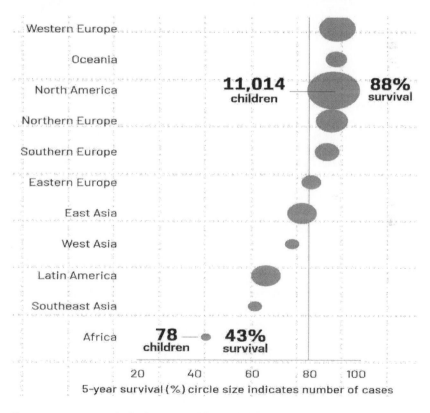

Figure 1. 5-year age-standardized net survival (percent) observed in the available cohorts of cases diagnosed with lymphoid leukemia
Reprinted with permission from Jemal, Torre, Soerjomataram, and Bray, *The Cancer Atlas*.

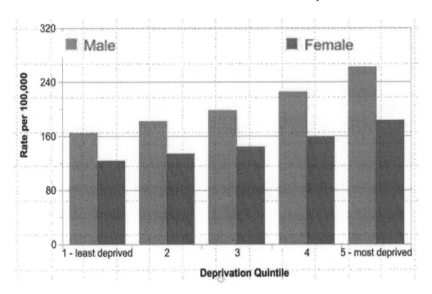

Figure 2. Age-standardized (Europe) mortality rates per 100,000 by deprivation quintile in England for all cancers combined (excluding non-melanoma skin cancers), 2007–2011
Reprinted with permission from Salvatore Vaccarella, Joannie Lortet-Tieulent, Rodolfo Saracci, David I. Conway, Kurt Straif, and Christopher P. Wild, ed., *Reducing Social Inequalities in Cancer: Evidence and Priorities for Research*, IARC Scientific Publications No. 168 (Lyon: International Agency for Research on Cancer, 2019). Also available at publications.iarc.fr.

of mortality to incidence strongly increases from high to low-income countries.[16]

Many more illustrations of social inequalities in cancer can be explored in the International Agency for Research on Cancer's *Reducing Social Inequalities in Cancer: Evidence and Priorities for Research*.[17] This publication is the outcome of an international workshop convened by the Agency in April 2018. The book introduces the concept of cancer as a disease of disparities and how global public health addresses social inequalities in cancer. The chapters provide an overview of social

---

[16] International Agency for Research on Cancer (IARC) and World Health Organization, "Cancer Today: Data Visualization Tools for Exploring the Global Cancer Burden in 2020," 2022, gco.iarc.fr/today/home.

[17] See Vaccarella, Lortet-Tieulent, Saracci, Conway, Straif, and Wild, *Reducing Social Inequalities in Cancer*.

inequalities in cancer between and within countries, factors and mechanisms contributing to these inequalities, and real-world examples of interventions that reduce these social inequalities. The workshop also recommended research priorities to reduce social inequalities in cancer: first, generating knowledge and monitoring progress; second, expanding research focused on prevention; and, third, focusing on equality when implementing and assessing cancer control measures.

At Boston College, **Kurt Straif**, MD, PhD., is currently Visiting Professor of Epidemiology and co-director of the Global Observatory on Pollution at Health with the Schiller Institute for Integrated Science and Society. Since 2001, he had leading positions at the International Agency for Research on Cancer (IARC), as a senior epidemiologist, Head of the IARC Monographs Programme, to classify carcinogenic hazards of all kinds of environmental exposures (chemical, biological, physical agents, and personal habits), Acting Head of a large epidemiological research group, and initiator of large international projects. In 2014, he relaunched the *IARC Handbooks of Cancer Prevention* with a broad perspective on prevention (i.e., breast cancer screening, avoidance of obesity, and colorectal cancer screening). Since 2017 he also supervises the World Health Organization's Classification of Tumours ("Blue Books"). In 2016, he received the Champion of Environmental Health Research Award in commemoration of fifty years of Environmental Health Research by the National Institutes of Health. In 2018, he presented the Distinguished Lecture in Occupational and Environmental Cancer at the U.S. National Cancer Institute.

Chapter 2: Driving Forces of the Epidemic: A Polluted and Polluting Planet

Philip J. Landrigan

Nearly 20 million new cancer cases are diagnosed across the world each year. By stressing that the majority of cancers can be prevented, Philip Landrigan focuses on the troubling consequences of pollution on individual, social, and planetary health. Since 1990, reduction has occurred in the traditional forms of pollution associated with deep poverty and in the numbers of deaths caused by these forms of pollution. But the modern forms of pollution—ambient air pollution and chemical pollution—are on the rise, as well as the numbers of deaths due to these forms of pollution. Moreover, the health consequences of pollution are inequitably distributed, with the most significant increases in cancer incidence and mortality occurring in low- and middle-income countries—i.e., the countries least capable of confronting the disease and least well able to afford costly therapies. Finally, the author suggests science-based strategies for pollution control and cancer prevention.

The world today is experiencing an unprecedented global pandemic of cancer. Cancer has become one of the top two causes of death in 134 countries, the leading cause of death in most high-income countries, and the leading cause of death by disease among children in high-income countries. Nearly 20 million new cancer cases are diagnosed across the world each year. By 2040, this number is expected to rise to nearly 30 million and to result each year in 16.4 million deaths.[1]

Cancer is very inequitably distributed. Most increases in cancer incidence and mortality are occurring in low-income and middle-

---

[1] See American Cancer Society, *Global Cancer Facts and Figures*, 4th ed. (Atlanta: American Cancer Society, 2018), www.cancer.org/content/dam/cancer-org/research/cancer-facts-and-statistics/global-cancer-facts-and-figures/global-cancer-facts-and-figures-4th-edition.pdf.

income countries—the countries least capable of confronting the disease and least well able to afford costly therapies. In the absence of intentional intervention, these disparities will widen further in coming decades. The majority of cancers can be prevented. Relatively few are of purely genetic origin. The great majority of cancers are due to dietary factors, personal behaviors, and hazardous materials in the environment that act either alone, or more commonly, in concert with each other and with variations in individual susceptibility. The purpose of this chapter is to explore the contribution of pollution to the global cancer pandemic, the global disparities in cancer morbidity and mortality, and, at the same time, the science-based strategies for pollution control and cancer prevention.

Pollution

Pollution—unwanted waste of human origin released to air, land, water, and the ocean without regard for cost or consequence—is an existential threat to human and planetary health.[2] Like climate change, biodiversity loss, and depletion of the world's fresh water supply, pollution endangers the stability of the earth's support systems and threatens the continuing survival of human societies. Pollution includes air contaminated by fine particulate matter ($PM_{2.5}$), ozone, and oxides of sulfur and nitrogen; biological and chemical contamination of fresh water; contamination of the ocean by plastic waste, petroleum-based pollutants, toxic metals, manufactured chemicals, pharmaceuticals,

---

[2] See Philip J. Landrigan, Richard Fuller, Nereus J. R. Acosta, Olusoji Adeyi, Robert Arnold, Niladri Nil Basu, Abdoulaye Bibi Balde, Roberto Bertollini, Stephan Bose-O'Reilly, Jo Ivey Boufford, Patrick N. Breysse, Thomas Chiles, Chulabhorn Mahidol, Awa M. Coll-Seck, Maureen L. Cropper, Julius Fobil, Valentin Fuster, Michael Greenstone, Andy Haines, David Hanrahan, David Hunter, Mukesh Khare, Alan Krupnick, Bruce Lanphear, Bindu Lohani, Keith Martin, Karen V. Mathiasen, Maureen A. McTeer, Christopher J. L. Murray, Johanita D. Ndahimananjara, Frederica Perera, Janez Potocnik, Alexander S. Preker, Jairam Ramesh, Johan Rockstrom, Carlos Salinas, Leona D. Samson, Karti Sandilya, Peter D. Sly, Kirk R. Smith, Achim Steiner, Richard B. Stewart, William A Suk, Onno C. P. van Schayck, Gautam N. Yadama, Kandeh Yumkella, and Ma Zhong, "The *Lancet* Commission on Pollution and Health," *Lancet* 391, no. 10119 (2018): 462–512.

pesticides, nitrogen, phosphorus, fertilizer, and sewage; and poisoning of the land by lead, mercury, pesticides, industrial chemicals, electronic waste, and radioactive waste.

The *Lancet* Commission on Pollution and Health found that pollution is responsible each year for an estimated nine million deaths—16 percent of all deaths globally—as well as for economic losses totaling US $4.6 trillion, 6.2 percent of global economic output.[3] The Commission noted pollution's deep inequity. Ninety-two percent of pollution-related deaths, as well as the greatest burden of pollution's economic losses, occur in low-income and middle- income countries (LMICs) (Figure 1).[4]

Table 1 presents the distribution of pollution-related deaths by pollution source and gender.[5]

Pollution is closely linked to climate change.[6] Fossil fuel combustion is the main source of both airborne fine particulate ($PM_{2.5}$) pollution and of the carbon dioxide, black carbon, and other greenhouse gases that drive climate change. Methane, released to the atmosphere in enormous volumes in the extraction of natural gas by hydraulic fracturing ('fracking') as well as from agricultural operations, is an additional potent driver of climate change.

The *Lancet* Commission on Pollution and Health observed that pollution and climate change can both be "directly attributed to the

---

[3] See Landrigan et al., "The *Lancet* Commission on Pollution and Health."

[4] The Figure 1 is from GBD Risk Factors Collaborators, "Global Burden of 87 Risk Factors in 204 Countries and Territories, 1990–2019: A Systematic Analysis for the Global Burden of Disease Study 2019," *Lancet* 396, no. 10258 (2020): 1223–1249. The acronym GBD means Global Burden of Disease. See also Institute for Health Metrics and Evaluation (IHME), "Global Burden of Disease (GBD)," *Institute for Health Metrics and Evaluation*, 2019, www.healthdata.org/gbd/2019.

[5] See GBD Risk Factors Collaborators, "Global Burden of 87 Risk Factors in 204 Countries and Territories, 1990–2019: A Systematic Analysis for the Global Burden of Disease Study 2019," *Lancet* 396, no. 10258 (2020): 1223–1249.

[6] See A. J. McMichael, Alistair Woodward, and Cameron Muir, *Climate Change and the Health of Nations: Famines, Fevers, and the Fate of Populations* (New York: Oxford University Press, 2017).

currently prevalent, linear, take-make-use-dispose- economic paradigm—termed by Pope Francis 'the throwaway culture'—in which natural resources and human capital are viewed as abundant and expendable and capital are viewed as abundant and expendable and the consequences of their reckless exploitation are given little heed.[7]

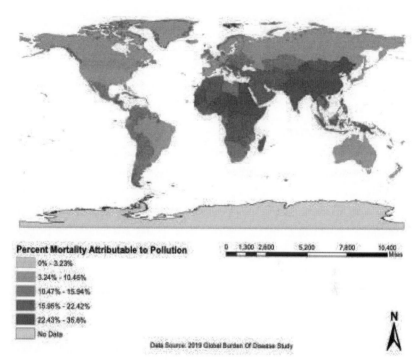

Figure 1. Global Inequity in the Distribution of Pollution-Related Deaths

Ninety-two percent of pollution-related deaths occur in low-income and middle-income countries. In all countries, pollution disproportionately affects the poor, the marginalized and minorities.

---

[7] See Landrigan et al., "The *Lancet* Commission on Pollution and Health," 465. The quote refers to Francis, *Laudato Si'*, nos. 16, 22, and 43. See e Raworth, *Doughnut Economics: Seven Ways to Think Like a 21st Century Economist* (White River Junction, VT: Chelsea Greens Publishing, 2017).

Table 1. Global deaths attributable to pollution by source and gender, 2019

	Female	Male	Total
	Number of Deaths (millions)	Number of Deaths (millions)	Number of Deaths (millions)
Air (Total)	2.92	3.75	6.67
Household air	1.13	1.18	2.31
Ambient particulate	1.70	2.44	4.14
Ambient ozone	0.16	0.21	0.37
Water (Total)	0.73	0.63	1.36
Unsafe sanitation+	0.40	0.36	0.76
Unsafe source+	0.66	0.57	1.23
Occupational (Total)	0.22	0.65	0.87
Carcinogens	0.07	0.28	0.35
Particulates (dust)	0.15	0.37	0.52
Lead	0.35	0.56	0.90
Total	3.92	5.09	9.01

Note: The total numbers of deaths for air, water and all pollution are less than the arithmetic sum of the individual risk factors within each of these categories because there are overlapping contributions—e.g., household air and ambient air pollution each can contribute to the same outcomes.

Pollution Trends

Reduction has occurred since 1990 in the traditional forms of pollution associated with deep poverty-household air pollution, unsafe drinking water, and inadequate sanitation—and in the numbers of deaths due to these forms of pollution. Thanks to the work of national governments, international organizations, private philanthropies, faith groups, and non-governmental organizations in introducing cleaner fuels, improving sanitation and water supplies, and providing new vaccines, antibiotics, and treatments, deaths from these ancient scourges continue slowly to decline.[8]

By contrast, the more modern forms of pollution—ambient air pollution and chemical pollution—are on the rise, and the numbers of deaths due to these forms of pollution have increased substantially over the past twenty years in all regions of the world, but most especially in South, East, and Southeast Asia. Ambient air pollution was responsible for 4.5 million deaths in 2019, up from 2.9 million in 2000. Deaths from chemical pollution doubled in this time from 0.9 million to 1.8 million.[9]

---

[8] See Landrigan et al., "The *Lancet* Commission on Pollution and Health."

[9] See Landrigan et al., "The *Lancet* Commission on Pollution and Health"; GBD Risk Factors Collaborators, "Global Burden of 87 Risk Factors in 204 Countries and Territories, 1990–2019: A Systematic Analysis for the Global Burden of Disease Study 2019."

Increases in deaths from the more modern forms of pollution are occurring as countries urbanize, build infrastructure, and develop their industrial bases. They are driven by rising levels of pollution together with demographic factors that include an aging global population and increased numbers of people exposed to pollution. The number of deaths due to ambient air pollution is on track to double by 2050.[10]

Chemical Pollution

Chemical pollution is a highly complex and particularly insidious threat (Table 2). It includes carcinogens, neurotoxicants, reproductive toxicants, and endocrine disruptors. Fossil fuels—mainly oil and natural gas—are the principal feedstocks to both chemical and plastic manufacture and thus the root source of chemical pollution.

Table 2. Key Facts on Chemical Pollution

• 350,000 chemicals in commerce.
• These are mostly new, fabricated chemicals invented since 1905. They never existed on Earth.
• Used in millions of consumer reports.
• Widely disseminated in the environment.
• Nearly universal human exposure, but disproportionately heavy exposure of the poor and minorities—environmental injustice.
• Global production is on track to double in the next 25–30 years.
• Two thirds of chemical production are now in developing countries.
• The majority of chemicals have never been tested for safety or toxicity.

A recent comprehensive study of 22 chemical inventories from 19 countries has identified over 350,000 manufactured chemicals, thus tripling previous estimates of the number of new synthetic chemicals

---

[10] See Jos Lelieveld, John S. Evans, Mohammed Fnais, Despina Giannadaki, and Andrea Pozzer, "The Contribution of Outdoor Air Pollution Sources to Premature Mortality on a Global Scale," *Nature* 525, no. 7569 (2015): 367–371.

invented since 1950.[11] Some are used in the manufacture of plastics. Others are incorporated into millions of consumer goods and industrial products ranging from foods and food packaging to clothing, building materials, electronics, motor fuels, cleaning compounds, pesticides, cosmetics, toys, and baby bottles.

Worsening chemical pollution is driven by relentless growth in the production, use, and disposal of industrial chemicals, heavy metals, pesticides, and plastics. Global chemical production is increasing at an annual rate of 3.0–3.5 percent, and it is on track to double in the next two to three decades. Plastic production is increasing in parallel (Figure 2). Approximately two-thirds of chemical and plastic production now takes place in low-income and middle-income countries where environmental and occupational safeguards are often weak. The consequence is disproportionally heavy and uncontrolled exposures of workers, children, and other vulnerable populations.

The great majority of manufactured chemicals have never been tested for safety or toxicity.[12] Because of major gaps in chemical policy, most chemicals (except pharmaceuticals and vaccines) are introduced into commerce without any pre- market safety assessments. Major gaps therefore exist in knowledge about the potential of many widely used chemicals to damage ecosystems or harm human health. Many manufactured chemicals have been found—sometimes only after years or even decades of use—to have caused grave damage to planetary support systems and to human health. Historical examples include asbestos, tetraethyl lead, chlordane, DDT, and the ozone-destroying chlorofluorocarbons. More recently developed chemicals such as phthalates, neonicotinoid insecticides, brominated flame retardants,

---

[11] See Zhanyun Wang, Glen W. Walker, Derek C. G. Muir, and Kakuko Nagatani-Yoshida, "Toward a Global Understanding of Chemical Pollution: A First Comprehensive Analysis of National and Regional Chemical Inventories," *Environmental Science & Technology* 54, no. 5 (2020): 2575–2584.

[12] Philip J. Landrigan and Lynn R. Goldman, "Children's Vulnerability to Toxic Chemicals: A Challenge and Opportunity to Strengthen Health and Environmental Policy," *Health Affairs (Millwood)* 30, no. 5 (2011): 842–850.

and perfluorinated substances (PFAS) appear repeat this dismal history. Even less is known about the possible combined effects of exposures to chemical mixtures.

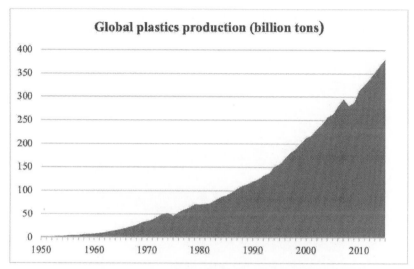

Figure 2. Global plastic production 1950–2015. The sum of annual global polymer resin, synthetic fiber, and plastic additive production. Most of this plastic still exists.
See Hannah Ritchie and Max Roser, "Plastic Pollution," *Our World in Data,* September 2018, ourworldindata.org/plastic-pollution.

Pollution and Cancer

Environmental pollutants have been recognized to be potent causes of human cancer for more than two centuries since Dr. Percivall Pott (1714–1788) of London discovered in 1776 that the cause of an epidemic of skin cancer of the scrotum among young boys employed as chimney sweeps was soot that became lodged in folds in the boys' skin when they were lowered naked into chimneys (Figure 3).[13] Later research has documented that

---

[13] See Percivall Pott, "Cancer Scroti," in P. Pott, *Chirurgical Observations Relative to the Cataract the Polypus of the Nose, the Cancer of the Scrotum, the Different Kin s of Ruptures, and the Mortification of the Toes and Feet* (London: T.J. Carnegy, for L. Hawes, W. Clarke, and R. Collins, 1775), 179–180.

chimney soot and other forms of smoke, including tobacco smoke, contain polycyclic aromatic hydrocarbons (PAHs)—a potent class of chemical carcinogens.

In recent decades, multiple links have been established between pollution and cancer, including air pollution, water pollution, and chemical pollution (Table 3).

Figure 3. London Chimney Sweep (a "Climbing Boy"), Mid-1700s Jessica Brain, "Chimney Sweeps and Climbing Boys," *Historic UK,* April 7, 2021, www.historic-uk.com/CultureUK/ History-Boy-Chimney-Sweep/.

Table 3. Pollution and Cancer—The Multiple Connections

Ambient air pollution
• Potent cause of lung cancer—responsible for an estimated 40 percent of all lung cancer deaths worldwide. It is more important than tobacco smoking as a cause of lung cancer in lower-middle and low-income countries.
• Constituents of air pollution are proven human carcinogens:

o Polycyclic aromatic hydrocarbons (PAH)—also known as black soot.
o Diesel exhaust.

Water pollution
- Arsenic in drinking water is responsible for massive outbreaks of skin and bladder cancer in Southeast Asia, Taiwan, northern Chile (Antofagasta), and northern Argentina.

Chemical pollution
- Multiple chemical pollutants are proven human carcinogens.

Chemicals and Cancer

Multiple chemical pollutants have been identified as causes of cancer. They include asbestos, benzene, the benzidine-based dyes, beryllium, 1,3-butadiene, chromium, ethylene oxide, ionizing radiation, nickel, nitrosamines, plutonium, radium, 2,3,7,8-tetrachlorodibenzo-dioxin, and wood dust. Most of the links between chemicals and cancer have been identified through astute clinical observation and confirmed through toxicological and epidemiological research. Many of the initial clinical observations linking toxic chemicals to cancer were made in heavily exposed occupational populations, and the findings were subsequently extended to community populations where exposures are generally lower but include highly vulnerable groups such as young children and pregnant women.

To systematically evaluate chemical pollutants for carcinogenic hazard, the International Agency for Research on Cancer (IARC), the cancer arm of the World Health Organization, established the IARC Monographs Programme in the early 1970s.[14] This exemplary global program applies rigorous procedures for the scientific review and evaluation of carcinogenic hazards. In reaching its overall evaluations of the carcinogenicity of chemical pollutants, the IARC Monographs

---

[14] See Robert A. Baan and Kurt Straif, "The Monographs Programme of the International Agency for Research on Cancer: A Brief History of Its Preamble," *ALTEX* (2021), 10.14573/altex.2004081.

Programme carefully examines epidemiological and toxicological data linking chemical exposures to human cancer as well as mechanistic evidence based on key characteristics of carcinogens. The IARC assessment process is based solely on data published in the peer-reviewed literature. It is fiercely independent of commercial interests. Since its inception in 1971, it has evaluated more an 1,000 chemicals and has assessed the carcinogenicity of these chemicals as follows:

- 121 proven human carcinogens (Group 1)
- 89 probable human carcinogens (Group 2a)
- 319 possible human carcinogens (Group 2b)
- 500 agents not classifiable (Group 3)

These IARC evaluations shape cancer control policies worldwide. They have helped to save tens of thousands of lives.

Trends in Childhood Cancer

In the past half century, mortality from childhood cancer has declined dramatically in high-income countries. This decline is the consequence of spectacular advances in medical and surgical treatments that, in turn, are based on great increases in understanding of cancer biology and therapeutics.

In this same time, however, the population-based incidence rate of childhood cancer has increased significantly and has offset the declines in mortality. Cancer is now the leading cause of death by disease among children under age 15 in the United States and other highly developed countries.

Increases in incidence have occurred for three major malignancies of children and young adults, in the United States according to data of the Surveillance, Epidemiology, and End Results Program (SEER) from the

National Cancer Institute.[15] Similar increases have been seen in other high-income countries. In the USA, they include:

- *Leukemia.* Leukemia is the most common childhood cancer. Incidence of leukemia in 0–14 years-old U.S. children increased from 3.3 per 100,000 in 1975 to 5.1 per 100,000 in 2005: <u>55 percent increase</u>. Acute lymphocytic leukemia increased in the same years from 2.2 to 4.0 per 100,000: <u>81 percent increase</u>.
- *Primary Brain Cancer.* This is the second leading cancer of children. Incidence of cancer of the brain and nervous system in 0–14 years-old children increased from 2.3 per 1000,000 in 1975 to 3.2 per 100,000 in 2005: <u>39 percent increase</u>.
- *Testicular Cancer.* Incidence of testicular cancer in white men (most of them adolescents and young adult males) increased from 4.3 per 100,000 to 7.0 per 100,000 in 2005: <u>51 percent increase</u>. Among n the same years, both the absolute incidence and the rate of increase were much lower—from 0.9 to 1.3 per 100,000.

These increases are far too rapid to be of genetic origin. Some have argued that they may reflect improved access to medical care or the increasingly widespread availability of newer diagnostic technologies such as magnetic resonance imaging (MRI) and computed tomography (CAT) scan. While those explanations might point to a one-time "bump" in reported incidence around the time that Medicaid was introduced (on July 30, 1965) or newer imaging techniques became available, they fail to account for the steady increase in incidence of three different types of childhood and young adult cancer in multiple countries over a span of three decades.

A key question is whether these increases could be due, at least in part, to exposures to pollution or other hazards in the environment. This question is particularly germane in the case of pediatric cancer, because

---

[15] See National Cancer Institute, "Surveillance, Epidemiology, and End Results Program," *National Cancer Institute,* 2021, seer.cancer.gov.

children are far more sensitive to most toxic environmental exposures than adults.

Children's Great Vulnerability to Chemical Carcinogens

A 1993 analysis undertaken by the U.S. National Academy of Sciences established that children's unique vulnerability to toxic exposures in the environment stems from four sources:[16]

- Children have disproportionately heavy exposures to many chemicals.
- Children's metabolic pathways, especially in fetal life and in the first months after birth, are immature. Infants and children are therefore to detoxify and excrete many environmental chemicals and thus more vulnerable to them.
- Human development is complex, delicate, and therefore all too easily disrupted by environmental exposures.
- Children have many years of future life and thus time to develop disease of long latency initiated by early exposures.

Pollution and Childhood Cancer

Recognition is growing that hazardous exposures in the environment are powerful causes of cancer in children. In recent years, medical researchers have identified a number of environmental causes of childhood cancer. For example, maternal exposure to ionizing radiation such as X-rays during pregnancy, and early childhood exposures to CAT scans, have been found to increase risk of childhood leukemia and brain tumors.[17] Prenatal exposure to the synthetic estrogen, diethylstilbestrol

---

[16] See National Research Council, Committee on Pesticides in the Diets of Infants and Children, *Pesticides in the Diets of Infants and Children* (Washington, DC: National Academy Press, 1993).

[17] See Alice Stewart, Josephine Webb, Dawn Giles, and David Hewitt, "Mlignant Disease in Childhood and Diagnostic Irradiation in Utero," *Lancet* 271, no. 6940 (1956): 447, 10.1016/s0140-6736(56)91923-7.

(DES) causes adenocarcinoma of the vagina in young women.[18] In more recent years, robust evidence has emerged for additional links between environmental exposures and childhood cancer. These include associations between traffic-related air pollution,[19] paints, and solvents and elevate risks of leukemia, lymphoma and brain tumors.[20] Prenatal exposures to pesticides are associated with increased incidence of leukemia.[21] Children living in communities surrounded by manufacturing facilities, refineries, or intensive agriculture—where residents are often low-income or people of color—may have particularly high exposures.

Yet these recognized causes of childhood cancer account for only a small fraction of cases. Known carcinogens are used throughout the economy to produce goods and services, but recent research suggests that many chemicals in addition to those known to be carcinogens may contribute to cancer. Because most of these chemicals have never been tested for safety or toxicity, we do not have a comprehensive list of those that may cause cancer in children.[22]

Pollution Control and Cancer Prevention

---

[18] See Arthur L. Herbst, Marian M. Hubby, Freidoon Azizi, and Michael M. Makii, "Reproductive and Gynecologic Surgical Experience in Diethylstilbestrol-Exposed Daughters," *American Journal of Obstetrics and Gynecology* 141, no. 8 (1981): 1019–1028.

[19] See Tommaso Filippini, Elizabeth E. Hatch, Kenneth J. Rothman, Julia E. Heck, Andrew S. Park, Alessio Crippa, Nicola Orsini, and Marco Vinceti, "Association between Outdoor Air Pollution and Childhood Leukemia: A Systematic Review and Dose Response Meta-Analysis," *Environmental Health Perspectives* 127, no. 4 (2019): 10.1289/Ehp4381.

[20] See Frolayne M. Carlos-Wallace, Luoping Zhang, Martyn T. Smith, Gabriella Rader, and Craig Steinmaus, "Parental, in Utero, and Early-Life Exposure to Benzene and the Risk of Childhood Leukemia: A Meta-Analysis," *American Journal of Epidemiology* 183, no. 1 (2016): 1–14.

[21] See Andrew S. Park, Beate Ritz, Fei Yu, Myles Cockburn, and Julia E. Heck, "Prenatal Pesticide Exposure and Childhood Leukemia: A California Statewide Case-Control Study," *International Journal of Hygiene and Environmental Health* 226 (2020): 113486, 10.1016/j.ijheh.2020.113486.

[22] See Landrigan and Goldman, "Children's Vulnerability to Toxic Chemicals: A Challenge and Opportunity to Strengthen Health and Environmental Policy."

A key principle is that pollution can be controlled, and pollution-related cancer can be prevented.[23] The proof of this principle is seen in the experience of the many high-income countries and the increasing number of mid-income countries are making good progress against pollution. These countries have implemented science-based control strategies based on law, policy, and technology backed by effective regulation. As a result of these interventions, pollution-related disease and death rates have fallen sharply. A powerful case study is seen in the declines in asbestos-related cancers in many countries that imposed bans on all import and use of all forms of asbestos.[24] The *Lancet* Commission concluded that these solutions are ready to be globally scaled. The Commission observed that pollution prevention will slow climate change, improve human health, prevent disease, and help build national economies.[25]

Interventions against pollution have proven to be highly cost-effective. They rebut the oft-heard but fallacious claim that pollution control stifles economic growth. In fact, pollution control stimulates growth, creates new jobs, and builds human capital, especially in low-income and middle-income countries by improving health, increasing children's intelligence quotient (IQ), and extending the life span, thus enhancing economic productivity, national security, and human well-being.[26]

Four specific actions needed for prevention of cancers caused by manufactured chemicals are these:

- mandatory premarket testing of chemicals for safety and toxicity before they come to market;

---

[23] See Landrigan et al., "The *Lancet* Commission on Pollution and Health."

[24] See Bengt Jarvholm and Alex Burdorf, "Emerging Evidence That the Ban on Asbestos Use Is educing the Occurrence of Pleural Mesothelioma in Sweden," *Scandinavian Journal of Public Health* 43, no. 8 (2015): 875–881.

[25] See Landrigan et al., "The *Lancet* Commission on Pollution and Health."

[26] See Landrigan et al., "The *Lancet* Commission on Pollution and Health."

- post-market testing of the safety and toxicity of chemicals already on the market starting with those most highly suspect of causing disease;
- deployment of a risk assessment paradigm for cancer prevention that explicitly recognizes the unique vulnerability of fetuses, infants, and e-scale deployment of a risk assessment paradigm that protects the most vulnerable will protect all members of society.
- acting on what we know: reduce exposures to known toxins. Presume that all new chemicals are toxic until they are proven to be safe, a proactive approach to chemical regulation known as the Precautionary Principle.[27]

Conclusion

Prevention of cancer caused by pollution will require ultimately that we confront the social, moral, and economic root causes of pollution—specifically the current, take-make-use-dispose economic paradigm that emphasizes short- term thinking, focuses single-mindedly on gross domestic product (GDP), and extols greed.[28] This worldview sees natural resources and human capital as abundant and expendable and gives little heed to the consequences of their reckless exploitation. It fails to link economic development to social justice or to maintenance of the Earth's resources. Pope Francis has termed this paradigm the "throwaway culture."[29] It is profoundly unethical, and it is not sustainable."[30]

At Boston College, **Philip J. Landrigan**, MD, MSc, FAAP, is Director of the Global Public Health and the Common Good program and director of the Global Observatory on Pollution and Health. He is a pediatrician, public health physician, and epidemiologist. In New York City, he worked for many years in the Icahn School of Medicine at Mount Sinai, and he was involved in the medical and epidemiologic

---

[27] See Jeanne Rizzo, "Cancer Prevention through a Precautionary Approach to Environmental Chemicals: Policy and Research Recommendations for Moving Forward," *Reviews on Environmental Health* 24, no. 4 (2009): 279–286.

[28] See Raworth, *Doughnut Economics.*

[29] See Francis, *Laudato Si'*, nos. 16, 22, 43.

[30] See McMichael, Woodward, and Muir, *Climate Change and the Health of Nations.*

follow-up of 20,000 9/11 rescue workers. From 2015 to 2017, he co-chaired the *Lancet* Commission on Pollution and Health.

Chapter 3: Ethical Spending in Addressing Cancer Treatment, Screening, and Prevention

Arvind Kumar, Raja M. Flores

Focusing on the U.S., Arvind Kumar and Raja Flores discuss the economic aspects that accompany cancer spending in case of prevention, screening, and treatment. While these three facets are all important in promoting patient health and safety, screening and prevention have been shown to have much lower cost compared with cancer therapeutics or in eliminating the health hazards in low- and moderate-income housing in New York City. The distribution of healthcare funds, however, does not accurately reflect the differences in impact on survival and quality of life. Finally, by focusing on treatments, they critically discuss how the increasing use of robotic-assisted surgery—expensive for healthcare facilities—may not be to the benefit of patients.

Lung cancer continues to be the leading cause of cancer-related death worldwide, with 18.0 percent of cancer deaths attributable to this disease.[1] In the U.S. alone, it is estimated that 131,880 people will die from lung cancer in 2021.[2] In light of this vast disease burden, the national government has placed great importance on the treatment and eventual eradication of cancer. From President Richard M. Nixon's (1913–1994) historic signing of the National Cancer Act of 1971, which founded the National Cancer Institute (NCI) and declared the "war on cancer," to President Barack Obama's Cancer Moonshot Task Force in 2016, which projected a pathway to double the rate of progress in cancer prevention,

---

[1] See Hyuna Sung, Jacques Ferlay, Rebecca L. Siegel, Mathieu Laversanne, Isabelle Soerjomataram, Ahmedin Jemal, and Freddie Bray, "Global Cancer Statistics 2020: GLOBOCAN Estimates of Incidence and Mortality Worldwide for 36 Cancers in 185 Countries," CA: A Cancer Journal for Clinicians 71, no. 3 (2021): 209–249.

[2] See Rebecca L. Siegel, Kimberly D. Miller, Hannah E. Fuchs, and Ahmedin Jemal, "Cancer Statistics, 2021," CA: A Cancer Journal for Clinicians 71, no. 1 (2021): 7–33.

diagnosis, and treatment, cancer research has consistently been a government priority. U.S. healthcare spending overall reached $3.8 trillion in 2019, accounting for 17.7 percent of the nation's gross domestic product (GDP), of which $6.56 billion was allotted specifically to the NCI.[3] Notably, this account excludes private sector funding and donations.

Cancer spending can be divided between three areas: treatment, screening (secondary prevention), and prevention (primary prevention). Balanced distribution of funding is crucial given the large sums of money that are invested, yet a number of external factors and competing interests—such as political agendas, private sector profits, and scientific goals—often dictate the direction of spending. This review analyzes the appropriation of funding to these three facets and assesses the cost effectiveness of these investments in the context of patient-related outcomes.

Treatment

Lung cancer treatment consists of a combination of surgery, chemotherapy, and/or radiation therapy, along with newer innovations such as targeted therapy and immunotherapy. For early-stage lung cancer, surgery alone can often be a curative treatment.[4] However, many cases are diagnosed at further stages of progression, requiring medical interventions that introduce associated costs.

Globally, sales of cancer drugs reached $145.4 billion in 2019, far surpassing diabetes drugs, the second highest market with $51 billion in sales. Furthermore, by 2026, this value is expected to more than double to $311.2 billion. The lung cancer drug market specifically is

---

[3] See Anne B. Martin, Micah Hartman, David Lassman, and Aaron Catlin, "National Health Care Spending in 2019: Steady Growth for the Fourth Consecutive Year," *Health Affairs (Millwood)* 40, no. 1 (2021): 14–24.

[4] See Vignesh Raman, Chi-Fu Jeffrey Yang, John Z. Deng, and Thomas A. D'Amico, "Surgical Treatment for Early Stage Non-Small Cell Lung Cancer," *Journal of Thoracic Disease* 10, Suppl. 7 (2018): S898–S904.

projected to generate $8.67 billion in 2021.[5] Cancer drug prices continue to become more expensive as initial list prices increase at an exponential rate and additional post-marketing costs are added on.[6] Between 2009 and 2019, the median price of cancer drugs in the U.S. increased by 152 percent, from $5,790 to $14,580, with certain cancer drugs costing as much as $35,000–$50,000 per month of treatment.[7]

While funds continue to be streamlined towards cancer therapeutics, and cancer drugs become increasingly expensive, we may be misrepresenting their benefit. A study of all cancer therapeutics that were approved by the Food and Drug Administration (FDA) over a five year period between 2008 to 2012 found that 67 percent (36/54) of drugs were approved based on a surrogate end point that was not overall survival, such as response rate or progression- free survival (PFS).[8] Similar findings were published by the *Milwaukee Journal Sentinel* based on an investigation that found 74 percent of cancer drugs over the past decade were approved without clear survival benefit.[9] Although there may be advantages to using

---

[5] See Evaluate Pharma, "Evaluate Pharma World Preview 2020, Outlook to 2026," *Evaluate,* July 16, 2020, www.evaluate.com/thoughtleadership/pharma/evaluatepharma-world-preview-2020-outlook-2026.

[6] See Michail Alevizakos, Apostolos Gaitanidis, and Leonard J. Appleman, "Quantification of the Financial Burden of Antineoplastic Agent Price Increases," Journal of Clinical Oncology 37, no. 15 (2019): doi.org/10.1200/JCO.2019.37.15_suppl.6519; Stacie Dusetzina, Haiden Huskamp, and Nancy Keating, "Specialty Drug Pricing and Out-of-Pocket Spending on Orally Administered Anticancer Drugs in Medicare Part D, 2010 to 2019," JAMA 321, no. 20 (2019): 2025–2027; "Monthly and Median Costs of Cancer Drugs at the Time of FDA Approval 1965–2016," Journal of the National Cancer Institute 109, no. 8 (2017): doi.org/10.1093/jnci/djx173.

[7] See Kerstin N. Vokinger, Thomas J. Hwang, Paola Daniore, ChangWon C. Lee, Ariadna Tibau, Thomas Grischott, Thomas J. Rosemann, and Aaron S. Kesselheim, "Analysis of Launch and Postapproval Cancer Drug Pricing, Clinical Benefit, and Policy Implications in the US and Europe," Jama Oncology 7, no. 9 (2021): doi.org/10.1001/jamaoncol.2021.2026.

[8] See Chul Kim and Vinay Prasad, "Cancer Drugs Approved on the Basis of a Surrogate End Point and Subsequent Overall Survival: An Analysis of 5 Years of US Food and Drug Administration Approvals," JAMA Internal Medicine 175, no. 12 (2015): 1992–1994.

[9] See John Fauber and Elbert Chu, "FDA Approves Cancer Drugs without Proof They're

surrogate end points for FDA approval, patients should be made aware that their new medication with a host of side effects has not been shown to extend their lives. Instead, extensive marketing campaigns use buzzwords such as "breakthrough," "game changer," "miracle," "cure," "revolutionary," "transformative," and "life saver," to promote these new therapeutics.[10]

Concurrently, treatment centers have also increased their direct public advertising, with the hope of increasing awareness and knowledge of available treatments and furthering patient-centered care. In 2014, $173 million was spent in advertising by cancer centers in the U.S. across television, magazines, radio, newspapers, billboards, and the internet, with 86 percent of the total advertising expenditure concentrated among twenty major cancer centers and 59 percent ($101.7 million) of the spending by Cancer Centers of America, a for-profit company with five hospitals.[11] Although such "direct-to-consumer" advertising encourages patient empowerment, research has shown that the advertisements focus on the benefits of therapies more often than the risks, and nearly half include curated patient testimonials that focus on survival or cures rather than typical results and potential disclaimers.[12]

One of the most heavily advertised innovations in cancer treatment is robotic surgery. New developments in minimally invasive surgery techniques in general have offered similar long-term survival, similar or decreased peri-operative mortality, and better patient experiences with complications, pain, hospital length of stay, and quality of life as compared

Extending Lives," *Milwaukee Journal Sentinel*, October 26, 2014, archive.jsonline.com/watchdog/watchdogreports/fda-approves-cancer-drugs-without-proof-theyre-extendinglives b99348000z1-280437692.html/.

[10] See Matthew V. Abola and Vinay Prasad, "The Use of Superlatives in Cancer Research," *JAMA Oncology* 2, no. 1 (2016): 139–141.

[11] See Laura B. Vater, Julie M. Donohue, Seo Young Park, and Yael Schenker, "Trends in Cancer-Center Spending on Advertising in the United States, 2005 to 2014," *JAMA Internal Medicine* 176, no. 8 (2016): 1214–1216.

[12] See Laura B. Vater, Julie M. Donohue, Robert Arnold, Douglas B. White, Edward Chu, and Yael Schenker, "What Are Cancer Centers Advertising to the Public? A Content Analysis," *Annals of Internal Medicine* 160, no. 12 (2014): 813–820.

to traditional open approaches.[13] Over the last 15 years, rates of robotic-assisted minimally invasive surgery have rapidly increased and leading institutions and providers are evaluated based on their use and proficiency with the robot.

Nevertheless, much like many new cancer therapeutics, the emphasis on robotic surgery may not be due to patient benefits. Many studies that support the use of robotic surgery over video-assisted thoracoscopic surgery advocate for benefits in surgical technique including improved visualization of anatomy and easier lymph node dissection, but these factors tend to be surgeon-specific.[14] On the contrary, in 2019, the FDA published a communication that robotic-assisted surgery was not granted marketing authorization for any cancer-related surgery due to unclear survival benefits to patients over other surgical modalities. "We want doctors and patients to be aware of the lack of evidence of safety and effectiveness for these uses so they can make better informed decisions about their cancer treatment and care."[15] Nevertheless, robotic surgeries continue to be performed under "off-label" use, and while this technique can be useful for the properly trained surgeon, patients may not be experiencing additional benefits.

In addition to the lack of supporting evidence that robotic surgery benefits patients, it is quite expensive for healthcare facilities to invest in this technology. Market competition may eventually drive down costs, but

---

[13] See Jacob Klapper and Thomas A. D'Amico, "VATS Versus Open Surgery for Lung Cancer Resection: Moving toward a Minimally Invasive Approach," Journal of the National Comprehensive Cancer Network 13, no. 2 (2015): 162–164.

[14] See Pierluigi Novellis, Marco Alloisio, Elena Vanni, Edoardo Bottoni, Umberto Cariboni, and Giulia Veronesi, "Robotic Lung Cancer Surgery: Review of Experience and Costs," Journal of Visualized Surgery 3(2017): 39, doi.org/10.21037/jovs.2017.03.05.

[15] Stephanie Caccomo, "FDA in Brief: FDA Cautions Patients, Providers About Using Robotically-Assisted Surgical Devices for Mastectomy and Other Cancer-Related Surgeries," U.S. Food & Drug Administration, February 28, 2019, www.fda.gov/news-events/fda-brief/fda-brief-fdacautions-patients-providers-about-using-robotically-assisted-surgical-devices.

at present, the primary manufacturer of surgical robots internationally is Intuitive Surgical, which generates nearly $4.5 billion annually with a market cap of about $120 billion. Research has conflicted on the long-term cost benefit of robotic surgery, and while large tertiary care centers may have the volume to justify expenditures on robotic surgery, adequately sustaining a surgical robot continues to be too expensive for many public hospitals in low-income areas of the world.[16]

Screening

Current screening guidelines for lung cancer, as per the U.S. Preventive Services Task Force, encourage annual screening with low-dose computed tomography (LDCT) in adults aged 50 to 80 years who have a 20 pack-year smoking history and currently smoke or have quit within the past 15 years.[17] Symptoms of lung cancer often present at later stages, but regular screening can identify the disease well before the onset of symptoms and while it is still curable. These screening guidelines are based on the results of two longitudinal studies: the National Lung Screening Trial (NLST) and the International Early Lung Cancer Action Project (I-ELCAP).

The NLST was founded in 2002 by the NCI to compare mortality from lung cancer in patients screened by LDCT versus chest radiography (CXR). 53,454 participants between the ages of 55 and 74 with high-risk smoking history were screened with either LDCT or CXR once per year for three years. Results demonstrated higher rates of positive screening tests amongst the LDCT group, with 12.6 percent more lung cancers diagnosed and a 20.0 percent reduction in lung cancer specific mortality over 7 years.[18]

---

[16] See Novellis et al., "Robotic Lung Cancer Surgery: Review of Experience and Costs."

[17] See U.S. Preventive Services Task Force, "Lung Cancer: Screening," *U.S. Preventive Services Task Force,* March 9, 2021, www.uspreventiveservicestaskforce.org/uspstf/recommendation/lung-cancer-screening#fullrecommendationstart.

[18] See National Lung Screening Trial Research Team, Denise R. Aberle, Amanda M. Adams, Christine D. Berg, William C. Black, Jonathan D. Clapp, Richard M. Fagerstrom, Ilana F. Gareen, Constantine Gatsonis, Pamela M. Marcus, and JoRean D. Sicks, "Reduced Lung-

Similarly, 31,567 asymptomatic at-risk participants were included in the I- ELCAP study and underwent LDCT screening for lung cancer between 1994 and 2005. Results demonstrated that 80 percent of patients with lung cancer diagnosed by screening CT had clinical stage I cancer. Early detection of the disease allowed the majority of these patients to be eligible for treatment, yielding a 10-year survival rate of 88 percent and an even higher 92 percent survival rate amongst the 91 percent of these patients who underwent surgical resection.[19]

The primary findings of these trials support the use of LDCT for lung cancer screening but acknowledge that screening may lead to additional costs for patients and the healthcare system. From the patient perspective, increased screening was shown to result in more frequent false positive results, which can lead to unnecessary further imaging and invasive testing for patients as well as increased anxiety and fear.[20] Studies have shown, however, that despite increased rates of incidental findings and false positives after LDCT screening, overall medical cost to patients remained similar to those screened with CXR.[21]

Medical institutions must also cross the barrier to entry for screening, requiring a well-equipped radiology department and the necessary budget to purchase and maintain CT machines. Funding for the NLST alone reached $250 million, creating hesitancy amongst many providers on the

---

Cancer Mortality with Low-Dose Computed Tomographic Screening," New England Journal of Medicine 365, no. 5 (2011): 395–409.

[19] See International Early Lung Cancer Action Program Investigators, Claudia I. Henschke, David F. Yankelevitz, Daniel M. Libby, Mark W. Pasmantier, James P. Smith, and Olli S. Miettinen, "Survival of Patients with Stage I Lung Cancer Detected on CT Screening," New England Journal of Medicine 355, no. 17 (2006): 1763–1771.

[20] See National Lung Screening Trial Research Team et al., "Reduced Lung-Cancer Mortality with Low-Dose Computed Tomographic Screening."

[21] See Ilana F. Gareen, William C. Black, Tor D. Tosteson, Qianfei Wang, JoRean D. Sicks, and Anna N. A. Tosteson, "Medical Care Costs Were Similar across the Low-Dose Computed Tomography and Chest X-Ray Arms of the National Lung Screening Trial Despite Different Rates of Significant Incidental Findings," Medical Care 56, no. 5 (2018): 403–409.

value of screening.[22] Nevertheless, unlike with robotic surgery, many studies have shown that lung cancer screening can be performed in a cost-effective manner that also benefits patients, largely due to the proven survival benefit.

Current estimates for the cost effectiveness of CT screening vary but remain within the limits of conventionally accepted cost-effectiveness threshold of $50,000–$109,000 per quality-adjusted life years (QALY) gained.[23] In analysis conducted by the NLST, LDCT cost an additional $1,631 per person and $81,000 per QALY, with additional variability amongst subgroups.[24] One study by Andrea Villanti and colleagues found that the cost of annual screening for a hypothetical population of eighteen million adults at high risk for lung cancer was about $1.85 billion per year over fifteen years and yielded a cost- utility ratio of $28,240 per QALY. This compares with the $8.67 billion generated by lung cancer drugs in 2021 alone. Increasing overall survival and QALY amongst this population was also estimated to increase the national GDP by $10.6

[22] See National Lung Screening Trial Research Team, Denise R. Aberle, Christine D. Berg, William C. Black, Timothy R. Church, Richard M. Fagerstrom, Barbara Galen, Ilana F. Gareen, Constantine Gatsonis, Jonathan Goldin, John K. Gohagan, Bruce Hillman, Carl Jaffe, Barnett S. Kramer, David Lynch, Pamela M. Marcus, Mitchell Schnall, Daniel C. Sullivan, Dorothy Sullivan, and Carl J. Zylak, "The National Lung Screening Trial: Overview and Study Design," Radiology 258, no. 1 (2011): 243–253; Katherine Bourzac, "Diagnosis: Early Warning System," Nature 513, no. 7517 (2014): S4–S6.

[23] See Andrea C. Villanti, Yiding Jiang, David B. Abrams, and Bruce S. Pyenson, "A Cost-Utility Analysis of Lung Cancer Screening and the Additional Benefits of Incorporating Smoking Cessation Interventions," PLoS One 8, no. 8 (2013): e71379, doi.org/10.1371/journal.pone.0071379. In healthcare literature, the QALY (quality-adjusted life year or quality-adjusted life-year) is a generic measure of disease burden, which depends on the assessment of the quality and length of life lived, combined in a single number.

[24] See William C. Black, Ilana F. Gareen, Samir S. Soneji, JoRean D. Sicks, Emmett B. Keeler, Denise R. Aberle, Arash Naeim, Timothy R. Church, Gerard A. Silvestri, Jeremy Gorelick, Constantine Gatsonis, and National Lung Screening Trial Research Team, "Cost-Effectiveness of CT Screening in the National Lung Screening Trial," New England Journal of Medicine 371, no. 19 (2014): 1793–1802.

billion and recover $0.38 per every one dollar spent on lung cancer screening.[25]

Prevention

Environmental exposures are directly linked to the incidence of lung cancer, with cigarette smoking as the most important risk factor.[26] Smoking has been shown to explain almost 90 percent of lung cancer risk in men and 70–80 percent in women.[27] In patients who do not smoke, there is still a high risk of developing lung cancer after exposure to second-hand smoke, radon, asbestos, and other environmental toxins. In 1964, the U.S. Surgeon General published the *Smoking and Health* report, the first public health advisory on the impact of cigarette smoking.[28] Since then, smoking rates have fallen from about 43 percent to about 14 percent (as of 2019). Nevertheless, the Centers for Disease Control and Prevention (CDC) reports that each day, 3,200 new youth start smoking, and with the introduction of alternative smoking methods, such as vaping and flavored tobacco products, lung cancer risk continues to be a prominent public health issue.[29]

---

[25] See Villanti, Jiang, Abrams, and Pyenson, "A Cost-Utility Analysis of Lung Cancer Screening and the Additional Benefits of Incorporating Smoking Cessation Interventions."

[26] See Tonya Walser, Xiaoyan Cui, Jane Yanagawa, Jay M. Lee, Eileen Heinrich, Gina Lee, Sherven Sharma, and Steven M. Dubinett, "Smoking and Lung Cancer: The Role of Inflammation," Proceedings of the American Thoracic Society 5, no. 8 (2008): 811–815.

[27] See Danny R. Youlden, Susanna M. Cramb, and Peter D. Baade, "The International Epidemiology of Lung Cancer: Geographical Distribution and Secular Trends," Journal of Thoracic Oncology 3, no. 8 (2008): 819–831.

[28] See United States, Surgeon General's Advisory Committee on Smoking and Health, Smoking and Health: Report of the Advisory Committee to the Surgeon General of the Public Health Service, Public Health Service Publication No. 1103 (Washington, DC: U.S. Department of Health, Education, and Welfare, Public Health Service, 1964).

[29] See National Center for Chronic Disease Prevention and Health Promotion, Office on Smoking and Health, *The Health Consequences of Smoking—50 Years of Progress: A Report of the Surgeon General* (Atlanta, GA: Centers for Disease Control and Prevention, 2014); National Center for Chronic Disease Prevention and Health Promotion, Office on Smoking and Health, "Current Cigarette Smoking among Adults in the United States," *Centers for*

Given that these environmental causes of lung cancer are preventable, the market size for cancer therapeutics and funding for screening begets the question, is the same level of concern and support given towards cancer prevention? From a financial perspective, many of the studies that highlighted the cost-effectiveness of lung cancer screening also show that the addition of smoking cessation programs results in reduced cost-utility ratios. Villanti and colleagues show a decreased price per QALY from $28,240 with screening alone   to $16,198–$23,185   after   adding smoking   cessation   programs.[30] Smoking cessation would also save the U.S. more than $300 billion per year in smoking-related illness expenses and lost productivity. Tobacco companies continue to profit, however, spending $8.2 billion in marketing in the U.S. in 2019 resulting in sales of nearly 250 billion cigarettes and a market size of over $900 billion.[31]

Low-income households are at especially high risk for developing adverse health effects due to increased exposure to second-hand smoke and other toxins. Many of these effects would be preventable with adequate maintenance and funding of public housing. While certain actions have been taken, especially with the 2018 U.S. Department of Housing and Urban Development rule that required smoke-free housing policies be implemented by all public housing authorities, there is still room to improve.

Case Analysis: New York City Housing Authority Public Housing

The New York City Housing Authority (NYCHA) is the oldest and largest public housing authority in the United States, with the goal of providing decent,   affordable   housing   for   low-   and   moderate-

---

Disease Control and Prevention, December 10, 2020, www.cdc.gov/tobacco/data_statistics/fact_sheets/adult_data/cig_smoking/index.htm.

[30] See Villanti, Jiang, Abrams, and Pyenson, "A Cost-Utility Analysis of Lung Cancer Screening and the Additional Benefits of Incorporating Smoking Cessation Interventions."

[31] See National Center for Chronic Disease Prevention and Health Promotion, Office on Smoking and Health, "Economic Trends in Tobacco," Centers for Disease Control and Prevention, March 25, 2021, www.cdc.gov/tobacco/data_statistics/fact_sheets/economics/econ_facts/index.htm.

income residents throughout New York City. NYCHA's 335 public housing developments house over 500,000 people across the five boroughs of New York City.[32] Unfortunately, deteriorating living conditions including, but not limited to, mold, asbestos, lead, pest infestation, and second- or third-hand cigarette smoke, marijuana, and/or vaping have resulted in unsafe living conditions for tenants for years.

Over the course of 2018, Community Voices Heard (CVH), a grassroots organization founded by NYCHA resident leaders, and Regional Plan Association (RPA) engaged in a door-to-door survey documenting health and living conditions in NYCHA housing in Far Rockaway, New York. Major takeaways from this survey were that 81 percent of residents needed immediate repairs to their apartment and that the poor living conditions negatively impacted physical health in 25 percent of respondents and mental health in 33 percent of respondents. When asked about the presence of various toxins in their apartments, 15 percent of respondents reported lead, 13 percent reported asbestos, 32 percent reported visible mold, and 31 percent reported leaks, with potentially more unaware. Little or incomplete efforts were provided by NYCHA management to address these issues, with residents having nowhere else to turn.[33]

New York State Department of Health's assessment of NYCHA housing had similar findings, with 83 percent of apartments and 75 percent of common areas inspected having at least one severe condition that could pose a health hazard to tenants. A majority of areas had more than one environmental quality issue including water intrusion damage, chipping and peeling paint, damaged plaster, mold, insect and/or

---

[32] See New York City Housing Authority, "NYCHA 2021 Fact Sheet," New York City Housing Authority, March 2021, www1.nyc.gov/assets/nycha/downloads/pdf/NYCHA-Fact-Sheet_2021.pdf.

[33] See Moses Gates, "The Impacts of Living in NYCHA: Needs for Resident Health in the Rockaways and Beyond," *Regional Plan Association,* July 2020, rpa.org/work/reports/nycha-resident-needs-assessment.

rodent infestations, inoperable appliances, and malfunctioning or missing smoke and carbon monoxide detectors.[34]

According to NYCHA estimates in 2020, of the 175,000 apartments, 62,000 are receiving full repairs, while $18 billion is required to stabilize the remaining 110,000 apartments. Only $3.3 billion had been secured by NYCHA at that time.[35] Despite public awareness efforts and reports to government organizations, NYCHA residents have been left to tend to the repairs by themselves. While the residents lead initiatives to improve their own housing quality, governmental organizations and NYCHA have largely only followed.

Conclusion

Breaking down expenditure on lung cancer identifies three areas of focus: treatment, screening, and prevention. While these three facets are all important in promoting patient health and safety, from a utility perspective, screening and prevention have been shown to have much lower cost per QALY added compared with cancer therapeutics. The distribution of funding, however, does not accurately reflect the differences in impact on survival and quality of life. Over the last decade, lung cancer screening has gained significant prevalence since the NLST and I-ELCAP trials indicated earlier detection of lung cancer and better long-term survival for at-risk patients who undergo annual LDCT scans. Studies have also shown that integrating preventive measures with screening trials is not only cost-effective but also beneficial for patient health.

While smoking rates have declined over the last fifty years, the tobacco industry still generates exorbitant amounts of money, spending over $8 billion annually on marketing. Meanwhile, environmental factors that further increase risk of lung cancer and other health outcomes continue

---

[34] See New York State Department of Health, "Assessment of New York City Housing Authority (NYCHA) Properties," March 2018, www.governor.ny.gov/sites/default/files/atoms/files/FINAL_Assessment_of_NYCHA_Report.pdf.

[35] See New York City Housing Authority, "A Blueprint for Change," *New York City Housing Authority,* 2020, www1.nyc.gov/site/nycha/residents/blueprint-for-change.page.

to plague our most at-risk populations. In NYCHA public housing, for example, blueprints have been created that indicate $18 billion would be needed to install repairs that would directly decrease rates of lung cancer as well as asthma, diabetes, obesity, heart disease, and infections, yet only $3.3 billion had been secured. In contrast, $8.67 billion is spent on the lung cancer drug industry worldwide (as part of the $150 billion spent on all cancer therapeutics), with patients unaware that some of these lauded drugs may not improve overall survival. This current misappropriation of funding towards initiatives that are driven by business, political, and scientific agendas, ignores the underlying causes of poor health outcomes and undermines our goals in addressing cancer.

Arvind Kumar is a medical student at the Icahn School of Medicine, in New York City, on a research fellowship year with the Mount Sinai Center for Clinical Informatics and Hasso Plattner Institute for Digital Health at the Mount Sinai.

Raja M. Flores, M.D., is the Chairman of the Department of Thoracic Surgery, and Steven and Ann Ames Professor in Thoracic Surgery at the Mount Sinai Medical Center. He is a recognized leader in the field of thoracic surgery for his pioneering efforts in the treatment of mesothelioma and implemented the current program for this procedure at Memorial Sloan-Kettering Cancer Center.

Chapter 4: Health Care Access and Coverage for Cancer Patients: An Ethical Imperative

Lilian Ferrer, Rodrigo López, Francisca López, María Isabel Catoni

The ethical imperative voiced by colleagues from the Universidad Católica de Chile stresses the urgency of providing universal access to healthcare services on a global scale because health is a social good and a social right. On the one hand, health systems should promote innovations because they will contribute to greater sustainability and foster the sharing of health benefits to the different communities in the world. On the other hand, in healthcare practice, it is necessary to create more inclusive models of care that reach out to larger sectors of the population. Finally, interdisciplinary work is necessary to provide comprehensive care, considering the social determinants of health in the diverse social contexts where people live.

Globalization allows us to be more connected and have a better access to information among different countries. By this, problems around the world are known and comparisons between different cultures, populations, and communities are ineluctable. Focusing solely on the people, we can see that each one has personal resources available, but, at the same time, the environment in which they live will determine the level of health and risk factors and daily habits, that is, the social determinants of health. Culture is a strong determinant in the health of the population, but there are diseases that are transverse to it, such as cancer. Today, cancer is one of the leading causes of death worldwide. When considering the population growth rate, new sedentary lifestyles and aging, an increase of approximately 60 percent in the number of cases is projected, being estimated up to 81 percent only in middle- and low-income countries by the year 2040.[1]

Aging is a great challenge given that oncological problems occur more frequently in older people and that there is a change in the form of treatment, because chemotherapy and radiotherapy are being preferentially performed through ambulatory care, which allows reducing the costs associated with hospitalization. However, this approach requires nursing care or management of side effects at home, which ultimately results in a constant technological advance in care or interventions.[2]

These aspects unveil global and local differences between countries and communities given that populations in situations of vulnerability present lower quality of life, which will translate into aging in unfavorable conditions. If we add that homes do not have basic services or are exposed to pollutants, it will be more difficult for patients to recover from their health condition in an ambulatory way.

In relation to technological advances, even if they are available, not all people will have access to them in a fair way because they are not available in their country or have a high cost, among other reasons. The above scenarios show us that inequities have serious consequences, even more so if we consider access to health as a right for all people in the world. This means that all people, despite their genetics and lifestyle, may have the possibility of accessing interventions for promotion, prevention, rehabilitation, diagnosis or treatment.

This right of the most vulnerable people is a fraternal duty of all of us who live together in this "common home."

---

[1] Solange Parra-Soto, Fanny Petermann-Rocha, María Adela Martínez-Sanguinetti, Ana María Leiva-Ordeñez, Claudia Troncoso-Pantoja, Natalia Ulloa, Ximena Díaz-Martínez, and Carlos Celis-Morales, "Cáncer en Chile y en el Mundo: Una Mirada Actual y Su Futuro Escenario Epidemiológico," Revista Médica de Chile 148, no. 10 (2020): 1489–1495.
[2] Sanchia Aranda, "Creating Innovation in Cancer Care Delivery," Asia-Pacific Journal of Oncology Nursing 5, no. 2 (2018): 134–136.

> The ethical relevance of the good of health is such as to motivate a strong commitment to its *protection* and *treatment* by society itself. It is a duty of solidarity that excludes no one, not even those responsible for the loss of their own health. The ontological dignity of the person is in fact superior: it transcends his or her erroneous or sinful forms of behavior. Treating disease and doing one's best to prevent it are ongoing tasks for the individual and for society, precisely as a tribute to the dignity of the person and the importance of the good of health.[3]

Health, as a social right, means that everyone should receive care according to their needs. The ethic of public health is to protect and provide coverage to the essential collective needs of people.[4] It also adds the fundamental ethical principles, including: protection, which ensures welfare, meaning that the state must respond to unpostponable needs; justice, which considers equity in the application of policies, strategies, and actions, with emphasis on the most vulnerable to avoid discrimination and unequal distribution of opportunities; reciprocity, considered as compensation for damages through a balance between benefits and burdens and as creating support measures for communities facing a situation of lower health protection; and accountability, being able to answer for the consequences of decisions.[5]

---

[3] John Paul II, "Letter to the President of the Pontifical Academy for Life on the Occasion of a Study Congress on 'Quality of Life and Ethics of Health,'" February 19, 2005, www.vatican.va/content/john-paul-ii/en/letters/2005/documents/hf_jp-ii_let_20050219_pont-acad-life.html.

[4] María Cristina Paredes, Karen Pesse, and Ximena Barros, "Ética de la Salud Pública: Propuesta Sobre los Principios Fundamentales Que Guían las Responsabilidades Éticas del Estado en el Contexto Pandemia COVID-19," *Revista Médica de Chile* 148, no. 10 (2020): 1481–1488.

[5] Paredes, Pesse, and Barros, "Etica de la Salud Publica: Propuesta Sobre los Principios Fundamentales Que Guian las Responsabilidades Eticas del Estado en el Contexto Pandemia COVID-19"; Fermin Roland Schramm and Miguel Kottow, "Principios Bioeticos en Salud Publica: Limitaciones y Propuestas [Bioethical Principles in Public Health: Limitations and Proposals]," *Cadernos de Saude Publica* 17, no. 4 (2001): 949–956; World Health Organization, "Guidance for Managing Ethical Issues in Infectious Disease Outbreaks," 2016, apps.who.int/iris/bitstream/handle/10665/250580/9789241549837eng.pdf?sequence=1&isAllowed=y.

Another relevant aspect is the difficult decision on where to put the focus. This is the classic dilemma of whether to spend more on health promotion and disease prevention or on the treatment of patients already diagnosed. It is a relevant problem since protecting tomorrow's potential patients at the cost of suffering or shortening the lives of today's patients is difficult to justify. It is necessary to find strategies that adequately combine both aspects, using human resources with advanced competencies at both the primary and secondary levels of care.

Positioning ourselves in the context of care for people with cancer, we can see that protection, justice, reciprocity, and responsibility are not fully achieved in many situations, since there is a delay in care concerning timely diagnosis and access to effective treatment. There is an unequal distribution of opportunities: there are countries where medical care is scarce or, within the same nation, urbanized areas concentrate the greatest supply of health services and benefits compared to more rural areas, generating differences that have a negative impact on health due only to where you live.

This is also contrasted with the characteristics of the communities. Culture is a significant factor when it comes to implementing care or proposing new behaviors, since cultural factors are immersed in life habits and personal beliefs. For example, environmental management, whether it is considered globally, aimed at pollution, or locally, utilizing resources or services available to communities, has cultural implications on health management.[6]

Tumas, Pou, and del Pilar Díaz point out that biological, genetic, and environmental factors cause differences in risk, incidence, diagnosis, treatment, survival, and mortality in people with breast cancer.[7] Other factors are aging, urbanization and fertility. In relation to urbanization,

---

[6] Aranda, "Creating Innovation in Cancer Care Delivery."

[7] Natalia Tumas, Sonia Alejandra Pou, and Maria del Pilar Diaz, "Inequidades en Salud: Analisis Sociodemografico y Espacial del Cancer de Mama en Mujeres de Cordoba, Argentina [Inequities in Health: Socio-Demographic and Spatial Analysis of Breast Cancer in Women from Cordoba, Argentina]," *Gaceta Sanitaria* 31, no. 5 (2017): 396–403.

we can see that the incidence rate of breast cancer is higher in urban areas, which is partly explained by a higher detection of cases. Urbanization leads to less healthy diets and less physical activities, and together with poverty, it is identified as a sociodemographic determinant of breast cancer incidence.

In Colombia, oral cancer has a higher incidence in the older adult population, in urban areas, and in situations of poverty or vulnerability. Moreover, this high incidence also highlights the presence of possible barriers of access to health services, which prevents timely diagnosis and treatment and frequently leads to finding the pathology in more advanced stages.[8]

In Chile, cancer is included in the program of Explicit Health Guarantees (GES), which assures access, opportunity, financial protection, and quality of care for certain types of cancer. However, this program focuses on treatment, not prevention. In addressing health problems, social responsibility has driven international research, and, at the same time, it allowed cross-cultural comparisons. Caring for affected people implies considering the people's culture, given that an understanding of the context is required for research, care, and for any type of advance that will have a beneficial impact on the population.[9]

Being a member of a society entails a mutual obligation to foster relationships between different people from all parts of the world. In addition, there are connected institutions and practices that are influencing each other in performing actions and having obligations of justice that arise between people by social processes. The social connectedness model points out that all agents contribute to the structural

---

[8] Adriana Posada-Lopez, Marta Aida Palacio-Correa, and Andres A. Agudelo-Suarez, Caracteristicas Sociodemograficas y Clinicas de los Pacientes Tratados por Primera Vez por Cancer Escamocelular Oral. Medellin, Colombia," *International Journal of Odontostomatology* 12, no. 3 (2018): 237–245.

[9] Margaret Lombe, Chrisann Newransky, Tom Crea, and Anna Stout, "From Rhetoric to Reality: Planning and Conducting Collaborations for International Research in the Global South," Social Work 58, no. 1 (2013): 31–40.

processes they produce.[10] This means that even if one lives in an area with abundant resources and services, including health, one must still contribute to social equality.

Within this responsibility, we can consider innovation as a resource to which people should contribute. This approach, when applied to healthcare, ensures that treatments and care should be available to all people, including the most vulnerable and hard-to-reach populations.[11] Belonging to a society, a nation or community makes us part of a collective where we are in constant contact with other people and have a responsibility to address the social problems we face, including health problems.

Hence, why are there differences in disease outcomes? For the Pan American Health Organization (PAHO), a population's health is linked to the socioeconomic situation, the cultural context, and the social values fostered by governmental and private actions.[12] Knowing the impact of socio-demographic factors and the environment, it is necessary to implement a preventive care model able to reduce the incidence of cancer and detect cancer in early stages to achieve a better cancer prognosis.

For health systems, on the one hand, it is fundamental to promote innovations because they will contribute to greater sustainability and foster the sharing of health benefits to the different communities in the world.[13] When we consider innovation in cancer care, we can refer to the initiative promoted by PAHO to support advanced practice nursing in Latin America. Moreover, it is essential to promote interdisciplinary work teams

---

[10] Iris Marion Young, "Responsibility and Global Justice: A Social Connection Model," *Social Philosophy & Policy* 23, no. 1 (2006): 102–130.

[11] Beatrice Halpaap, Rosanna W. Peeling, and Francois Bonnici, "The Role of Multilateral Organizations and Governments in Advancing Social Innovation in Health Care Delivery," *Infectious Diseases of Poverty* 8, no. 1 (2019): 81, 10.1186/s40249-019-0592-y.

[12] Organización Panamericana de la Salud, ed., La Salud y los Derechos Humanos: Aspectos Éticos y Morales, Publicacíon Científica No. 574 (Washington, DC: Organización Panamericana de la Salud, 1999).

[13] Halpaap, Peeling, and Bonnici, "The Role of Multilateral Organizations and Governments."

that could address all aspects of people's lives and thus make possible a care that is adapted to people's particular reality.

On the other hand, there are efforts to create more inclusive models of care that reach out to larger sectors of the population. In Chile, advanced practice nursing centered on oncology was promoted in order to reduce problems of access and coverage, by training healthcare professionals with the ability to diagnose, treat, and follow up. This approach helps to reduce the current gap in oncology specialists. Working complementarily with a consolidated oncology medical team, nurses expand care opportunities for patients. In Chile, the contributions of the nursing profession have been incorporated in the National Cancer Plan 2018–2028 and in the National Cancer Law, enacted on October 2, 2020.[14]

Within the problems of access and coverage, the great territorial extent of Chile makes having oncology care centers in all regions of the country strategically impossible. This limitation requires that people travel from one region to another to have access to treatment options, with greater difficulty for the elderly or people with disabilities. Therefore, it is expected that promoting nurses with advanced skills and expertise will facilitate a greater distribution of specialized care throughout Chile and, at the same time, will contribute to diagnosis in early stages of the disease, which will improve the life expectancy of patients.

More generally, interdisciplinary work is necessary to provide comprehensive care, considering the people's social context for determining the level of health care required. Poverty inhibits access to basic resources, like housing and food, that, in the case of an oncology patient, must be in optimal condition to avoid complications associated with the treatments. Likewise, poor people are caught in a vicious circle: Poverty generates ill health and ill health maintains poverty.[15] An appeal by Mother

---

[14] Ministerio de Salud, "Ley N. 21.258: Crea La Ley Nacional del Cancer, Que Rinde Homenaje Postumo al Doctor Claudio Mora," 2020, www.bcn.cl/leychile/navegar?idNorma=1149004.

[15] Adam Wagstaff, "Pobreza y Desigualdades en el Sector de la Salud," *Revista Panamericana de la Salud Publica* 11, nos. 5–6 (2002): 316–326.

Teresa of Calcutta states that poverty has not been created by God but by us because of our selfishness. In today's globalized world, in which diseases that affect poorer or less developed countries can affect the entire planet, we must care about the health of the most vulnerable as a matter of social justice and care for our home, the common home.

It is necessary to consider the cost-effectiveness of preventive programs, given that by investing in health promotion and disease prevention, they reach a large number of the population and fewer resources are spent at the hospital level. For the measures to be effective, they must be carried out with cultural competence. The health professional must consider the beliefs of the community to which he/she has to deliver health care since personal ideas in relation to the disease have a strong impact on adherence to treatment or healthy lifestyle habits.

Interesting is the perspective of Donald Berwick. He proposes that the major investment should be made in correcting the social determinants of health and not in continuing to build and provide care in large and expensive "repair workshops." These do not address low investment in health promotion and so fail to change human well-being.[16] Thus, he proposes to base the motivation to change human well-being in health on what he calls the moral determinants of health, among which the most important is a strong sense of social solidarity in which people understand that they depend on each other to ensure the health of all.

In summary, globalization has allowed us to have a great connection between countries and communities, which has allowed us to know the impact that some diseases like cancer have around the world, and at the same time, has generated international collaboration through research, being able to know different realities, differentiating people according to their culture. However, as there are differences, we can see that not all people have the same access to health care at any level, violating fundamental ethical values. By having a social responsibility in the face of these disparities,

---

[16] Donald M. Berwick, "The Moral Determinants of Health," *JAMA* 324, no. 3 (2020): 225–226.

we hope to continue contributing through innovation to better health care and the reduction of gaps in access and coverage. Among the countries following this line of action is Chile with the advanced practice nursing initiative.

It is expected that models of care will be created with preventive and intercultural approaches, while considering sociocultural factors. This motivation is aligned with the words of Pope Francis: "It is impossible to be 'local' in a healthy way without being sincerely open to the universal, without feeling challenged by what is happening in other places, without openness to enrichment by other cultures, and without solidarity and concern for the tragedies affecting other peoples" (*Fratelli Tutti*, no. 146).

Lilian Ferrer, RN, MSc, PhD, FAAN, is Vice President for International Affairs at the Pontificia Universidad Católica de Chile. She is a UC midwife and earned a Master of Science in Nursing and a doctorate in Public Health from the University of Illinois, Chicago.

Rodrigo López, MD, MSc, PhD, Associate Professor in the Faculty of Medicine of the Pontificia Universidad Católica de Chile. He is also member of Institutional Review Board and Director of the Cardiovascular Anesthesiology Scholarship Program.

Francisca López, MSc(c) is pursuing a master's in nursing at the Pontificia Universidad Católica de Chile.

María Isabel Catoni, RN, MA, is Professor and Director of the Nursing School at the Pontificia Universidad Católica de Chile.

Part 2
Social Concerns
and
Strategies

Chapter 5: Cancer, Global, Pandemic, Health, Ethics, and Social Justice: A Meditation on Some Five-Letter Words that Are Pervasive Accelerants

Richard J. Jackson

In reflecting on cancers, Richard Jackson stresses the serious social harms caused by inadequate prevention and, within the social fabric, he examines what he calls the "cancer accelerants:" water, power, money, and greed. They are four specific factors that require ethical attention. Water powerfully influences past and future health and well-being, for human beings and for the planet. Water conflicts are ethically troubling. Powers at play within the medical/industrial complex lead to further power imbalances in the social fabric, which are increased and worsened by structural racism and systemic impoverishment. Money further complicates any attempt to promote greater social justice whether one considers, on the one hand, financial interests and, on the other hand, lack of financial resources and poverty. Finally, greed poisons human and social interactions by inhibiting virtuous behaviors and choices, both at the personal and social level.

Billions of dollars have been spent investigating the genetic and biological causes of cancer. The National Cancer Institute alone has funded $27 billion over the last five years, and far more is spent on treatment.[1] These expenditures are understandable. Cancer kills 600,000 Americans a year and brings immense suffering as well as social and economic costs.[2] At the same time, the narrow focus on, and support of, the model of "the brilliant researcher in a well- funded laboratory working to save lives" is an overly narrow and badly diversified

---

[1] See National Cancer Institute, "NCI Funding Trends," January 12, 2021, www.cancer.gov/about-nci/budget/fact-book/historical-trends/funding#funding.

[2] See Center for Disease Control and Prevention, "Leading Causes of Death," *National Center for Health Statistics,* October 19, 2021, www.cdc.gov/nchs/fastats/leading-causes-of-death.htm. See also Christian Cintron's chapter in this volume.

investment. Reflecting on the broad agenda of the global cancer pandemic, with its many strands of causation and approaches, I propose there are some five-letter words that weave these strands and approaches together.

I affirm this as a physician with a long public health career committed to reducing risks to health from the environment, including tracking and reducing exposure to carcinogens. As my admired colleague Dr. Kenneth Olden, former Director of the National Institute of Environmental Health Sciences, observed: "The genes load the gun, but the environment pulls the trigger." I worked hard in establishing childhood cancer and birth defect registries, on reducing health risks from pesticides, and in reducing chemical exposures by measuring the levels of chemicals in the bodies of a large sample of Americans. More recently, I have focused on the ways the built environment—how we build our homes, neighborhoods, and transportation systems—influences our health, often in ways we barely perceive.

It may seem that to improve the health of all we need more and better science. This is only partially true. Quadrupling health expenditures from one to nearly four trillion dollars a year has failed both for those who need care and those who provide care. More harmful are the science deniers, the disease- and vaccine-deniers and political and internet manipulators, who have harmed us and our neighbors. This was clearly the case with COVID-19. Look at the death rates in refuser communities. The serious harm from inadequate prevention is also true for cancer. I suggest that the triggers common to and accelerating both of these failures can be explained in a few five letter words.

Water

The first of the five letter words is *water*. This is a reflection on my living in the western United States where water powerfully influences past and future health and well-being. While the Northeast and the Gulf Coast of the U.S. are coping with too much water, we in the Southwest must confront too little drinking water, not enough for bathing, irrigating fields, and raising livestock. Los Angeles, the immense, second-largest city in the U.S., was founded in part because of its location on the Los Angeles River. As with all other great cities, early civic leaders realized that the city would languish without vast supplies of water from distant places, in this case, the Colorado River, the Owens Valley, and the western slope of the Sierra. California spent billions in capturing freshwater runoff and delivering it to Los Angeles and to the state's farms. California now directs 20 percent of its electrical power merely to pump water. Diminished West Coast precipitation and a reduced snowpack are making fresh water far more precious. Now, as you drive the major north-south freeway in California, you see newly desertified fields and dead orchards.

Water challenges foreshadow planetary collapse. At the time of the first moon walk in 1969, there were 3.5 billion people on the planet. Today there are 7.6 billion.[3] The planet's level of CO_2 in the atmosphere has gone from about 324 to 414 ppm,[4] causing the earth to become hotter with droughts. Wildfires and storms are becoming increasingly more lethal with "once in a century storms" becoming nearly annual events. When I speak about this, I try not to use the word *warming*. It does not capture the malignant power of a 2-degree C° increase in average global temperature. This increase is just the beginning. Water access will become a powerful trigger worldwide for political conflicts, often because of too little water, as from the melting of glaciers on the planet's "third pole," namely the Himalayan Hindu Kush that supplies water to 1.3 billion people.[5] As great a threat that drought is, too much water will be life

---

[3] See United Nations Department of Economic and Social Affairs and Population Division, "World Population Prospects 2019: Online Edition. Rev. 1," 2019, population.un.org/wpp/Download/Standard/Population/.

[4] See CO2-Earth, "Latest Daily Co2," 2021, www.co2.earth/daily-co2.

[5] See Arnico K. Panday, "Melting Glaciers, Threatened Livelihoods: Confronting Climate Change to Save the Third Pole," *United Nations Development Programme, Regional Bureau for Asia and the Pacific: Strategy, Policy and Partnerships,* June 3, 2021, www.asia-

destroying, with seawater inundation and submersion of productive agricultural areas, for example in Bangladesh and other areas in Southeast Asia. The United States Intelligence Report asserts that drought and flooding resulting from climate heating are threat multipliers and anticipates that they will lead to political conflicts and immense population migrations.[6]

Power

I believe the second five letter word is *power*. I have often thought about how water and power in California are nearly synonymous. Power, especially the lack of it, relates to cancer. The continued use of carcinogenic chemicals over the years and in many geographic areas is the product of the political power of the manufacturers and distributors and the agriculture industry.

While considering powerful industries in the United States, I must include the medical/industrial complex, which accounts for 18 percent the U.S. Domestic Product and employs about 9 percent of its workforce. It also produces about 8 percent of the U.S. climate-forcing greenhouse gases. A different form of power shapes cancer mortality, and the rates are higher in areas with limited economic power, which are often marginalized because of race. Those with less power and resources have higher smoking levels and poorer quality food and are more likely to work in hazardous settings and to have earlier disabilities. Medicine has known for two hundred years that exposure to coal tars raises the risk of cancer, and yet as we speak, there are increasing political efforts globally to return to high rates of mining of cancer-causing agents like asbestos.

Power imbalance by using more advanced weapons facilitated colonialist expansion and was enabled by racist tropes to deny humanity

---

pacific.undp.org/content/rbap/en/home/library/human_development/policy-brief-confronting-climate-change-to-save-the-third-pole.html.
[6] See Office of the Director of National Intelligence, "2021 Annual Threat Assessment of the U.S. Intelligence Community," April 9, 2021, www.dni.gov/files/ODNI/documents/assessments/ATA-2021-Unclassified-Report.pdf.

to those seen as "the other." When working conditions were intolerable—for example in sugarcane and cotton harvesting in the tropics—colonial power created a demand for economic and legislative human exploitation in the form of slavery. The cancer rates of those with low power are always higher than those of the plantation or factory owner. A leading destroyer of our health, and of capital and happiness, is structural racism and structural impoverishment. Think of the massacre and fires in 1921 of the "Black Wall Street" in Tulsa,[7] and of generationally impoverished families deprived of access to decent homes, neighborhoods, jobs, and family farms. Since 1980, the United States there has seen an acceleration in the assets of the very wealthy,[8] but no adjusted improvement of wages for the middle class, and a near flat line for the poor. Poverty remains pervasive and the condition of nearly 1 in 7 of our children.[9] In 1970, health care costs were about 7 percent of the Gross Domestic Product (GDP) and today they exceed 17.7 percent.[10] And while we have made scientific progress, I and many of my clinical colleagues are more concerned today than in the past about loved ones who must enter the "health system" than we were 40 years ago. It breaks my heart to see primary care physicians pushed to care for more than five patients an hour and dedicated nurses who need their unions to bargain for properly apportioned patient loads. The local hospital near where I live was taken

---

[7] See Yuliya Parshina-Kottas, Anjali Singhvi, Audra D.S. Burch, Troy Griggs, Mika Grondahl, Lingdong Huang, Tim Wallace, Jeremy White, and Josh Williams, "What the Tulsa Race Massacre Destroyed," *New York Times*, May 24, 2021, www.nytimes.com/interactive/2021/05/24/us/tulsa-race-massacre.html.

[8] See Thomas Piketty, Emmanuel Saez, and Gabriel Zucman, "Distributional National Accounts: Methods and Estimates for the United States," November 2016, gabriel-zucman.eu/files/PSZ2018Slides.pdf.

[9] See Children's Defense Fund: Leave No Children Behind, "The State of America's Children 2021," 2021, www.childrensdefense.org/wpcontent/ uploads/2021/04/The-State-of-Americas-Children-2021.pdf.

[10] See Rabah Kamal, Daniel McDermott, Giorlando Ramirez, and Cynthia Cox, "How Has U.S. Spending on Healthcare Changed over Time?," *Peterson-KFF Health System Tracker,* December 23, 2020, www.healthsystemtracker.org/chart-collection/u-s-spending-healthcare-changedtime/#item-usspendingovertime_2.

over by a large chain that reduced nurse staffing while increasing patient-loads even for the sickest patients. Even early in the pandemic the hospital business leaders were cost-cutting personal protective equipment and paying the healthcare system's CEO $18 million per year.

Money

The third five letter word is *money*. During my fourth year at Jesuit-run St. Peter's College in Jersey City, I traveled for medical school application interviews. At least three times during my interviews, I was asked, "Do you want to go to medical school to make a lot of money?" The first time I was asked I mumbled that I wanted to have a meaningful life, but it forced me to think about what I did not want. I did not want to be poor. I grew up that way, and I did not want constant worry about food, heating, and rent and have a desperate fear about medical bills. Frank McCourt's 1996 memoir, *Angela's Ashes*, reflected on the pain of being marginalized and ridiculed because he was poor.[11] I think of one in seven children in my country growing up in poverty, the pain of those fears, and the erosion of self-confidence. Having too little money meant too little power over one's life.

Greed

The last five letter word is *greed*. The saying "Behind every great fortune there is a crime" is ascribed to many writers. Lawrence James's history, *The Rise and Fall of the British Empire*, outlines the degree to which colonialist military incursions were the political partner to immense trade operations such as the East India Company and the Hudson's Bay Company.[12] The British Navy, along with sometimes surprisingly small armies, were the operating arms of these corporations. Early on, Portugal and Spain extracted enormous amounts of gold and other wealth from South America, but feeding addictions and human trafficking was an even greater moneymaker.

---

[11] See Frank McCourt, *Angela's Ashes: A Memoir* (New York: Scribner, 1996).

[12] See Lawrence James, *The Rise and Fall of the British Empire* (London: Little, Brown, 1994).

Harvesting sugarcane throughout the Caribbean basin—to make lucrative, easily transported, rum—required disease-resistant heat-tolerant populations and fueled the transatlantic slave trade from Africa. The tobacco trade, the opium wars, and the drug wars follow this pattern. The more profitable an industry—for example, easy extraction of a ready resource and sale at premium prices—the more those who profit aggressively guard their positions in legal, legislative, and physical battles. While water, money, and power affect the mind, greed erodes moral boundaries. Self-interest is at the core of capitalism, but greed has become a global malignancy with omnipresent metastases, and the medical industrial complex is not greed-free.

The overselling of alcohol, tobacco, and unhealthy food—along with dangerous workplaces and vehicles—is a byproduct of greed. At these moments, we need the best of medicine with caring clinicians in organizations where health is a core value rather than a billboard slogan. I grew up in New Jersey, a state profoundly impacted by the petroleum, chemical, and pharmaceutical industries, which has affected the lives of family and friends. A few times each year, a friend or family member calls me about a recent diagnosis of cancer and looking for advice. I almost always give same advice (and this is the right advice for all "curbside consults"): "find the best possible physician and care setting you possibly can."

The Lown Institute, named after renowned medical leader Dr. Bernard Lown, offers its Lown awards to role-model physicians like Don Berwick and Mona Hanna-Attisha.[13] The Institute's other efforts include the Shkreli Awards for individuals and organizations who disgrace the title "caregiver."[14] The Shkreli Award is named after the "Pharma-Bro" who cranked up the price of a long-standing essential anti-parasitic medication for children by fifty-six-fold. He eventually was sentenced to seven years in prison. I worry that we suffer a prison deficiency for powerful crooks.

---

[13] See Lown Institute, "About," 2021, lowninstitute.org/about/.

[14] See Lown Institute, "Shkreli Awards," 2021, lowninstitute.org/projects/shkreli-awards/.

Few if any tobacco industry CEOs have faced prison. I predict no prison for the CEOs of the Texas electric power companies who reaped great profits while exploiting a vulnerable power grid that failed in 2021 February's ice storm and led to over two hundred deaths.[15] Some hospital system CEOs are similarly self-serving. Even at the most prestigious healthcare institutions in Boston and New York City, published stories report the failure of their leaders to disclose outside corporate board memberships and extraordinarily lucrative retainers.[16] When I was a child, I thought that greed was personified by a villainous old man exulting in his diamonds and gold. Greed has become a systemic disease not merely in individuals but a blood cancer of the modern world reaching across societies and right to the top of all world governments. When you first looked at the table of contents of this volume, it might have seemed to have many disparate strands, but they weave together in a fabric that suffocates public health progress and covers many avoidable and, yes, moral threats.

The U.S. has been at "War with Cancer" for over fifty years, but cancer threats will always reside in living cells. I would suggest that the cancer accelerants of water, power, money, and greed must be brought to justice so that humanity can prevent and control this cursed disease rather than merely continue to amplify it.

Richard J. Jackson, MD, MPH, is Professor emeritus at the Fielding School of Public Health at the University of California, Los Angeles. A pediatrician, he served in many leadership positions with the California Health Department, including the highest as the State Health Officer. For

---

[15] See Jeremy Schwartz, Kiah Collier, and Vianna Davila, "'Power Companies Get Exactly What They Want': How Texas Repeatedly Failed to Protect Its Power Grid against Extreme Weather," *The Texas Tribune*, February 22, 2021, www.texastribune.org/2021/02/22/texas-power-gridextreme-weather/.

[16] See Charles Ornstein and Katie Thomas, "Memorial Sloan Kettering Leaders Violated Conflict-of-Interest Rules, Report Finds," *New York Times*, April 4, 2019, www.nytimes.com/2019/04/04/health/memorial-sloan-kettering-conflicts-.html.

nine years he was Director of the National Center for Environmental Health at the Center for Disease Control and Prevention (CDC), and he received the Presidential Distinguished Service award. He was also elected to the Institute of Medicine of the National Academy of Sciences.

Chapter 6: The Role of Policy in Prevention: Protecting People and the Environment

Nsedu Obot Witherspoon

While the role of governments in promoting health policies and regulations to protect and support all its citizens, particularly those more vulnerable, needs to be reaffirmed, the work of non-profit organizations should be highlighted. Nsedu Obot Witherspoon discusses the mission, contributions, and actions of a national non-profit organization—the Children's Environmental Health Network—that strives to foster equity, protect all children from environmental hazards, and promote safe and healthy environments for children to thrive in. This commitment is challenged by the traditional approach to environmental health laws and regulations that is based on proving harm from environmental hazards, such as carcinogens, before measures are taken to protect all, especially the most vulnerable. The goal of fostering a cancer free society is a collective and shared endeavor, which requires to acknowledge and address the troubling effects of systemic discrimination and racism on low wealth, Black, Indigenous, and People of Color communities.

The Children's Environmental Health Network (CEHN) is a national non-profit organization dedicated to protecting all children equitably from environmental hazards and promoting safe and healthy environments for children to thrive in. In 2015, CEHN released *A Blueprint for Protecting Children's Environmental Health: An Urgent Call to Action.*[1] As the leading national U.S. based non-profit organization, focused on protecting all children equitably from environmental hazards, CEHN led a multi-disciplinary process that prioritized where collective effort is needed in order to change the current paradigm. The traditional approach to environmental health laws

---

[1] See Kristie Trousdale, Rachel Locke, Nsedu Witherspoon, Carol Stroebel, Brie Sleezer, and Brenda Afzal, "A Blueprint for Protecting Children's Environmental Health: An Urgent Call to Action," *Children's Environmental Health Network,* October 2015, cehn.org/wpcontent/uploads/2015/11/BluePrint_Final1.pdf.

and regulations is that harm must be proven before measures are taken to protect all, especially our most vulnerable, such as children.

> The *Blueprint* emphasizes urgent action to make children's health a priority for our nation. It outlines the steps that are necessary for progress towards protecting children's environmental health, and for developing a solid foundation to support future commitments moving forward. The *Blueprint* is a high-level resource that is available to assist community leaders and the children's environmental health field in prioritizing the needs of our children. Key recommendations include: to mobilize society to take action on children's environmental health, to create knowledge essential for effective action and make use of the knowledge we currently have, to marshal the engine of the

economy to achieve environments where children can thrive and enjoy a sustainable and economically secure future, and to build political will for child- centered policies.

In genuine efforts to protect all, especially the most vulnerable, from environmental hazards such as carcinogens, inequities need to lead to solutions. Achieving health equity requires assessment of cumulative environmental health burdens within a social determinants of health framework.[2] It is necessary to address environmental justice as a structural public health challenge. A "health in all policies" approach must be coupled with thoughtful integration of social, economic, and political indicators, and affected communities must be an integral part of the process.

---

[2] See the policy statement American Public Health Association, "Addressing Environmental Justice to Achieve Health Equity," Policy Number 20197, November 5, 2019, www.apha .org/policies-and-advocacy/public-health-policy-statements/policy- database/2020/01/14/addressingenvironmental-justice-to-achieve-health-equity.

Promoting a Cancer Free Society

There are some specific examples of approaches working toward equitable systems change in the cancer prevention arena. The Cancer Free Economy Network combines the efforts of leaders within impacted communities, public health and science, market shift, and policy/legal sectors. All are working to lift the burden of cancers and other diseases by driving a dramatic and equitable transition from toxic substances in our lives, communities, and economy to safe and healthy alternatives for all.[3] Our collective work is organized across teams that include focus on building power, health science, shifting markets, communication, and policy/legal strategies.

Building power aims to assist, strengthen, and mobilize vulnerable community members in their daily fights to promote prevention. Health science provides the evidence of chemical exposures upon health and well-being, while leading to the creation of a multidisciplinary cancer prevention research agenda. Shifting markets implies creating demand for and supply of healthy and safe alternatives. Through effective communications, building public awareness fosters demand for change. There is also a focus on the promotion of policy and legal strategies to protect the health of all.

Actions that the Cancer Free Economy (CFE) Network supports include, first, changing the public narrative to promote acceptance of the fact that exposures to harmful chemicals may increase risk for cancer diagnosis. Second, there is emphasis on mobilizing communities around cancer prevention. Third, there is a push for interdisciplinary cancer prevention research. Fourth, there is a focus on coordinating supply and demand strategies to reinforce progress on healthy alternatives.

---

[3] See Cancer Free Economy Network, "About Us," *Cancer Free Economy Network*, 2020, www.cancerfreeeconomy.org.

One of many key actions of the CFE was the development of the Joint Statement on Cancer Prevention.[4] This call-to-action results from an unprecedented collaboration of cancer and health leaders calling for the reduction of the burden of cancer by addressing environmental risk factors. The intersections between the climate crisis and toxic chemical exposures are also acknowledged, resulting in targeted work within the CFE to indicate the co-benefits of addressing both. With warmer temperatures comes increased exposure to toxic chemicals, and increased weather events result in concentrated releases of chemicals.[5] Climate change exacerbates the health impacts from air pollution,[6] and toxic chemicals increase the vulnerability communities have to climate change effects.[7]

The Effects of Systemic Discrimination and Racism

The same generations of systemic discriminations and racism that have resulted in Black, Brown, and low wealth communities disproportionately suffering from the COVID-19 pandemic are also driving the stark racial inequities in several types of cancer and disease outcomes.[8] Fenceline, low wealth, Black, Indigenous, and People of Color (BIPOC) communities have been plagued by economic

---

[4] See Cancer Free Economy Network, "Cancer and Health Leaders Call for Action to Reduce the Burden of Cancer by Addressing Environmental Risk Factors," *Cancer Free Economy Network,* September 2020, www.cancerfreeeconomy.org/joint-statement/.

[5] See Renee Cho, "Climate Change May Be Hazardous to Your Health," *State of the Planet, Columbia Climate School: Climate, Earth, and Society,* March 12, 2018, news.climate.columbia.edu/2018/03/12/climate-change-may-hazardous-health/.

[6] See American Public Health Association, U.S. Department of Health and Human Services, and Centers for Disease Control and Prevention, "Climate Change Decreases the Quality of the Air We Breathe," *Centers for Disease Control and Prevention*, 2021, www.cdc.gov/climateandhealth/pubs/air-quality-final_508.pdf.

[7] See Aneesh Patnaik, Jiahn Son, Alice Feng, and Crystal Ade, "Racial Disparities and Climate Change," *Princeton Student Climate Initiative,* August 15, 2020, psci.princeton.edu/tips/2020/8/15/racial-disparities-and-climate-change.

[8] See Brett Milano, "With COVID Spread, 'Racism—Not Race—Is the Risk Factor,'" *The Harvard Gazette,* April 22, 2021, news.harvard.edu/gazette/story/2021/04/with-covid-spread-racism-not-race-is-the-risk-factor/.

disinvestment and have served as primary dumping grounds for polluting facilities.[9] These extremely high risk communities have suffered for decades due to the zip codes that they live in, the occupations that afford the ability to provide for their families, the homes that they reside in, and the early learning/K-12 schools where they learn.

Fenceline communities are also where live most of our essential workers, whom we depend on greatly for the daily functions of community life. These community members have paid and continue to pay the ultimate price for existence, their health. Generation after generation, BIPOC communities absorb the impacts that lack of investment, capacity, and human decency have created. Living among high levels of pollution has created U.S. communities with some of the highest occurrences of asthma, cancer, lead poisoning, obesity, mental health, and learning disabilities.[10] While overall cancer mortality has been declining, cancer health disparities continue to present increased risk of developing or dying from cancer, particularly among Black populations.[11] To address this situation the Cancer Free Economy Network developed an agenda for the Biden-Harris Administration that aligns with the Build Back Better concept, encouraging that steps toward cancer prevention and environmental equity are urgent and possible.[12]

---

[9] See Katherine Bagley, "COVID-19 Worsens the Role Environmental Injustice Already Plays in Marginalized Communities," *PBS News Hour,*
May 12, 2020, www.pbs.org/newshour/health/covid-19-worsens-the-role-environmental-injustice-already-plays-in-marginalized-communities.

[10] See Shava Cureton, "Environmental Victims: Environmental Injustice Issues That Threaten the Health of Children Living in Poverty," *Reviews on Environmental Health* 26, no. 3 (2011): 141–147.

[11] See National Cancer Institute, "Cancer Disparities," *National Cancer Institute,* November 17, 2020, www.cancer.gov/about-cancer/understanding/disparities.

[12] "The Building Back Better (BBB) is an approach to post-disaster recovery that reduces vulnerability to future disasters and builds community resilience to address physical, social, environmental, and economic vulnerabilities and shocks." Global Facility for Disaster Reduction and Recovery, "Building Back Better in Post-Disaster Recovery," *Global Facility for Disaster Reduction and Recovery,* 2021, 2, www.recoveryplatform.org/assets/tools_guidelines/GFDRR/Disaster Recovery Guidance Series- Building Back Better in Post-DisasterRecovery.pdf. See also United Nations Office for Disaster Risk Reduction, "Build

The Need to Especially Protect Children

In September 2020, the report *Childhood Cancer: Cross Strategies for Prevention*[13] was released by a collaboration of over sixty partners and leaders in the health, science, business, policy, and advocacy sectors, including members of the Cancer Free Economy Network. This report stresses that childhood cancer incidence has increased each year since 1975. While mortality from childhood cancers has decreased due to advancements in medicine and treatment protocols, genetics cannot explain the steady annual increase in incidence. The National Cancer Institute's Surveillance, Epidemiology, and End Results Program demonstrates that incidence has increased 41 percent with an annual percent increase of 0.8 percent.[14] Compelling scientific evidence of increased risk identified environmental contributions to childhood cancer trends, including exposures to pesticides, vehicular air pollution, paints, and solvents.[15] With the release of the report also came the public launch of the Childhood Cancer Prevention Initiative.[16]

With this initiative, organizations within the childhood cancer community, advocates, health professionals, faith leaders, business investors, and researchers have come together to create awareness of the

---

Back Better in Recovery, Rehabilitation, and Reconstruction: Consultative Version," *United Nations Office for Disaster Risk Reduction*, 2017, ww.unisdr.org/files/53213_bbb.pdf.

[13] See Polly Hoppin, Molly Jacobs, Bobbi Wilding, Howard Williams, David Levine, Mary Ryan, and Marilyn Markle, "Childhood Cancer: Cross-Sector Strategies for Prevention," *Cancer Free Economy Network,* September 23, 2020, www.cancerfreeeconomy.org/wpcontent/uploads/2020/09/CFE_ChildhoodCancerPrevention_Report_F2.pdf.

[14] See National Cancer Institute, "Surveillance, Epidemiology, and End Results Program," *National Cancer Institute,* 2021, seer.cancer.gov.

[15] See Todd P. Whitehead, Catherine Metayer, Joseph L. Wiemels, Amanda W. Singer, and Mark D. Miller, "Childhood Leukemia and Primary Prevention," *Current Problems in Pediatric and Adolescent Health Care* 46, no. 10 (2016): 317–352; Rosana E. Norman, Alexander Ryan, Kristen Grant, Freddy Sitas, and James G. Scott, "Environmental Contributions to Childhood Cancers," *Journal of Environmental Immunology and Toxicology* 2, no. 2 (2014): 86–98.

[16] See Cancer Free Economy Network, "Childhood Cancer Prevention Is Possible," *Cancer Free Economy Network*, 2020, www.cancerfreeeconomy.org/childhood_cancer_prevention/.

environmental connections while the nature of some forms of childhood cancer are identified. Collectively, cases are made for childhood cancer prevention within the scientific, business, economic, and policy sectors. This Initiative works to prioritize the fact that childhood cancer is the leading cause of death among children with forty-six cases diagnosed daily, 16,000 annually, and $1.9 billion spent each year on related hospitalizations.[17] In addition to the call for a childhood cancer prevention research agenda, this Initiative also strives to advance public policy to incentivize producing safer chemicals and products, while also supporting the expansion of regulations to reduce known childhood cancer contributors.

In order to address cancer prevention overall, and childhood cancer prevention specifically, a systems approach is required to achieve the largest impact and to foster the opportunity to address multiple exposure pathways.[18] This comprehensive approach depends on the assumption that the breaking down of complex concepts into simple, easy to understand units helps in better addressing such complexity and facilitates articulating effective solutions. In this context, it is critical to ascertain the exposure pathways that place children at risk for cancer and other long-term illness. Within the existing systems, it is also important to identify, understand, and consider the influences, circumstances, beneficiaries, and implications that concern the proposed systemic shifts while possible actions are considered.

In the past, successful policies promoting public health standards have been implemented. As examples, vehicle seat belt laws have reduced mortality rates from accidents, tobacco cessation efforts have helped to reduce lung disease, food subsidy programs have been shown to reduce

---

[17] See Hoppin, Jacobs, Wilding, Williams, Levine, Ryan, and Markle, "Childhood Cancer: Cross-Sector Strategies for Prevention."
[18] See Gordan K. C. Chen, "What Is the Systems Approach?," *Interfaces* 6, no. 1 (1975): 32–37.

health inequalities,[19] and the removal of lead from paint and gasoline in the 1970s dramatically reduced childhood blood lead levels.[20] These successes should encourage timely and urgent policies to reduce the factors leading to cancer in children.

Government's Role in Cancer Prevention

With an obligation to promote public health, the government's role should include safeguarding existing federal laws with evidence of equitable protection of communities from rollbacks and alterations. The U.S. Environmental Protection Agency should be held accountable for enforcing existing regulations, while air quality and water protections need to be expanded. Among state and federal supported offices and programs, the reduction or elimination of pesticide use should be required. Overall, the goals of eliminating toxics, using safer materials in children's products and our built environments, and promoting innovation and advancements in non-regrettable substitution options need to be required.

The role of responsible governments also includes using government and institutional dollars to purchase nontoxic options, ensuring children's spaces are sited safely, requiring transparent disclosure of chemicals of concern in children's products and in areas intended for use by children (e.g., artificial turf), and increased funding for research on cancer prevention.

Governments have a fundamental obligation to provide for the general well-being of the public and our shared environment, both of which are profoundly at risk due to the ways in which chemicals are manufactured, used, and released. Policies that restrict harmful chemicals

---

[19] See Katie Thomson, Frances Hillier-Brown, Adam Todd, Courtney McNamara, Tim Huijts, and Clare Bambra, "The Effects of Public Health Policies on Health Inequalities in High-Income Countries: An Umbrella Review," *BMC Public Health* 18, no. 1 (2018): 869, doi.org/10.1186/s12889-018-5677-1.

[20] See American Academy of Pediatrics Committee on Environmental Health, "Lead Exposure in Children: Prevention, Detection, and Management," *Pediatrics* 116, no. 4 (2005): 1036–1046.

and drive our economy toward safer solutions are essential if we are serious about preventing debilitating, deadly diseases like cancers.

Our Collective Role in Cancer Prevention

As the demand for sustainable markets continues to gain traction and grow, the question still remains whether we collectively will meet the urgent opportunity before us to add our voices to the children's environmental health movement so that we can adequately and equitably protect our most vulnerable. The Children's Environmental Health Network (CEHN) welcomes partnerships with citizens, relying on their time and energy, as the Network continues to mobilize and leverage the children's environmental health movement. CEHN offers a variety of ways in which people can lend their voices to the fight for equitable protection of all children from known harmful carcinogens and toxics. One way to step up is to participate in action alerts that target elected leaders, community leaders, and decision-makers, asking them to put children first. Another way to actively participate in this vital work is to participate in the Children's Environmental Health Day.[21]

Children's Environmental Health Day is the second Thursday of every October, which is Child Health Month. It is a day of assessment, re-alignment, networking, and opportunity to share effective strategies, resources, and lessons learned in the field. Partner events, which aim to promote education and action around the protection of children's health, are tracked and available to support people's motivations and encourage to replicate events in other areas of the country. Children's Environmental Health Day Proclamations are also encouraged and secured at the state and local levels.[22] These resources become critical tools for advocacy and engagement among partners and community members, with elected representatives and community leaders. This collective work

---

[21] See Children's Environmental Health Network, "Children's Environmental Health Day," *Children's Environmental Health Network*, 2021, cehday.org.
[22] See Children's Environmental Health Network, "Obtain a Proclamation," *Children's Environmental Health Network*, 2021, cehn.org/cehmovement/cehday/proclamation/.

to change the current paradigm centered on treatment to also include a focus on prevention is a key priority in CEHN's effectiveness strategy, not only to protect the lives of children living today but for generations to come.

Nsedu Obot Witherspoon, MPH, serves as the Executive Director for the Children's Environmental Health Network (CEHN), where her responsibilities include successfully organizing, leading, and managing policy, education/training, and science-related programs. For the past eighteen years, she has served as a key spokesperson for children's vulnerabilities and the need for their protection, conducting presentations and lectures across the country.

Part 3
Ethical Issues
and
Practical Approaches

Chapter 7: Talking God and Talking Cancer: Why Womanist Ethics Matters for Breast Cancer Prevention and Control among Black Women

Elizabeth A. Williams

Elizabeth Williams, first, articulates a Womanist approach that denounces the racial disparities and inequities in access to preventive, diagnostic, and therapeutic services for Black women in the United States. Second, she highlights how grassroots organizations empower women and allow them to take back their health. Moreover, Womanist theology and spirituality, and particularly Womanist ethics, serve Black women in making sense of and responding to breast cancer by promoting breast cancer control and prevention for Black women and by supporting Black women in dealing with the crises breast cancer brings in their lives and in society.

The activist, feminist, and poet Audre Lorde, who herself died of breast cancer, once said, "Each woman responds to the crisis that breast cancer brings to her life out of a whole pattern, which is the design of who she is and how her life has been lived. The weave of her every day existence is the training ground for how she handles crisis."[1] This in many ways describes how Black women with breast cancer respond to the troubles breast cancer brings, as well as how Black women respond to a broader world that does not value their Blackness or femaleness.

Black women, particularly those who subscribe to Womanist theology, respond to breast cancer out of a whole pattern of their constructions of God and how God responds to them and the troubles they face. Black women's lives and how they live their lives in struggle against breast cancer disparities are reflected in Black women's breast cancer control and prevention activities. These activities reflect Black women's ethics, and

---

[1] Audre Lorde, *The Cancer Journals*, special ed. (San Francisco: Aunt Lute Books, 1997), 7.

how their identities as Black women provide the training ground for handling troubles Black women face. This chapter describes breast cancer disparities experienced by Black women in the United States. It further examines how Womanist theology serves Black women in making sense of and responding to breast cancer. Womanist ethics as an outgrowth of Womanist theology and spirituality will be considered. Lastly, this chapter highlights how Black women employ Womanist ethics in addressing breast cancer control and prevention for Black women and the crises breast cancer brings.

Black Women and Breast Cancer Disparities

In 2020, it was estimated by the World Health Organization that 2.3 million women were diagnosed with breast cancer globally.[2] Of these newly diagnosed cases, Black women comprised more than 33,000 of these cases, making breast cancer the most diagnosed cancer among Black women in the United States.[3] Furthermore, of the more than 600,000 deaths that occurred in 2020 from breast cancer around the world,[4] more than six thousand were among Black women in the United States.[5]

While advances in medical technologies to detect and treat breast cancers have occurred, these advances do not fully reflect the breast cancer experience of Black women in the United States. Black women have a lower breast cancer incidence rate than their white counterparts.[6] However, Black women under 45 years of age have a higher breast cancer incidence rate than other ethnic groups, and on average experience a 40 percent higher breast cancer mortality rate than white women.[7]

[2] World Health Organization, "Breast Cancer," *World Health Organization*, March 26, 2021, www.who.int/news-room/fact-sheets/detail/breast-cancer.

[3] American Cancer Society, "Cancer Facts & Figures for African Americans, 2019–2021," 2019, www.cancer.org/content/dam/cancer-org/research/cancer-facts-and-statistics/cancer-facts-and-figures-for-african-americans/cancer-facts-and-figures-for-africanamericans-2019-2021.pdf.

[4] World Health Organization, "Breast Cancer."

[5] American Cancer Society, "Cancer Facts & Figures for African Americans, 2019–2021."

[6] American Cancer Society, "Cancer Facts & Figures for African Americans, 2019–2021."

[7] American Cancer Society, "Cancer Facts & Figures for African Americans, 2019–2021."

The overall mortality rate from breast cancer among Black women in the United States is significantly higher than that of white women.[8] From 1989 to 2012, total breast cancer death rates decreased by 36 percent, which amounts to approximately a quarter of a million breast cancer deaths averted over this period in the United States. The decrease in death rates were experienced among all ethnic groups in the country, except for American Indians/Alaskan Natives and African Americans. The disparity in breast cancer age-adjusted mortality has continued to widen between Black women and white women, with more than six thousand Black women succumbing to breast cancer in the United States in 2020, representing more than 18 percent of cancer deaths among Black women that year.[9]

Although not fully understood, several risk factors are cited as explanations for higher breast cancer mortality among Black women in the United States. Among these factors, Black women are at greater risk of being diagnosed with advanced stage breast cancers.[10] Contributing to these advanced stage breast cancers is the higher risk Black women experience from specific cancer types, particularly triple-negative breast cancer (TNBC). Black women have a twofold greater risk for being diagnosed with triple-negative breast cancer versus white women.[11] Triple-negative breast cancer refers to those cancers that lack estrogen, progesterone, and the human epidermal growth factor receptor.[12] Due to the invasive makeup of the triple-negative breast cancer tumor type, fewer options are available for treating triple-negative breast cancers.[13] Due to this risk factor and others, the overall 5-year survival rate for Black women

---

[8] American Cancer Society, "Cancer Facts & Figures for African Americans, 2019–2021."

[9] American Cancer Society, "Cancer Facts & Figures for African Americans, 2019–2021."

[10] American Cancer Society, "Cancer Facts & Figures for African Americans, 2019–2021."

[11] American Cancer Society, "Cancer Facts & Figures for African Americans, 2019–2021."

[12] American Cancer Society, "Cancer Facts & Figures for African Americans, 2019–2021."

[13] Tomi Akinyemiju, Justin Xavier Moore, and Sean F. Altekruse, "Breast Cancer Survival in African-American Women by Hormone Receptor Subtypes," *Breast Cancer Research and Treatment* 153, no. 1 (2015): 211–218.

is lower at 81 percent compared to 91 percent for white women (2008–2014).[14]

While the statistics regarding breast cancer survival among Black women in the United States are sobering, there remains a ray of hope on the cancer front in the United States. Based on 2020 estimates, nearly 1.3 million Black people were cancer survivors in the United States.[15] This is encouraging news. Nevertheless, there are not enough Black women counted among these cancer survivors. Therefore, the factors that put Black women at increased risk for breast cancer incidence and mortality are important to examine.

Advances in cancer treatment have resulted in breast cancers being treated at earlier stages. However, too many Black women in the United States continue to experience disparities in access to quality breast cancer care. These healthcare disparities increase Black women's susceptibility to poorer breast cancer outcomes. Compared to white women, Black women are more likely to have lower insurance rates or have inadequate healthcare insurance coverage even with increased access to healthcare under the Affordable Care Act.[16] Although the Affordable Care Act has increased access to cancer treatment, uninsured and underinsured women are less likely to receive core biopsies, lumpectomies, adjuvant therapy, and hormonal treatment.[17] Women lacking health care insurance and underinsured are also more likely to be diagnosed with later stage breast cancers and have diminished rates of breast cancer survivorship compared to those with insurance.[18]

---

[14] American Cancer Society, "Cancer Facts & Figures for African Americans, 2019–2021."

[15] American Cancer Society, "Cancer Facts & Figures for African Americans, 2019–2021."

[16] Jie Chen, Arturo Vargas-Bustamante, Karoline Mortensen, and Aexander N. Ortega, "Racial and Ethnic Disparities in Health Care Access and
Utilization under the Affordable Care Act," *Medical Care* 54, no. 2 (2016): 140–146.

[17] Shaofei Su et al., "The Quality of Invasive Breast Cancer Care for Low Reimbursement Rate Patients: A Retrospective Study," *PLoS One* 12,
no. 9 (2017): e0184866, doi.org/10.1371/journal.pone.0184866.

[18] Yefei Zhang, Luisa Franzini, Wenyaw Chan, Hua Xu, and Xianglin L. Du, "Effects of Health Insurance on Tumor Stage, Treatment, and Survival in Large Cohorts of Patients with

Beyond diminished access to quality care, poverty puts Black women at increased risk of negative breast cancer outcomes in other ways. Lower socioeconomic status puts Black women at increased risk for breast cancer by making these women more susceptible to forms of structural racism, including living in communities with more dilapidated housing, increased concentrations of environmental pollutants, and limited opportunities for high-quality education and employment with living wages and benefits.[19] Identified risk factors for breast cancer—including lack of physical activity, smoking, poor nutrition, and obesity—also tend to be more prevalent among those living in poverty.[20] Because of poor nutrition and lack of physical activity Black women are particularly susceptible to weight gain, which has been linked to the development of breast cancers and diminished breast cancer survival rates.[21]

Black women are also exposed to racism and other forms of bias, including sexism in the broader society. This situation also has an impact on their breast cancer risk. Higher levels of exposure to discrimination function as chronic stressors, which alter immune function and endogenous hormone levels, thereby increasing breast cancer risk among Black women.[22] Black women constitute a socially marginalized group in

Breast and Colorectal Cancer," *Journal of Health Care for the Poor and Underserved* 26, no. 4 (2015): 1336–1358.

[19] Zinzi D. Bailey, Nancy Krieger, Madina Agenor, Jasmine Graves, Natalia Linos, and Mary T. Bassett, "Structural Racism and Health Inequities in the USA: Evidence and Interventions," *Lancet* 389, no. 10077 (2017): 1453–1463.

[20] Philippe Irigaray, John A. Newby, Richard Clapp, Lennart Hardell, Vyvyan Howard, Luc Montagnier, Samuel Epstein, and Dominique Belpomme, "Lifestyle-Related Factors and Environmental Agents Causing Cancer: An Overview," *Biomedicine & Pharmacotherapy* 61, no. 10 (2007): 640–658.

[21] Melinda Stolly, Lisa Sharp, Anita Wells, Nolanna Simon, and Linda Schiffer, "Health Behaviors and Breast Cancer: Experiences of Urban African American Women," *Health Education and Behavior* 33, no. 5 (2006): 604–624.

[22] Irigaray et al., "Lifestyle-Related Factors and Environmental Agents Causing Cancer: An Overview."

the United States, who as a result of their intersecting identities of race, class, and gender face social disempowerment and violence.[23]

Controlling Images

One of the ways Black women have been disempowered and victimized is through "controlling images" or negative constructions of Black womanhood and femininity.[24] These controlling images erase Black women's complexity and reduce them to gendered tropes that impact their health. One of these controlling images is the "Strong Black Woman" schema.[25] According to this schema, Black women are expected to be fearless, silent, and emotionally unaffected in the face of adversity or everyday challenges. Reinforced by their faith in God, Black women who conform to this controlling image are perceived as unaffected by traumas or emotional upheavals.[26]

The "Strong Black Woman" schema serves as double-edged sword for Black women. Whereas the image may serve as a source of pride and strength for many Black women within their communities, the image is also problematic. Black women who subscribe to this schema are less likely to seek support from others or be emotionally vulnerable for fear of being perceived as weak. The inability of Black women to be themselves or seek help increases Black women's risk for psychological distress, depressive symptoms, obesity, and cardiovascular disease.[27] Black women with breast cancer may be further at risk of the negative health consequences of this

---

[23] Patricia Hill Collins, *Black Feminist Thought: Knowledge, Consciousness, and the Politics of Empowerment*, rev. 10th anniversary ed. (New York: Routledge, 2000), 4–5.

[24] Hill Collins, *Black Feminist Thought*, 5.

[25] Jasmine A. Abrams, Morgan Maxwell, Michell Pope, and Faye Z. Belgrave, "Carrying the World with the Grace of a Lady and the Grit of a Warrior: Deepening Our Understanding of the 'Strong Black Woman' Schema," *Psychology of Women Quarterly* 38, no. 4 (2014): 503–518.

[26] Elizabeth A. Williams, *Black Women and Breast Cancer: A Cultural Theology* (Lanham, MD: Lexington Books, 2019), 9–10.

[27] Tamara Beauboeuf-Lafontant, "Listening Past the Lies That Make Us Sick: A Voice-Centered Analysis of Strength and Depression among Black Women," *Qualitative Sociology* 31, no. 4 (2008): 391–406.

image because breast cancer culture at large further reinforces concealment of survivors' true feelings about cancer out of fear that these feelings may be considered socially unacceptable or contrary to societal ideas about how cancer survivors should behave.[28] Breast cancer survivors, including Black cancer survivors, are often expected to be brave and strong in the face of breast cancer, not fearful or vulnerable.

Challenges and Resources

Breast cancer presents numerous challenges for Black women. These troubles include the racial, economic, and social vulnerabilities Black women face that increase their risk of disease and types of the breast cancer they are more likely to be diagnosed with. Breast cancer brings troubles to Black women due to poverty and discrimination increasing the likelihood they will receive poorer quality care and die at higher rates from breast cancer. Breast cancer is also trouble for Black women because it forces them to remain silent about what hurts them, further compromising their health to live up to controlling images of their humanity.

Yet, instead of succumbing to the troubles breast cancer presents, Black women do not give into these challenges. Instead, Black women use their reliance on God as a source of strength and resolve in dealing with breast cancer. This reliance on God is evidenced among Black women by their spirituality. Drawing on a deep cultural tradition of spirituality drawn from the history of Black people in the United States, Black spirituality is about faith in a transcendent force that is both felt internally and externally as an interconnected relationship with God, a higher power, and others. This faith is evidenced as transformative power and freeing succor for handling life's adversities. Strength and inspiration are drawn from belief in the unlimited potential of this benevolent source.[29]

---

[28] Annette Madlock Gatison, "The Pink and Black Experience: Lies That Make Us Suffer in Silence and Cost Us Our Lives," *Women's Studies in Communication* 38, no. 2 (2015): 135–140.

[29] Kelley Newlin, Kathleen Knafl, and Gail D'Eramo Melkus, "African-American Spirituality: A Concept Analysis," *Advances in Nursing Science* 25, no. 2 (2002): 57–70.

Black women use spirituality to cultivate hope in times of despair and challenge. For Black women with breast cancer, adversities highlight the tension between reality and desire, the way things are, and the way things can be. Black women breast cancer survivors' spirituality functions as a transcendent counterweight that gives them the capacity to create alternative conceptualizations of life's possibilities.[30] While Black women are aware of social, economic, and medical limitations they face confronting breast cancer (even their own mortality), through their faith in God, Black women transcend life circumstances by using their relationship with God to (re)appraise their thoughts and experiences and (re)envision and (re)create their destinies.

Black women's relationship with God is part of their Christian theology.[31] Christian theology is a story about those who are in trouble. God intervenes and responds to those in trouble. God not only intervenes. God prevails over trouble. Black women with breast cancer see themselves in this theological narrative. They see the triune God as active with them to overcome the troubles breast cancer brings. As a creative, transcendent, and ever-present force, the triune God works with Black women to reappraise the situations they face and influences how they respond to breast cancer.[32] How Black women with breast cancer think about God and who they are in relationship to God form Black women's constructive theology.[33] This constructive theology also informs Black women's theological anthropology or how they respond to breast cancer and others in practical, everyday ways.[34]

Black women's reappraisal of the breast cancer experience results in intentionally using their agency to make situations better for themselves and others.[35] This purposeful desire to improve situations is what the Womanist ethicist Stacey Floyd-Thomas refers to as "moral anthropology"

---

[30] Williams, *Black Women and Breast Cancer*, 9–10.
[31] Williams, *Black Women and Breast Cancer*, 9–10.
[32] Williams, *Black Women and Breast Cancer*, 9–10.
[33] Williams, *Black Women and Breast Cancer*, 19–21.
[34] Williams, *Black Women and Breast Cancer*, 19–21.
[35] Williams, *Black Women and Breast Cancer*, 99.

or the "epistemological privilege of Black women knowing themselves and [that] their world stands under the moral imperative of making themselves and their world morally better."[36]

Womanist

The Womanist ethics Black female breast cancer survivors enact is an outgrowth of "Womanist" first defined by the writer Alice Walker.[37] Serving as a counterpoint to white feminism, a Womanist is "a black feminist or feminist of color," whose intersectional identities as Black and female create a unique cultural and social standpoint, particularly in relation to oppression. The experience of oppression (i.e., racism, sexism, and breast cancer disparities) allows Black women to see the world through a prism called double consciousness, an awareness of how they are viewed by the larger, white, and patriarchal world and how they view themselves within a Black cultural ethos.[38] Using their Black female standpoint as an epistemological lens to understand the world, Womanists are "committed to the survival and wholeness of entire people, male *and* female."[39] Black women with breast cancer struggle against the troubles breast cancer brings and reject the suffering caused by it through a Womanist ethics of love.[40]

This commitment to survival and wholeness indicative of Womanist ethics views Blackness and femaleness as valuable and the starting point for

---

[36] Stacey M. Floyd-Thomas, "Womanist Ethical Language Handout," April 19, 2019. Personal communication.

[37] Alice Walker, "In Search of Our Mothers' Gardens," in *Black Theology: A Documentary History*, ed. J. H. Cone and G. S. Wilmore, Vol. 1: 1966–1979, 2nd ed. (Maryknoll, NY: Orbis Books, 1993), 339–348.

[38] W. E. B. Du Bois, "The Souls of Black Folk," in W. E. B. Du Bois, *Writings*, The Library of America (New York: Literary Classics of the United States, distributed by Viking Press, 1986), 357–548.

[39] Alice Walker, *In Search of Our Mothers' Gardens: Womanist Prose* (San Diego: Harcourt Brace Jovanovich, 1983), xi–xii.

[40] See Phillis Isabella Sheppard, *Self, Culture, and Others in Womanist Practical Theology*, Black Religion/Womanist Thought/Social Justice (New York: Palgrave Macmillan, 2011), 71.

love in action.[41] This love in action is distilled into a Womanist ethics which includes radical subjectivity, traditional communalism, redemptive self-love, and critical engagement.[42] Radical subjectivity involves Black women taking themselves seriously enough to exert their agency and craft lives in response to (and even beyond) a world that repeatedly limits and pigeonholes Black womanhood.[43] Traditional communalism stresses that Womanists are Black women who unapologetically love and prefer Blackness in its varied forms and use cultural assets to affirm and support each other.[44] Redemptive self-love is the purposeful act of Black people reclaiming stereotypes used to shame Black people by loving aspects of Black culture that Black people possess.[45] Finally, critical engagement describes using one's intersectional identities as a Black woman to understand and critique all forms of intersectional oppression with the intent of achieving survival and wholeness.[46] As a consequential ethics that seeks the greatest good over what harms life, this Womanist ethics offers a helpful framework to consider Black women's organized breast cancer control and prevention activities.

Cancer Control

As the World Health Organization defines it, "Cancer control aims to reduce the incidence, morbidity, and mortality of cancer and to improve the quality of life of cancer patients in a defined population, through the systematic implementation of evidence-based interventions for prevention, early detection, diagnosis, treatment, and palliative care."[47]

---

[41] See Stacey M. Floyd-Thomas, "Writing for Our Lives: Womanism as an Epistemological Revolution," in *Deeper Shades of Purple: Womanism in Religion and Society*, ed. S. M. Floyd-Thomas, Religion, Race, and Ethnicity (New York: New York University Press, 2006), 1–16.
[42] Floyd-Thomas, "Writing for Our Lives," 7.
[43] Floyd-Thomas, "Writing for Our Lives," 8.
[44] Floyd-Thomas, "Writing for Our Lives," 9.
[45] Floyd-Thomas, "Writing for Our Lives," 9–10.
[46] Floyd-Thomas, "Writing for Our Lives," 10.
[47] World Health Organization, "Cancer Control Knowledge into Action: WHO Guide for Effective Programmes: Prevention," *World Health Organization*, 2007, iv, www.ncbi.nlm.nih.gov/books/NBK195368/pdf/Bookshelf_NBK195368.pdf.

Effective breast cancer control activities include basic principles like leadership, which entails creating clarity and unity of purpose, by encouraging team building, ownership of the process, and continuous learning, as well as responding to people affected by breast cancer, in order to meet their physical, psychosocial, and spiritual needs.[48] Through the Womanist ethical principles of radical subjectivity, traditional communalism, and redemptive self-love, Black women with breast cancer are engaged in cancer control activities to support the physical, psychosocial, and spiritual needs of Black women with breast cancer. Sista Strut is as an example of a breast cancer control intervention that employs the tenets of Womanist ethics.

Sista Strut is a cause marketing campaign to raise awareness about breast cancer among women of color in the United States.[49] The campaign includes an organized walk which provides information about community resources and benefits local non-profit breast cancer organizations. Organized twenty years ago in Louisiana to bring attention to breast cancer disparities among Black women in the state, the event has spread to cities across the country including New Orleans, Memphis, Jacksonville, St. Louis, Chicago, and Louisville.[50]

In addition to raising awareness about community resources, Sista Strut explicitly draws on the strength of survivors and their families and friends to heighten awareness, promote early detection, and work for breast cancer cures.[51] The walk encourages breast cancer survivors and supporters to walk as a health promoting activity that reduces breast cancer risk.[52] Survivors wear brightly colored t-shirts to highlighting they are survivors.

---

[48] World Health Organization, "Cancer Control Knowledge into Action."

[49] Sista Strut, "Sista Strut," *Sista Strut: Breast Cancer Walk*, 2021, www.sistastrut.org.

[50] LSU Health Foundation New Orleans, "Sista's Strut against Breast Cancer," *LSU Health Foundation New Orleans*, 2021, www.lsuhsc.edu/ newsroom/Sistas Strut Against Breast Cancer.html.

[51] Sista's Strut, "Sista Strut."

[52] National Cancer Institute, "Causes and Prevention," *National Cancer Institute*, 2021, www.cancer.gov/about-cancer/causes-prevention.

The walk is a tangible display of strength in unity for Black breast cancer survivors and cancer survivorship.

The campaign's walk subverts the "Strong Black Woman" image by challenging what "strength" as a cultural attribute means. Redefining Black women's strength reflects radical self-love by reclaiming the strong Black woman stereotype used to hurt Black women to save Black women's lives from breast cancer. Rather than "strength" meaning Black women suffer in silence, the Sista Strut encourages Black women to love and take themselves seriously as breast cancer survivors as an act of radical subjectivity.[53] By dressing in bright colors for the walk, Black women affirm their collective identities as cancer survivors and supporters by coming out of the shadows to celebrate cancer survivorship as an act of traditional communalism.[54]

Bringing cancer survivors and supporters together, the walk additionally reinforces critical engagement by demonstrating that breast cancer is a threat to all Black women. Therefore, it is a matter that Black women, those with breast cancer and those at risk, must collectively struggle against for Black women's survival and wholeness.[55] The walk supports cancer survivors' physical, psychosocial, and spiritual well-being by reinforcing that Black women do not face breast cancer alone. Instead, the strength of Black women to survive breast cancer is found in Black women's organized efforts against disease.

Cancer Prevention

Cancer prevention, defined as action taken to lower the risk of getting cancer, includes engaging in activities that lessen cancer susceptibility, including supporting medical research for cures.[56] Practical ways this occurs for Black women is through organized efforts to educate Black women about breast cancer disparities and by reducing stigma around the

---

[53] Floyd-Thomas, "Writing for Our Lives," 8.
[54] Floyd-Thomas, "Writing for Our Lives," 9.
[55] Floyd-Thomas, "Writing for Our Lives," 10.
[56] National Cancer Institute, "Causes and Prevention."

disease.[57] Reflective of radical subjectivity, traditional communalism, and critical engagement, Sisters Network Inc. is an example of these type of cancer prevention activities.

Sisters Network Inc. (SNI) was founded in 1994 and serves as a leading voice and the only national Black breast cancer survivorship organization in the United States. Governed by an elected board of directors and informed by an appointed medical advisory committee, SNI has a membership of 3,000 and includes more than 25 affiliate survivor-run chapters nationwide.[58] The organization's purpose is to save lives and educate the Black community and others about the breast cancer crisis affecting Black women around the country.[59] As a leading advocacy organization, SNI serves as a source of information for Black women affected by breast cancer and promotes cancer prevention in Black communities.

In 1999, SNI hosted the nation's first national breast cancer conference to examine the impact of breast cancer disparities among Black women. The conference, now in its twelfth year, attracts hundreds of participants, including nationally recognized medical experts. Given the pervasive nature of breast cancer disparities among Black women, the conference has been hosted in metropolitan cities including Houston, Atlanta, Detroit, and Chicago.[60] The organization has several trademark community outreach programs, including "STOP THE SILENCER"—a national branding campaign which challenges resistance to discussing cancer or life-threatening conditions in Black communities. SNI's efforts focus on raising breast cancer awareness and increasing survivorship in Black communities.[61]

---

[57] Diana Price, "Black American Women and Breast Cancer Disparity," *CancerConnect,* September 2020, news.cancerconnect.com/breast-cancer/black-american-women-and-breast-cancer-disparity.

[58] Sisters Network Inc., "Sisters Network Inc. History," *Sisters Network Inc.: A National African American Breast Cancer Survivorship Organization,* 2020, www.sistersnetworkinc.org/history.html.

[59] Sisters Network Inc., "Sisters Network Inc. History."

[60] Sisters Network Inc., "Sisters Network Inc. History."

[61] Sisters Network Inc., "Sisters Network Inc. History."

Karen Eubanks Jackson, Founder/CEO of SNI, a 28-year four-time breast cancer survivor, founded the organization in 1994 during her personal journey with breast cancer.[62] As she sought support, Jackson recognized a lack of "sisterhood" in traditional organizations, namely the lack of Black breast cancer survivors or distinct Black cultural esthetics in these organizations.[63] Additionally, Jackson learned during her breast cancer treatment about the higher breast cancer mortality rate of Black women and breast cancer disparities Black women experience.[64] What additionally prompted Jackson to establish SNI was the limited availability of culturally sensitive materials for Black women with breast cancer.[65]

Jackson's actions in founding SNI reflect radical subjectivity because Jackson took seriously her need as a Black woman with breast cancer to exert her agency to create breast cancer resources for Black women that did not exist.[66] Wanting resources for herself and other Black women affected by breast cancer, Jackson took her advocacy to the next level, thereby reflecting the ethics of traditional communalism and critical engagement by creating an organization that uses the intersectional identities of Black women with breast cancer to critique oppressions that put Black women at risk for higher breast cancer mortality.[67]

As Jackson's biography further underscores, as a breast cancer champion, Jackson's primary motivation for creating SNI was to "break through the silence and shame of breast cancer that immobilizes African American women, restricts their ability to receive support services, interferes with early detection, and ultimately affects their survival rates."[68] Jackson's actions further reflect the ethic of redemptive self-love in that

---

[62] Sisters Network Inc., "Sisters Network Inc. Founder and Ceo Karen Eubanks Jackson," *Sisters Network Inc.: A National African American Breast Cancer Survivorship Organization,* 2020, www.sistersnetworkinc.org/founder.html.
[63] Sisters Network Inc., "Sisters Network Inc. Founder and Ceo Karen Eubanks Jackson."
[64] Sisters Network Inc., "Sisters Network Inc. Founder and Ceo Karen Eubanks Jackson."
[65] Sisters Network Inc., "Sisters Network Inc. Founder and Ceo Karen Eubanks Jackson."
[66] Floyd-Thomas, "Writing for Our Lives," 8.
[67] Floyd-Thomas, "Writing for Our Lives," 9, 10.
[68] Sisters Network Inc., "Sisters Network Inc. Founder and Ceo Karen Eubanks Jackson."

Jackson reclaimed the stereotypes of silence and shame in the Black community about discussing cancer and confronted them head-on in one of the organization's signature initiatives, "STOP THE SILENCER®" This signature initiative encourages Black breast cancer survivors to use their survivorship stories to educate and encourage other Black women to have mammograms and engage in early detection activities.[69] Again, redefining what strength means for Black women, SNI's national creed emphasizes "In Unity there is Strength, In Strength there is Power, In Power there is Change."[70] For both the Sista Strut walk and Sisters Network Inc., strength for Black women is in unity and organizing in service of love, survival, and wholeness for Black women. This is where the transcendent power to struggle against breast cancer comes from for Black women.

Conclusion

Black women face troubles of which breast cancer is but one. Christian theology tells Black women that trouble does not last always. Troubles necessitate a response. Grounded in the primacy of Black women's lives, experiences, thoughts and creative action, Black women have developed a Womanist theology and Womanist ethics in response to troubles. Womanist ethics matters to breast cancer control and prevention because it provides a framework for understanding the ways Black women use the weave of their lives by putting their faith into action to address breast cancer disparities and meet the practical control and prevention needs of Black women with breast cancer.

At Tennessee State University, **Elizabeth A. Williams** is Interim Dean in the College of Public Service and Urban Affairs and Professor of Public

---

[69] Sisters Network Inc., "Sisters Network Inc. History."
[70] Sisters Network Inc., "Home," *Sisters Network Inc.: A National African American Breast Cancer Survivorship Organization*, 2021, www.sistersnetworkinc.org.

Health in the Department of Public Health, Health Administration and Health Sciences. She earned her Ph.D. from the University of Kentucky and an M.Div. from Vanderbilt University. Noted for her work in eliminating cancer health disparities, cultural competence, and community-engaged research, she is the author of *Black Women and Breast Cancer: A Cultural Theology* (2019).

Chapter 8: Social Inequities and Social Justice: Crafting Ethical Priorities for a Global Journey with Cancer

Conor M. Kelly

Conor Kelly examines social inequities and, by strongly advocating for social justice, frames ethical priorities. In particular, he invites to focus not only on what we do not know about cancer (e.g., in terms of scientific understanding and medical know-how), but also on what we already know about cancer regarding its toll on human beings and societies, as well the continuing and even increasing inequities in cancer care across the planet. Hence, new ethical priorities for the ongoing global journey with cancer require a greater emphasis on combatting the disparities that shape peoples' experiences of cancer, expand access to the cancer treatments that are known to work and work well, and increase access to palliative care for patients with cancer.

There is a lot we do not know about cancer. Granted, the scientific understanding of cancer has come a long way, and the medical know-how needed to treat cancer has ballooned in the last fifty years (and truly exploded in the last twenty), but one cannot shake the feeling that we are still only seeing the proverbial tip of the iceberg when it comes to the human understanding of cancer. This is why so many contemporary cancer treatments are experimental, why the United States spends billions of dollars on cancer research every year, and why patients facing cancer diagnoses regularly seek out second opinions. There is much we do not know about cancer, and these knowledge gaps leave us searching for new answers.

This instinct—to search for understanding—is a good one. As a theologian grounded in a tradition that insists that an innate "desire to know the truth" (*Fides et Ratio*, Introduction) is a quintessential mark of our shared humanity, I would never deny the intrinsic good to be found in the pursuit of knowledge and understanding, nor would I gloss over of the pragmatic benefits that emerge when more accurate assessments of a given problem lead us to more meaningful solutions. Nevertheless, as a theologian and ethicist, I believe our search for answers in the sphere of cancer, while commendable, has skewed our priorities and therefore left us ill-equipped to address the rising global cancer pandemic. We have let our thirst for knowledge get the better of us, and consequently we now put so much energy into what we do not know about cancer that we are losing sight of what we do know. This shift in focus is intolerable because what we do know about cancer reveals dramatic ethical insufficiencies.

The point of this chapter is to correct this imbalance, chiefly by articulating the ethical insufficiencies involved and then describing a new path forward that would allow us to avoid replicating the current injustices while we come to 63 terms with the fact that cancer is not a Global North problem but a human one. To achieve these ends, the chapter has three parts. The first part emphasizes some of the most poignant "knowns" of cancer, including and especially what is known about the disparities in cancer rates and cancer treatments, because these facts reveal both our current priorities in the so-called fight against cancer and the inadequacy of those priorities from an ethical perspective. The second part explores how the framing of this approach as a fight dictates the priorities and contributes to the disparities, even though this framing builds upon a doubly false narrative that we must correct. The final part describes an alternative framing that can help us refocus on what we do know, stimulating new ethical priorities for the global cancer pandemic before us.

The Ethical Insufficiencies behind the Known Facts about Cancer's Disparities

Consider some of the basic facts that we know about cancer at this moment. One thing we know is that the incidence of cancer is on the rise and will continue to rise, not only in the wealthier nations of the Global North but also throughout the Global South. As a result, we know that cancer is and will continue to be an ever more common cause of death across the globe. This simple fact offers one concrete way to capture the notion of a rising global cancer pandemic: there will be more people dying from cancer across the globe as time wears on.

Significantly, we also know something about how the burden of these deaths will be distributed. Deaths from certain forms of cancer will be concentrated almost exclusively in the wealthier nations of the Global North because they will be tied to affluence, either directly—as a result of behavioral factors such as sedentary lifestyles, red meat consumption, and obesity that are more common with more resources—or indirectly—for instance, if they primarily develop as a result of aging and are therefore more common in nations with the highest life expectancies, because this measure is highly correlated with Gross Domestic Product (GDP) per capita.[1] Deaths from other types of cancer, meanwhile, will be concentrated in the less economically rich nations of the Global South, or in the poorer communities found within the economically powerful nations of the Global North, because the mortality rates of some cancers are closely tied to socio-economic status.[2] In these latter cases, two distinct trends impact mortality.

---

[1] See Susan J. Curry, Tim Byers, Maria Elizabeth Hewitt, and National Cancer Policy Board (U.S.), eds., *Fulfilling the Potential of Cancer Prevention and Early Detection* (Washington, DC: National Academies Press, 2003), 41–86. On the link between red meat and certain cancers, see Cheryl L. Rock, Cynthia Thomson, Ted Gansler, Susan M. Gapstur, Marjorie L. McCullough, Alpa V. Patel, Kimberly S. Andrews, Elisa V. Bandera, Colleen K. Spees, Kimberly Robien, Sheri Hartman, Kristen Sullivan, Barbara L. Grant, Kathryn K. Hamilton, Lawrence H. Kushi, Bette J. Caan, Debra Kibbe, Jessica Donze Black, Tracy L. Wiedt, Catherine McMahon, Kirsten Sloan, and Colleen Doyle, "American Cancer Society Guideline for Diet and Physical Activity for Cancer Prevention," *CA: A Cancer Journal for Clinicians* 70, no. 4 (2020): 245–271, at 254. For the links between cancer and age, see Mary C. White, Dawn M. Holman, Jennifer E. Boehm, Lucy A. Peipins, Melissa Grossman, and S. Jane Henley, "Age and Cancer Risk: A Potentially Modifiable Relationship," *American Journal of Preventative Medicine* 46, no. 3 Suppl. 1 (2014): S7–15. For the correlation between income and life expectancy, see Samuel H. Preston, "The Changing Relation between Mortality and Level of Economic Development," *International Journal of Epidemiology* 36, no. 3 (2007): 484–490.

[2] See Francis P. Boscoe, Christopher J. Johnson, Recinda L. Sherman, David G. Stinchcomb, Ge Lin, and Kevin A. Henry, "The Relationship between Area Poverty Rate and Site-Specific Cancer Incidence in the United States," *Cancer* 120, no. 14 (2014): 2191–2198.

First, because the "lack of options" is one of the key features of poverty, people living in poverty often find themselves facing conditions that increase their risk of cancer even as they simultaneously have fewer opportunities to extricate themselves from these circumstances.[3] Thus, although the lifestyle risk factors identified a moment ago are accurately associated with the choices of luxury, they are also experienced by those in poverty, but usually by force of imposition rather than election. For example, the "poor diet" of someone in poverty can often be traced to the fact that food deserts are heavily concentrated in the poorest neighborhoods in the United States, limiting access to the fruits and vegetables known to reduce cancer risk and instead forcing people with lower incomes to rely on processed foods that expose them to carcinogens and contribute to other risk factors like obesity.[4] In these ways and more, the lack of options accompanying poverty shapes cancer burdens for the poor.

Second, in addition to the increased exposures to risk factors that influence whether someone develops cancer, poverty also influences what happens after cancer arrives, because access to early diagnosis and treatment is directly correlated with wealth.[5] People living in poverty,

---

[3] Sandra M. Schneiders, "A Vow of Poverty," in *Poverty: Responding Like Jesus*, ed. K. R. Himes and C. M. Kelly (Brewster, MA: Paraclete Press, 2018), 41–48, at 46.

[4] See Andrew Deener, "The Origins of the Food Desert: Urban Inequality as Infrastructural Exclusion," *Social Forces* 95, no. 3 (2017): 1285–1309. For a metanalysis of the diets known to have the most preventative impact on cancer, see Mark T. Williams and Norman G. Hord, "The Role of Dietary Factors in Cancer Prevention: Beyond Fruits and Vegetables," *Nutrition in Clinical Practice* 20, no. 4 (2005): 451–459. Notably, the environmental injustices of concentrating green spaces in richer areas and concentrating polluting industries in poorer ones offer a second illustration of the structural influences shaping the lifestyle "choices" of individuals living in poverty. Philip Landrigan's work highlights these unjust tendencies. See, for instance, Philip J. Landrigan, et al., "The *Lancet* Commission on Pollution and Health," *Lancet* 391, no. 10119 (2018): 462–512, at esp. 474 and 487-492.

[5] See Paul C. Pearlman, Rao Divi, Michael Gwede, Pushpa Tandon, Brian S. Sorg, Miguel R. Ossandon, Lokesh Agrawal, Vinay Pai, Houston Baker, and Tiffani Bailey Lash, "The National Institutes of Health Affordable Cancer Technologies Program: Improving Access to Resource-Appropriate Technologies for Cancer Detection, Diagnosis, Monitoring, and Treatment in Low- and Middle-Income Countries," *IEEE Journal of Translational*

then, are less likely to benefit from the new technologies and new treatment plans that have sprung from our perennial fixation on what we do not know about cancer. As a result, the cancers that are concentrated among those in conditions of poverty are much deadlier than those that are concentrated in higher-income areas, a trend that holds both within nations and between nations.[6]

The best way to express the influence of all these trends on the disparate experiences of the burden of cancer is to recognize that, "when it comes to cancer, the poor are more likely to die of the disease, while the affluent are more likely to die with the disease."[7] This is the state of affairs that has emerged from pouring so much time, energy, and money into the question of what we do not know about cancer at the expense of what we do. Those efforts have translated into an increased attention on the cancers concentrated in richer nations and richer communities while limiting the attention paid to cancers concentrated in less wealthy nations and less wealthy communities. This has, helpfully, lowered mortality rates in those wealthier regions but at the cost of a growing gap that reflects implicit priorities that we cannot maintain if we are going to confront the rising global cancer pandemic appropriately.

The fundamental flaw in our current set of priorities, as reflected in these disparate burdens, is that they are unethical. In concrete terms, they represent a violation of social justice. Our current set of priorities transgresses social justice because it maintains a state of affairs in which the burden of cancer's mortality is distributed not just unevenly but unfairly. Norman Daniels, the philosopher and bioethicist, provides the theoretical

---

Engineering in Health and Medicine 4 (2016): 2800708, doi.org/10.1109/JTEHM.2016.2604485.

[6] See Boscoe et al., "The Relationship between Area Poverty Rate and Site-Specific Cancer Incidence in the United States," 2194; Mahshid Ghoncheh and Hamid Salehiniya, "Inequality in the Incidence and Mortality of All Cancers in the World," *Iranian Journal of Public Health* 45, no. 12 (2016): 1675–1677.

[7] Dr. Francis Boscoe, quoted in Hematology Times Staff, "Wealth Appears to Affect Distribution of Cancer Types," *MD Edge*, May 28, 2014, www.mdedge.com/hematology-oncology/article/185896/lymphoma-plasma-cell-disorders/wealth-appears-affect-distribution-cancer.

resources to justify this claim, for he explains in *Just Health* that "a health inequality is an inequity if it is the result of an unjust distribution of the socially controllable factors affecting population health and its distribution."[8] Appealing to John Rawls's famous *Theory of Justice*, Daniels further clarifies that a just distribution of these burdens would be one that leaves the least well-off in their best absolute position.[9] Unquestionably, the current situation of disparate cancer burdens is not the best we can achieve for the least well-off. There is little room to assert that the "socially controllable factors affecting population health and its distribution" are shared in what Rawls would describe as a fair and equitable fashion when it comes to cancer. It is hard to imagine an abstracted moral agent behind the "veil of ignorance" agreeing to a system in which environmental carcinogens are the almost inevitable lot of communities of color and people with the smallest incomes and lowest educational attainments.[10] Likewise, the current distribution of income (a key social determinant of health) between the Global North and the Global South is hardly to the benefit of the least well-off. On the contrary, there is an injustice to our current social inequalities, and thus they constitute social inequities violating social justice. Insofar as our current priorities for responding to cancer reinforce these connections, they are unethical.

The violations identified by Daniels's procedural account of social justice are not, however, the only flaws in our existing priorities. They are similarly indicted by a substantive account of social justice, like the one found in the Catholic theological tradition, which describes social justice

---

[8] Norman Daniels, *Just Health: Meeting Health Needs Fairly* (New York: Cambridge University Press, 2008), 101.

[9] See Daniels, *Just Health: Meeting Health Needs Fairly*, 92–97. He refers to John Rawls, *A Theory of Justice* (Cambridge, MA: Belknap Press of Harvard University Press, 1971).

[10] For one study into the clustering of pollution in relation to race, poverty, and educational attainment, see Michelle L. Bell and Keita Ebisu, "Environmental Inequality in Exposures to Airborne Particulate Matter Components in the United States," *Environmental Health Perspectives* 120, no. 12 (2012): 1699–1704. For the importance of the "veil of ignorance" in Rawls's theory of justice, see Rawls, *A Theory of Justice*, 118–123.

in relation to participation and insists *"that persons have an obligation to be active and productive participants in the life of society and that society has a duty to enable them to participate in this way"* (USCCB, *Economic Justice for All*, no. 71). According to this definition, social justice can be measured against people's ability to contribute productively to the common good of their communities. This has immediate implications for the disparate burdens of cancer that result from our current priorities because, as anyone who has accompanied someone with cancer can attest, cancer has a dramatic effect on a person's ability to engage in social life.[11] Notably, Daniels alludes to this idea when he describes health as "necessary to protect opportunity" and explains that good health is a prerequisite to pursuing one's life projects and engaging in society more broadly.[12] Insofar as our current priorities in relation to cancer treatment reinforce the limited participation of certain groups in social life, they undermine society's duty to enable all its members to participate in an active and productive way and thus violate the substantive norms of social justice. They are unethical.

Root Causes behind the Warped Priorities to Date

Granted, it is easy to cast stones, but the real value of a critical diagnosis like this can be measured by its ability to contribute to the development of an alternative, and improved, approach. Such a contribution can emerge from this analysis, provided we are willing to explore what has allowed us to respond to cancer in a way that violates both procedural and substantive accounts of social justice. While the astute reader already has some sense of where I think the roots of this problem lie, given my comments about the

---

[11] Researchers note these trends and highlight the fact that their impact extends far beyond the person with cancer: "The burden of cancer extends beyond mortality. Individuals who are affected by a diagnosis of cancer experience physical suffering, distress, and diminished quality of life associated with disease-related symptoms, diagnostic procedures, cancer therapies, and long-term/late adverse effects of treatment. Moreover, quality of life can also be substantially reduced for family, caregivers, and friends of patients with cancer." Rock et al., "American Cancer Society Guideline for Diet and Physical Activity for Cancer Prevention," 245.

[12] Daniels, *Just Health: Meeting Health Needs Fairly*, 30. See also 31–46 more broadly.

impact of our focus on the unknowns of cancer over its knowns, this second part of the chapter will push that point even further. It is not simply that we are focusing on a narrow set of questions to the exclusion of others, it is also that we are approaching those questions with a narrow set of assumptions about what we should be trying to achieve by asking them. Specifically, we have let unethical priorities shape our approach to cancer because we are framing the appropriate response almost exclusively in the combative terms of a war that must be won instead of using a more honest analogy.

I am, of course, not the first person to raise concerns about the use of war metaphors for the "fight" against cancer. Physicians and bioethicists have long raised alarm about the impact of military metaphors in medicine, arguing in both scholarly contexts and popular publications that it is problematic to describe a patient's treatment process as a battle because of the disassociations this language evokes.[13] Psychologists, meanwhile, have shown that military metaphors can increase apprehension and fatalistic thinking and decrease a person's overall willingness to pursue treatment.[14] These important criticisms, however, tend to focus on patients' experiences, and what I want to highlight is that this framing extends far beyond the doctor-patient relationship and actually influences the priorities of our collective approach to cancer more broadly, causing us to overemphasize some of the costliest pathways for addressing cancer while shying away from the ones that might do the most good.

At this broader level, the problem is that envisioning humanity's engagement with cancer as a war to be won undergirds an entire system

---

[13] See, for instance, Abraham Fuks, "The Military Metaphors of Modern Medicine," in *The Meaning Management Challenge: Making Sense of Health, Illness and Disease*, ed. Z. Li and T. L. Long (Oxford: Inter-Disciplinary Press, 2010), 57–68; Dhruv Khullar, "The Trouble with Medicine's Metaphors," *The Atlantic*, August 7, 2014, www.theatlantic.com/health/archive/2014/08/the-trouble-with-medicines-metaphors/374982.

[14] See David J. Hauser and Norbert Schwarz, "The War on Prevention II: Battle Metaphors Undermine Cancer Treatment and Prevention and Do Not Increase Vigilance," *Health Communication* 35, no. 13 (2020): 1698–1704.2

dedicated not so much to the wellbeing of individual persons with cancer but to the eradication of cancer as an abstract cause of death. While this may not seem particularly problematic at first glance, the truth is that it has led to the priorities that support our current system of social inequities instead of social justice. This framing simply is not sufficient for crafting the priorities we need to manage the rising global cancer pandemic ahead of us.

Here it will be useful to mine the war imagery a little more deeply. In modern warfare, victory typically belongs to the most technologically advanced nations with the greatest economic resources to pour into their war effort, yielding the concomitant assumption that loss is inevitable for anyone who lacks these tools. Describing cancer in military terms encourages us to translate these assumptions into the "war on cancer," where we similarly imagine that investment in the newest technologies is the only way to make any real progress, and we likewise accept that some nations (and, although we are loath to admit it, maybe even some patients) will get left behind as a matter of necessity. Thus, we arrive at the current unjust state of affairs, where novel treatments make big differences for those nations and patients with the most resources, while other cancers and other cancer patients fade from view.

If this process were ultimately to propel us to that final miracle cure—the silver bullet technology that would allow us to treat every form of cancer in every patient—perhaps we would be able to say that the sacrifices were worth it. In fact, we might even use Rawls's difference principle to insist that these sacrifices were just.[15] But as with real-life wars, this military framing assuages our consciences far too quickly, glossing over real losses with an appeal to the same *dulce et decorum est* assertions that the poet Wilfred Owen savaged after World War I.[16] Much like that "old Lie" (to borrow Owen's description of the phrase), the analogical allusions to "the greater good" found in the war against cancer similarly fall apart upon further review, for two reasons.

---

[15] See Rawls, *A Theory of Justice*, 72.
[16] "Dulce et Decorum Est," in Wilfred Owen, *Poems* (New York: Viking Press, 1921), 15.

First, the military framing misunderstands the human condition, prioritizing the annihilation of mortality despite the fact that death is a fundamental part of our human experience. Appeals to transhumanism aside, this is a quixotic quest, for even if we eliminated cancer as a cause of mortality, we would still die of something. The military metaphors obscure this reality, causing us to pursue the prolongation of life at all costs. Certainly, i have theological reasons for interpreting this as an untenable outcome, but I am fundamentally asserting a human point rather than a theological one: mortality is a defining feature of our human condition and any approach that fails to grapple honestly with our mortality is not an approach that will lead to good human priorities.[17]

The second shortcoming of the military framing is that it overstates the value of our resources. In part, because there is a limit to the benefits we can expect to achieve as mortal beings, there is a real limit to what our money can buy. On this point, I want to speak from a personal perspective and share that in the span of approximately fourteen months (from 2019 to 2020), I lost both my mother-in-law and my mother to two different types of cancer. Both women had the benefits of some of the most positive social determinants of health leading up to their diagnoses and both had access to the highest levels of cancer care available in this country. By all accounts, they had tremendous advantages in their "battles" with cancer. They were the ones who, based on the disparities described earlier, should have died with cancer, not from it, and yet they both died as a direct result of their disease. Their stories are, of course, anecdotal, but their particulars reveal a more universal truth, namely that however much superior firepower may prove decisive in actual warfare, there is no guaranteed way to "win" a "war" with cancer.

---

[17] For one explanation of the theological rationale for critiquing the tendency to fight mortality at all costs, see the republished Pius XII, "The Prolongation of Life: An Address to an International Congress of Anesthesiologists, November 24, 1957," *National Catholic Bioethics Quarterly* 9, no. 2 (2009): 327–332, at 329.

Toward Renewed Ethical Priorities

The sooner we can come to terms with both these realities—the inevitability of mortality and what can be described as the nonlinear relationship between resources and outcomes—the sooner we will be able to respond to the global cancer pandemic in a more just and equitable fashion. One way to start this shift is to re-envision the framing for our response. One reason for our current unjust prioritization of treatments for the cancers that have the highest prevalence in the richest areas (again, defined comparatively between nations and within nations) is our reliance on military metaphors, which allow us to accept that certain fronts in the war (and certain types of "soldiers") are worth fighting for while others simply are not. If we swapped out metaphors, however, and envisioned humanity's relationship with cancer as a journey, just as practitioners, patients, and researchers advocate, then we would be less apt to build our response around the assumption that exclusions are an inevitable, and therefore acceptable, cost of success.[18] Instead, we would be better able to acknowledge the contours of our present condition and thus would have a more honest engagement with what we do know about cancer, especially what we know about its disparate impact.

In practical terms, I think this shift in focus can lead to new ethical priorities for our ongoing global journey with cancer, and so I conclude with a brief outline of the two that I think are the most important. First, a journey built around an honest appreciation of what we do know about cancer should put greater emphasis on combatting the disparities that shape peoples' experiences of cancer and not just combatting the cancer itself. Certainly, the rebalancing of prevention and treatment should be one part of this expanded project, but this is not the only option. Another avenue includes social interventions designed to increase access to the social determinants that have the most positive impact on health outcomes. Public policies promoting things like education can have a

---

[18] For the comparative benefits of journey metaphors in cancer treatment, see Hauser and Schwarz, "The War on Prevention II: Battle Metaphors Undermine Cancer Treatment and Prevention and Do Not Increase Vigilance," 1701–1702.

dramatic impact on health and well-being, even in the poorest nations.[19] In other words, the first priority must be to increase the attention paid to the structural factors undergirding the disparate burden of cancer so that we can began to tackle the inequities and violations of social justice that we have tolerated for so long under our present paradigm.

Second, building further on what we do know about cancer, another priority that must be included in our global journey is to expand access to the cancer treatments that are known to work and work well, so that they are no longer the exclusive property of the richest patients and the richest nations. Importantly, I want to acknowledge that most of these treatments only came about as a result of research into the unknowns about cancer. We should not abandon cancer's unknowns altogether, but we should ensure that we do not ignore the ethically impactful knowns in the process. A related way in which we can do this is to increase access to palliative care for patients with cancer. As Alexandre Martins has argued persuasively, "Palliative care is not a privilege of high-income countries but a global health commitment that must be part of the agenda of public health actions and advocacy for health care as a human right."[20] In fact, this might be the most important priority to come out of the revised framing, for if we truly see the experience of cancer as a journey, then palliative care's holistic approach will be an essential tool. After all, if fighting against mortality is no longer the main goal, then accompanying one another in a rejection of isolation must become our top priority.[21]

Undoubtedly, there are other priorities we can add, but if we make these two shifts, we will go a long way in developing a more ethical, and more effective, response to the rising global cancer pandemic, in large part

---

[19] See Daniels, *Just Health: Meeting Health Needs Fairly*, 142–143.

[20] Alexandre A. Martins, "Non-Communicable and Chronic Diseases in Developing Countries: Putting Palliative Care on the Global Health Agenda," in *Catholic Bioethics and Social Justice: The Praxis of US Health Care in a Globalized World*, ed. M. T. Lysaught and M. P. McCarthy (Collegeville, MN: Liturgical Press Academic, 2018), 329–341, at 332.

[21] For the contrast between mortality and isolation as the fundamental challenge of human existence, see Samuel Wells, "Rethinking Service," *The Cresset* 76, no. 4 (2013): 6–14.

because we will be accounting for and attending to what we do know about cancer and not just what we do not yet understand.

....

Conor M. Kelly, Ph.D., is associate professor and chair of the department of theology at Marquette University in Milwaukee, WI. In 2020 he published the volume *The Fullness of Free Time: A Theological Account of Leisure and Recreation in the Moral Life* in the Moral Traditions series published by Georgetown University Press. Forthcoming is a co-edited volume on the moral theology of Pope Francis.

Chapter 9: Navigating the Continuum of Care: Common Goods and Uncommon Experiences

Christian Cintron

In light of his experience as clinical bioethicist in a healthcare institution in the U.S.A. (Anne Arundel Medical Center in Annapolis, MD), Christian Cintron reflects on concrete challenges—from the COVID-19 pandemic to the increasing costs of cancer care for individuals and families—that test the ability of providing care to cancer patients. Hence, policy reforms are urgent. They should aim at transforming practices in prevention and in providing care, while avoiding what he calls "financial toxicity." The stories of three patients exemplify both the ethical concerns and the needed structural solutions to foster prevention. The equitable participation of cancer patients through solidaristic practices exemplifies one approach leading to systemic improvements.

In late 2020, as the United States experienced a pre-holiday season lull in COVID-19 cases, a team of medical oncologists practicing in New York expressed their concerns for cancer patients whose care had been and would continue to be disrupted by COVID-19.[1] They argued that their patients, predominantly racial and ethnic minorities, were more likely to have jobs as essential workers that increased their risk of COVID-19, to work lower income jobs with minimal or no health insurance, to experience fractured care related to the various technological requirements and personal desire for effective telemedicine and transportation resources, and to demonstrate inadequate levels of health care literacy. These concerns were largely validated by a COVID-19 and cancer outcomes study that reported a decrease in all visits by Hispanic cancer patients when

---

[1] See Onyinye D. Balogun, Vivian J. Bea, and Erica Phillips, "Disparities in Cancer Outcomes Due to COVID-19: A Tale of 2 Cities," *JAMA Oncology* 6, no. 10 (2020): 1531–1532.

compared to White patients, and that both Black and Hispanic patients were less likely to use telehealth during the pandemic.[2] Both the results from the study and the warnings from Drs. Balogun, Bea, and Phillips highlight some of the everyday challenges in the provision of comprehensive cancer care. Without categorizing their concerns, the oncologists identify exemplary ways in which health care is influenced by the social determinants of health that effectuated an inequitable distribution of health for persons who suffer from those social factors disproportionately. In addition to the educational, socioeconomic, and transportation factors noted by the oncologists, other social, health system, and economic factors influence health. The interrelated dimensions of health and health care affect people's participation in health care, their ability to contribute to family and communal needs, and ultimately their promotion of the common good. Cancer care, particularly for the marginalized populations about which the COVID-19-worried oncologists were concerned, is an important context for examining the conditions necessary for health that are not only related to the cause of disease but also to its remediation.

The common cancer care protocol of surgery, chemotherapy, and radiation has been relatively unchanged in recent decades.[3] Though personalized for each individual, the efficacy of the protocol is influenced by genetic and biologic variations, as well as influential social variations that contribute to or inhibit the remediation of cancer. Common among the social influences leading to personalized adjustments in plans of care are the short and long-term financial consequences of cancer care. Much

---

[2] See Andrew L. Schmidt, Ziad Bakouny, Sheena Bhalla, John A. Steinharter, Douglas A. Tremblay, Mark M. Awad, Alaina J. Kessler, Robert I. Haddad, Michelle Evans, Fiona Busser, Michael Wotman, Catherine R. Curran, Brittney S. Zimmerman, Gabrielle Bouchard, Tomi Jun, Pier V. Nuzzo, Qian Qin, Laure Hirsch, Jonathan Feld, Kaitlin M. Kelleher, Danielle Seidman, Hsin-Hui Huang, Heather M. Anderson-Keightly, Sarah Abou Alaiwi, Talia D. Rosenbloom, Penina S. Stewart, Matthew D. Galsky, Toni K. Choueiri, and Deborah B. Doroshow, "Cancer Care Disparities During the COVID-19 Pandemic: COVID-19 and Cancer Outcomes Study," *Cancer Cell* 38, no. 6 (2020): 769–770.

[3] See Azra Raza, *The First Cell: And the Human Costs of Pursuing Cancer to the Last* (New York: Basic Books, 2019).

attention has been paid to alleviating the financial burden experienced by patients, their families and, by extension, society over the last decade, but the challenges created by the totality of costs remain. Because of the ways in which cancer care is influenced by the social determinants of health,[4] attention to the costs and the manner they disproportionately affect some groups helps illuminate the interdependent nature of the social determinants of health within the experiences of cancer care. Not being able to maintain participation in care because one cannot afford co-pays, utility bills, adequate housing, or quality food, among other financial responsibilities, reminds us that there are innumerable, interrelated, socially-mediated obstacles to overcome as we look to create the necessary conditions for all persons to participate equitably in cancer care.

The Social Determinants of Health

The influence of the social determinants of health, and in particular the crosscutting determinant of socioeconomic status, is known to disproportionately affect the delivery of health care to racial and ethnic minorities. In cancer care, the effects of lower socioeconomic status upon racial and ethnic minorities are amplified because of the high costs of cancer care generally and, more specifically, because of the exceptionally high costs relative to the timing of diagnosis, the type of cancer, and treatment. While the challenges emanating from the social determinants of health are widely known, the societal acceptance of those challenges is most alarming. Failure to address the root causes responsible for the disparate experiences in cancer care demonstrates a lack of commitment to establishing and maintaining the conditions necessary for individuals to pursue their own health and well-being. In so doing, the collective malaise undermines not only the potential for the health of Navigating the Continuum of Care: Common Goods and Uncommon Experiences marginalized patients but also the totality of the health care system as cancer care costs go unfettered and the deleterious financial consequences distress families and healthcare institutions.

---

[4] See Schmidt et al., "Cancer Care Disparities During the COVID-19 Pandemic."

The systemic effects of the social determinants that undermine or inhibit the health of certain individuals demonstrate myriad challenges to achieving the common good, understood as "the sum of those conditions of social life which allow social groups and their individual members relatively thorough and ready access to their own fulfillment" (*Gaudium et Spes*, no. 26). While appeals to the common good may not resonate with the responsible institutions and the persons comprising them (as evidenced by the lack of change in the face of known disparities and their causes), it is more likely that exploring the particular ways in which the lives individual cancer patients are affected by the costs and interrelated social determinants of health will inspire much-needed change. Several inpatient vignettes will highlight the ways in which the current approach to the provision of cancer care and its related costs limit the ability for individuals and society writ large to achieve the common good.

Three Patients' Stories

A 61-year-old male presents with a 6-week history of jaundice, fatigue, weight loss, anorexia, nausea, and dry skin. During a telemedicine visit six weeks prior to his hospitalization, his primary care provider suggested that he likely had an infection. The patient is known to have a family history of cancer, including his deceased mother and father and sisters who were diagnosed in their late 30s. During his inpatient evaluation, a pancreatic mass is discovered. Regarding the course of events for this patient, the collective healthcare system's (i.e., U.S. healthcare as guided by the Centers for Disease Control and Prevention, CDC) focus on preventative cancer care was somehow unfulfilled, particularly in light of his family history. Sadly, delays in diagnosis are known to contribute to higher costs. The average cost of initial diagnosis and treatment across all sites is $43,516 according to the National Cancer Institute's (NCI) 2020 estimates, with pancreatic cancer costs averaging $108,165. An additional burden of delaying the diagnosis is the increased risk of mortality, which obviously affects how individuals are able to participate in the lives of their families, workplaces, and communities.

Another patient has been admitted to the intensive care unit for complications related to her metastatic bladder cancer. The 79-year-old woman has a history of hypertension, diabetes mellitus II, and atrial fibrillation with rapid ventricular rate. Her computed tomography (CT) scan showed possible fluid collection in her anterior abdominal wall and extensive metastatic disease in her chest, abdomen, and pelvis. As she moves forward with the necessary procedures to treat her symptoms, her comorbidities and disease progression will likely trap her in a cycle of post-acute care with each repeat admission taking its toll on her health, resulting in longer and costlier stays in hospitals and post-acute care facilities. Research has shown that health-related Navigating the Continuum of Care: Common Goods and Uncommon Experiences quality of life is negatively impacted by the financial distress of health care.[5] Financial distress has outranked physical, emotional, social, and family distress, all of which can be exacerbated by the totality of consequences from the cycle of inpatient and post-acute treatment. For patients like this one, there exists a possibility for financial distress to feature prominently in perception of health-related quality of life as the new diagnosis cost for bladder cancer averages $26,442 with continuing (yearly) costs of $6,350. Considering the additional psycho-social supports and indirect cancer care costs suggests that a more comprehensive effort will need to be made to facilitate or make possible her overall well-being.

Finally, a 62-year-old female admitted to the oncology unit for abdominal pain and elevated sodium is known to have a history of liver cirrhosis with recurrent ascites, diabetes mellitus II, alcohol abuse, Chronic Obstructive Pulmonary Disease (COPD), hypertension, and lung cancer that required a lobectomy four years ago. During her admission, her liver pathology demonstrates findings consistent with moderatelyt o poorly differentiated hepatocellular carcinoma that is determined to be unresectable. She was not able to complete the first line

---

[5] See PDQ Adult Treatment Editorial Board, "Financial Toxicity and Cancer Treatment (PDQR): Health Professional Version," *PDQ Cancer Information Summaries* (Bethesda, MD: National Cancer Institute, 2021), www.ncbi.nlm.nih.gov/books/NBK384502/.

therapy because of her worsening liver function and has been told that she has reached the end stages of her disease process. The cost of liver cancer in the last year of life averages $92,133. In light of the median household income of $62,843, the treating end-stage liver cancer is largely cost-prohibitive for a majority of Americans. In most cases, costly life-prolonging treatments or clinical trials are pursued despite the fact that there is not a significant commensurate benefit (i.e., cure, aplliation, significant lief-extension, or improvement in health-related quality of life). Aggressive care plans at the end-of-life test the limits of health insurance (i.e., approval of therapies and interventions) and personal financial health often pushing patients toward the potential for bankruptcy.

Cancer Care and Its Costs

The downstream financial consequences for persons and families who are already socioeconomically disadvantaged are manifold. It is not uncommon that collective lost wages, depleted savings, and the brink of bankruptcy can lead to persons and families being displaced from housing. Additionally, the inability to absorb the continued costs, particularly in the end-of-life, proves deleterious for subsequent generations as the concomitant socioeconomic factors may continue to inhibit the possibility of financial health in the wake of aggressive cancer care. Though it is possible that portions of the financial burden can be mitigated through various cancer foundations and philanthropic organizations, the criteria for receipt of those funds are such that persons and their families must be close to dire financial straits. The reasons for the financial burden, aside from the direct costs of cancer care, are multifarious and linked to the social determinants of health and their causes. Unfortunately, authorized housing utility and food assistance through hospital foundations, and other assistance through private philanthropic organizations, cannot entirely mitigate the financially toxic burden of cancer care for individuals, their families, and by extension, their communities.

The totality of costs, direct and indirect, related to cancer care is staggering. With medical service and oral prescription drug costs in the U.S. approaching $166,000 in direct care costs, the attention to the causes and remedies for financial distress is needed. That need is further amplified because of the challenges in quantifying the indirect costs of care incurred by individuals and families resulting from lost wages, transportation costs, and the costs of additional caregivers. The detrimental cumulative effects of cancer care costs are often described using the term financial toxicity. Financial toxicity describes the ways in which the total financial burden of cancer care affects patients and their families, having first been used in 2013.[6] The term encompasses many of the above-mentioned challenges, including adhering to treatment, quality of life, bankruptcy, and an increased risk of mortality.

While the experience of shockingly high billed charges is shared, the aggregate effects of the social determinants contributing to the inability to pay for cancer care are known to disproportionately affect marginalized persons and communities. Census data reveal that racial and ethnic minorities are more likely to be socioeconomically disadvantaged, live in substandard housing, and have less access to high quality health care. The data also reveal that they are more likely to have poorer health and specifically cancer-related outcomes.[7] For example, unreliable transportation, which is directly related to time to diagnosis and adherence to treatment plans, can lead to increased costs associated with late-stage diagnosis (i.e., aggressive treatment and resulting inability to participate in daily activities).[8]

Not having adequate savings depends on one's employment status. Similarly, one's home environment can infringe upon one's ability to pay

---

[6] See S. Yousuf Zafar and Amy P. Abernethy, "Financial Toxicity, Part I: A New Name for a Growing Problem," *Oncology (Williston Park)* 27, no. 2 (2013): 80–81, 149. See also S. Yousuf Zafar, Jeffrey M. Peppercorn, Deborah Schrag, Donald H. Taylor, Amy M. Goetzinger, Xiaoyin Zhong, and Amy P. Abernethy, "The Financial Toxicity of Cancer Treatment: A Pilot Study Assessing out-of-Pocket Expenses and the Insured Cancer Patient's Experience," *Oncologist* 18, no. 4 (2013): 381–390.

[7] See PDQ Adult Treatment Editorial Board, "Financial Toxicity and Cancer Treatment (PDQR): Health Professional Version."

[8] See Samina T. Syed, Ben S. Gerber, and Lisa K. Sharp, "Traveling Towards Disease: Transportation Barriers to Health Care Access," *Journal of Community Health* 38, no. 5 (2013): 976–993.

for cancer care as individuals and families choose between costly safe and health promoting homes or other less advantageous options. Additionally, healthcare literacy is linked to increased costs in cancer care. Choosing not to maintain routine wellness checks as a result of misinformation, lack of information, or a wellfounded distrust directed toward medicine almost certainly leads to increased costs later in the cancer care journey. Thus, the experience of financial burden is linked to additional social determinants of health. Financial toxicity and the distress born out of fear of financial hardship that plague individuals, families, and communities, often inter-generationally, will exacerbate the disproportionate burdens of those who unwittingly suffer from the systemic injustices that perpetuate the social determinants of health.

Prevention as Treatment

In order to achieve better health outcomes and mitigate the financial burdens associated with cancer care, cancer treatment is currently oriented toward prevention as the *treatment* for cancer. Much of the design of cancer care in the U.S. originates from the CDC's National Comprehensive Cancer Control Program (NCCCP).[9] States are tasked with adapting the national framework to their local population needs and collaborating with local hospital systems and other agencies and organizations.

In Maryland, for example, lung cancer is one of the most commonly diagnosed cancers. From 2012 to 2016, lung cancer was the leading cause of cancer deaths, accounting for more than one quarter (25.1 percent) of all cancer deaths in the state. Thus, in Maryland, preventative efforts for reducing the occurrence of and deaths from lung cancer is a priority aligned to the NCCCP's goal of targeting cancers with the highest rates of incidence and mortality. With further refinement, state-based plans such as that of Maryland uncover who will benefit most from targeted preventative intervention. Secondary analysis in Maryland demonstrates

---

[9] See Centers for Disease Control and Prevention, "National Comprehensive Cancer Control Program (NCCCP)," July 30, 2021, www.cdc.gov/cancer/ncccp/index.htm.

that lung cancer disproportionately affects African Americans, and specifically African American men. Therefore, efforts in Maryland, reflecting the goal of the NCCCP and state-based Maryland Comprehensive Control Plan,[10] are directed toward reducing the incidence and mortality in lung cancer among African Americans. Supported by additional census and public health data, specific efforts to implement strategies aimed at mitigating the effects of the social determinants of health on this community were made. Secondary and tertiary aims such as reducing financial toxicity are outlined in the NCCCP.

Unfortunately, there are not specific mandates within the NCCCP for reducing financial toxicity, so it is incumbent upon the states to monitor and mitigate financial toxicity as best they can. In order to ensure success in mitigating cancer in a given community, coordination among various public and private institutions is required. The public-private and health system community partnerships are central while also highlighting opportunities for improvement.

Recently, Anne Arundel Medical Center[11] completed a lung cancer mitigation and treatment program in collaboration with local health departments and a private grant sponsor. The program was designed to improve the experience across the continuum of cancer care for at risk or diagnosed individuals in three counties by providing a multi-faceted approach to primary and secondary lung cancer prevention that integrated smoking avoidance and cessation, lung cancer screening services, and a Rapid Access Chest and Lung Assessment Program (RACLAP) intended to avoid delays in evaluation and consultation, cut down on unnecessary

---

[10] See Maryland Department of Health, "Maryland Comprehensive Cancer Control Plan 2021–2025," 2021, health.maryland.gov/phpa/cancer/cancerplan/SiteAssets/Pages/publica tions/ Cancer-MD-Maryland_FINAL -1.pdf.

[11] Anne Arundel Medical Center, part of Luminis Health, is a 385-bed community hospital serving Annapolis (MD) and the surrounding area. In 2020, the medical center contributed more than $61 million in community benefit, including subsidized programs and charity care, health education, and research activities.

procedures, provide timely feedback and information to the referring primary provider, and ensure patient and provider satisfaction.[12]

The RACLAP initiative offered interdisciplinary teams to patients and their families so that education, care planning, treatment, and support were provided in an individualized manner. Increased coordination in screening and care-plan development through RACLAP enabled the expansion of the program to minority patient populations whose use rate was incredibly low (10 percent) when compared to Whites (90 percent). In so doing, time-to-diagnosis was decreased, and more early-stage cancers were found when compared to historical marginalized group data.

These improvements likely resulted from increased awareness on behalf of providers who were motivated to refer to RACLAP patients with incidental findings. Cessation initiatives in inpatient care were also implemented during the program and have continued to include bedside interventions and substance abuse center collaboration. Mitigation or avoidance strategies also included education in schools, physician practices, community centers, campuses of large employers, and other venues. While the program was successfully based on the established participant, education, screening, and early identification goals, this program was only able to address one dimension of cancer care that contributes to marginalized groups not participating in cancer prevention or cancer care. The interrelated causes of financial toxicity and associated fear that weigh heavily in the community were reported but not resolved through the program's expanded use of nurse navigators and financial counselors. The health system's work to increase the number of free screenings, obtain co-payment assistance, coordinate transportation, and contribute to living expenses—common among cancer centers—were nominally effective in reducing certain financial burdens and related barriers to care. Surely, there are additional programs that have been

---

[12] See Bristol Myers Squibb, "Bristol Myers Squibb Foundation: Specialty Care for Vulnerable Populations," 2015, www.bms.com/about-us/responsibility/bristol-myers-squibb-foundatio n/our-key-initiatives/specialty-care-for-vulnerable-populations.html. Thanks to Catherine Brady Cupertino and Stephen Cattaneo, MD, and to Maria Christina M. Geronimo for her support in providing grant-funded program details.

equally or more successful in implementing strategies for reducing financial toxicity; however, the multifarious nature of the social determinants of health that influence financial toxicity presents an obstacle that likely exceeds the capacity of local hospital systems.

Addressing Financial Toxicity

Unfortunately, letting cancer patients experience severe financial distress or go into bankruptcy is part of the current healthcare system. Researchers have noted that this is simply not good for patients, physicians, and society,[13] yet it remains the responsibility of local health systems to *fix* it. Enabling the participation of all persons—particularly persons whose cancer care experience is disproportionately burdensome because of the social determinants of health—is not attainable through the work of local health systems alone. Instead, a more comprehensive and systematic approach is needed to both identify the contributing causes of financial toxicity and propose trial remedies for them on a national scale.

The complex problem of financial toxicity requires an equally expansive strategy that includes all contributing persons and institutions. That strategy necessarily begins with the recognition that there is a shared responsibility in promoting the health and well-being of all persons—especially those who suffer disproportionately—and remediating the systemic causes of those burdens. In acknowledging and engaging the interrelated causes in interpersonal (i.e., provider-patient) and institutional (i.e., systemic forces that influence the cancer care experience) relationships, all persons can participate in cancer care. This systemic turn toward a health care delivery model that embodies truly solidaric practices and policies would be capable of generating the requisite changes in cancer care relative to the social determinants of health and financial toxicity.

---

[13] See Diane Mapes, "Cancer, Bankruptcy and Death: Study Finds a Link," *Hutch News Stories,* January 25, 2016, www.fredhutch.org/en/news/center-news/2016/01/cancer-bankruptcy-death-study-financial-toxicity.html.

Dr. Scott Ramsey of the Hutchinson Institute for Cancer Outcomes and Research[14] has earnestly begun the work of enabling the equitable participation of all cancer patients through solidaric practices that offer systemic improvements.[15] In collaboration with the National Cancer Institute's Community Oncology Research Program (NCORP) affiliated clinics, Ramsey's program is attempting to highlight and realize the importance of local and national (i.e., institutional) practices. In coordination with the NCI, the program, complete with dedicated financial counselors, is intended to provide data on the effects of financial toxicity and offer potential corrective measures in the form of new policies or practices. The belief is that open dialogue about cost concerns will illuminate the underlying causes of financial toxicity—causes that can then be remediated through policy and practice change across the healthcare system. A national project such as this reflects the importance of learning from persons and communities affected by current institutional policies and practices, and the need to enlist additional resources to the systemic sources of healthcare inequity.[16] Should Dr. Ramsey's program, partnering with some 900 NCORP clinics, prove impactful in raising awareness and generating more substantive reforms, it will be the first step toward creating a more just healthcare system that enables equitable participation in cancer care.

---

[14] The Hutchinson Institute for Cancer Outcomes Research (HICOR) is a research institute at Fred Hutch in Washington State. HICOR's mission is to improve cancer prevention, detection, and treatment in ways that will improve the clinical and economic outcomes of cancer care. HICOR hosts researchers, clinicians, patients, payers, and policymakers in the collaborative practice of data sharing to improve the totality of the clinical experience for all stakeholders. See Fred Hutch, "Hutchinson Institute for Cancer Outcomes Research," 2021, www.fredhutch.org/en/research/institutes-networks-ircs/hutchinson-institute-for-cancer-outcomes-research.html.

[15] See Diane Mapes, "NIH Grant to Fund New Financial-Toxicity Intervention," *Hutch News Stories,* May 8, 2020, www.fredhutch.org/en/news/center-news/2020/05/nih-grant-funds-financial-toxicity-study.html.

[16] See Diane Mapes, "How to Achieve Equity in Cancer Care, Research and Beyond," *Hutch News Stories,* September 25, 2020, www.fredhutch.org/en/news/center-news/2020/09/how-to-achieve-equity-in-cancer-care--research-and-beyond.html.

Conclusion

It will be important for other healthcare systems to design and implement similar programs with national scope, particularly not-for-profit systems that are known to provide care to underserved areas and persons. Obvious partners include Catholic health systems that frequently espouse the importance of honoring the dignity of persons, caring for the poor and marginalized, and facilitating the common good. Honoring the dignity of persons not only requires attention to and remediation of the systemic forces that contribute to the inequitable experience of financial toxicity but also more concerted effort on behalf of providers during their patient encounters. The social determinants of health may be outside the control of patients and providers but providing empathic care during individual patient encounter is well within the reach of all providers. This means providing culturally competent care that is attentive to personal values, beliefs, and concerns, which can subsequently ameliorate certain social determinants such as health literacy. It also means inquiring about various non-health influences that contribute to the health and well-being of patients. Doing so can help to identify and address the social determinants of health that have contributed to the patient's illness or the patient's inability to participate in care. Re-centering the provider-patient relationship in community programs such as Dr. Ramsey's can further contribute to the necessary systemic changes as local health systems collaborate with national systems and structures. In such a way, more persons who have been marginalized can join in their cancer care. Structural reforms and a renewed focus on the person in context will better facilitate the promotion of the common good.

Christian Cintron received his Ph.D. in Theological Ethics from Loyola University Chicago in 2017. He currently serves as a clinical bioethicist at Anne Arundel Medical Center (Annapolis, MD), and adjunct lecturer in theology and ethics at Fairfield University (Fairfield, CT).

Part 4
International Perspectives:
Major Cancer Problems
and
Prospects for Prevention

Chapter 10: Major Cancer Problems and Prospects for Prevention in Asia

Rengaswamy Sankaranarayanan

Rengaswamy Sankaranarayanan discusses major cancer problems and prospects for prevention in Asia by showing, on the one hand, the diverse cancer incidence in various countries and, on the other hand, strategies to prevent, screen, diagnose, and treat that are implemented in various nations. To address, reduce, and eliminate the glaring inequities in cancer prevention and care between states, political commitments should allow to allocate adequate resources, implement targeted programs, improve health infrastructures, strengthen human resources, provide universal healthcare, promote efficient and socially conscious public-private partnerships, and develop efficient monitoring systems.

Cancer has become an important health problem in Asia due to aging, growing populations, and changes in lifestyle associated with economic development and epidemiologic transition. Asia accounts for almost two-thirds of the global population and almost half the world burden of cancer. The incidence of cancer cases is estimated to have increased from 6.1 million in 2008 to 9.5 million in 2020.[1] Striking variations in cancer patterns are seen in this vast continent due to different ethnicity, sociocultural practices, human development index, habits, and dietary practices. Seven cancers—namely in lung, breast, large bowel, stomach, liver, prostate, and oral cavity—account for 59 percent of the total burden in Asia. The prevention and early detection linked with appropriate

---

[1] Hyuna Sung, Jacques Ferlay, Rebecca L. Siegel, Mathieu Laversanne, Isabelle Soerjomataram, Ahmedin Jemal, and Freddie Bray, "Global Cancer Statistics 2020: GLOBOCAN Estimates of Incidence and Mortality Worldwide for 36 Cancers in 185 Countries," *CA: A Cancer Journal for Clinicians* 71, no. 3 (2021): 209–249.

treatment of these cancers will have a telling effect on the cancer burden in Asia.[2]

Given the massive disease burden, prevention and control of cancer require urgent political action and commitment of resources to implement a phased time-bound action plan for improving public and professional awareness, cancer healthcare infrastructure, and human resources.[3] Prevention as well as early detection of cancers lead to both better health outcomes and considerable savings in treatment costs. The still evolving or stagnant cancer health services require substantial investments to ensure equitable access to cancer care for all sections of the population.

The Status of Cancer Healthcare Services in Asia

Cancer management requires a comprehensive framework and multidisciplinary care. The cancer health services encompass mechanisms for awareness creation, appropriate referral pathways, patient and subject navigation integrated in primary, secondary, and tertiary hospitals, comprehensive cancer centers, and apex centers. These services should provide advanced care, trained human resources to staff the preventive and clinical services, procurement services for drugs, mechanisms for healthcare financing that reduce or avoid catastrophic out-of-pocket expenditure, data systems including cancer registries, quality assurance, on-going monitoring and evaluation of services rendered, and improved services based on the outcome. The main drivers of cost across the cancer continuum of care are the cancer workforce, medical devices and technology, cancer medicines, infrastructure utilization costs, and capital investments.

There are substantial differences in the adequacy and responsiveness of availability, affordability, and access of cancer health services between Asian countries as well as between different regions in vast countries such

[2] Sung et al., "Global Cancer Statistics 2020."

[3] Rengaswamy Sankaranarayanan, Kunnambath Ramadas, and You-lin Qiao, "Managing the Changing Burden of Cancer in Asia," *BMC Medicine* 12 (2014): doi.org/10.1186/1741-7015-12-3.

as China, India, Indonesia, and the Philippines. Cancer health services are still evolving in most Asian low- and middle-income countries (LMICs). A substantial variation in the development of the various cancer control components is observed between and within countries, corresponding to their level of income and development. Whereas all components of cancer care are well developed in high-income countries (HICs) such as Singapore and the Republic of Korea, services are underdeveloped in many LMICs such as Bangladesh, Cambodia, China, India, Indonesia, Laos, Myanmar, Pakistan, Vietnam, and Yemen. In high-income countries such as Singapore and South Korea, a low mortality to cancer incidence ratio is seen as opposed to a high ratio in countries like India, Mongolia, the Philippines, Tajikistan, and Kyrgyzstan due to lack of adequate health financing, substantial out-of-pocket costs by patients, and widening gap between affordable cancer care and increased cancer mortality.

In many countries, cancer diagnostic infrastructure—particularly high-quality pathology including immunohistochemistry, molecular markers, imaging, and endoscopy—is woefully inadequate. Cancer surgery facilities and cancer surgeons are few and are overstretched. There is considerable disparity and inequity in the distribution of radiotherapy services across LMICs. The "barriers to the accessibility of anticancer medicines include the lack of government reimbursement, budget allocation for healthcare and quality-assured generic and biosimilar medicines, as well as shortages and patient rights."[4]

Achieving the United Nations (UN) 2030 Sustainable Development Goal 3.8 on Universal Health Coverage (UHC) requires that everyone, everywhere can access needed healthcare without experiencing financial ruin as a result of that care.[5] Currently, Thailand and South Korea have

---

[4] Alexandru Eniu, Nathan I. Cherny, Melanie Bertram, Sumitra Thongprasert, Jean-Yves Douillard, Gracemarie Bricalli, Malvika Vyas, and Dario Trapani, "Cancer Medicines in Asia and Asia-Pacific: What Is Available, and Is It Effective Enough?," *ESMO Open* 4, no. 4 (2019): doi.org/10.1136/esmoopen-2018-000483.

[5] "Target 3.8: Achieve universal health coverage, including financial risk protection, access to quality essential health-care services and access to safe, effective, quality and affordable essential medicines and vaccines for all." sdgs.un.org/goals/goal3.

implemented effective UHC. Countries such as China, India, Indonesia, Malaysia, and the Philippines are in various stages of progress towards achieving UHC.

Cancer Prevention in Asia

Of the estimated 12 million new cancer cases by 2030 in Asia, at least 30–40 percent are avoidable with cancer prevention, which means nearly three or four million lives could be saved. Indeed, the implementation of cancer prevention strategies would result in the reduction of global cancer mortality, supporting the fulfilment of the United Nations 2030 Sustainable Development Goal 3.4 to reduce cancer deaths by one-third by 2030.[6] In Asia, substantial lives saved would be in low- and middle-income countries. Moreover, in the continent, more than 20 percent of all malignant tumors can be attributed to tobacco and human papilloma virus, respectively.

Tobacco control is a major cancer preventive action for lung and head and neck cancers among others that needs a complex undertaking of awareness, weaning of tobacco production, and reducing the consumption of tobacco. The World Health Organization Framework Convention on Tobacco Control (WHO FCTC) is an evidence-based public health treaty developed and implemented in response to the growing global tobacco epidemic. Except for Indonesia, all countries in Asia have ratified the WHO FCTC.[7] FCTC focuses on the implementation and evaluation of key measures to reduce the demand for tobacco: monitoring tobacco use; smoke-free laws; tobacco cessation interventions; health warnings; tobacco advertising, promotion, and sponsorship bans; and tobacco tax increases. In most Asian countries, the

---

[6] "Target 3.4: By 2030, reduce by one third premature mortality from non-communicable diseases through prevention and treatment and promote mental health and well-being." sdgs.un.org/goals/goal3.

[7] Thomas Stubbs, "Commercial Determinants of Youth Smoking in ASEAN Countries: A Narrative Review of Research Investigating the Influence of Tobacco Advertising, Promotion, and Sponsorship," *Tobacco Induced Diseases* 19 (2021): doi.org/10.18332/tid/139124.

FCTC has increased the implementation of measures across several policy domains, in both demand and supply side. These implementations have resulted in measurable impacts on tobacco consumption, prevalence, and other outcomes.[8] However, FCTC implementation must be accelerated to meet all the treaty obligations and consider measures that exceed minimum requirements. In Asia, tobacco is grown in an area of around 2.2 million hectares (ha) with the production of 4084 million kg of tobacco, which accounted for 63 percent of global tobacco production, with China and India producing 52 percent and 22 percent of tobacco in Asia respectively. While Singapore has excelled in implementing FCTC regulations, FCTC implementation has not impacted the amount of tobacco produced in Asia, and this needs particular attention. In 1970, Singapore banned tobacco advertising, as well as smoking in the auditoria of cinemas and theatres and on public buses, and, in 1991, Singapore was the first country to ban duty-free incoming cigarettes. Hong Kong banned manufacture, importation, and sale of smokeless tobacco in 1987, being only the second jurisdiction to do so.

In the last two decades, Asia has been highly successful in controlling the hepatitis B virus (HBV). Forty-eight countries in WHO Southeast Asia and in the Western Pacific regions have endorsed regional action plans for eliminating hepatitis. All Asian countries incorporated HBV vaccination into their national infant immunization programs, and two-thirds of Asian countries had achieved more than 90 percent coverage of completed (three doses) HBV vaccination. The implementation of the hepatitis B vaccination (HepB) has led to substantial decline in carrier states and hepatitis B related morbidity.[9]

Since perinatal transmission is a major route of HBV infection in endemic Asian countries or regions, the administration of a birth dose

---

[8] Janet Chung-Hall, Lorraine Craig, Shannon Gravely, Natalie Sansone, and Geoffrey T. Fong, "Impact of the WHO FCTC over the First Decade: A Global Evidence Review Prepared for the Impact Assessment Expert Group," *Tobacco Control* 28, no. Suppl. 2 (2019): s119–s128.

[9] Jade Pattyn, Greet Hendrickx, Alex Vorsters, and Pierre Van Damme, "Hepatitis B Vaccines," *Journal of Infectious Diseases* 224, no. 12 Suppl. 2 (2021): S343–S351.

(HepB-BD) of the HBV vaccine (within 24 hours after delivery) is the key to preventing perinatal HBV infection. However, timely HepB-BD coverage is still low in many places, especially in LMICs of Asia where the burden is concentrated, and this is the major impediment to eliminating HBV.[10] Unfortunately, such initiatives have been delayed due to the impact of the COVID-19 pandemic. Since unsafe injections and blood transfusions are an important route of transmission of HBV, promoting safe injections (defined as injections that do not harm the recipient, the healthcare worker, or the community) and safe blood banking are critical to prevent HBV infection.[11]

The world's first universal HBV vaccination program was introduced in Taiwan in 1984, reducing the prevalence of HBV infection to one-tenth of the original prevalence. The incidence of hepatocellular carcinoma (HCC) was reduced by 69 percent in the vaccinated birth cohorts of 6–19 year-old children and young adults.[12] The risk of developing HCC for vaccinated cohorts was associated with incomplete HBV vaccination, prenatal maternal hepatitis B surface antigen (HBsAg) seropositivity, and prenatal maternal HBeAg seropositivity.

Cervix cancer is highly preventable by combining human papillomavirus(HPV) vaccination and early detection and treatment of cervical cancer precancerous lesions such as cervical intraepithelial neoplasia Grades 2 and 3 (CIN 2/3) and adenocarcinoma *in-situ* (AIS). Currently licensed HPV vaccines target two to nine HPV types. HPV vaccine is a prophylactic vaccine and to be effective should be given to

---

[10] Margaret J. de Villiers, Shevanthi Nayagam, and Timothy B. Hallett, "The Impact of the Timely Birth Dose Vaccine on the Global Elimination of Hepatitis B," *Nature Communications* 12, no. 1 (2021): 6223, doi.org/10.1038/s41467-021-26475-6.

[11] Shan Shan, Fuqian Q. Cui, and Jidong D. Jia, "How to Control Highly Endemic Hepatitis B in Asia," *Liver International* 38 (2018): 122–125.

[12] Mei-Hwei Chang, "Hepatitis B Virus and Cancer Prevention," *Recent Results in Cancer Research* 188 (2011): 75–84; Mei-Hwei Chang, San- Lin You, Chien-Jen Chen, Chun-Jen Liu, Chuan-Mo Lee, Shi-Ming Lin, Heng-Cheng Chu, Tzee-Chung Wu, Sheng-Shun Yang, Hsu-Sung Kuo, and Ding-Shinn Chen, "Decreased Incidence of Hepatocellular Carcinoma in Hepatitis B Vaccinees: A 20-Year Follow-up Study," *Journal of the National Cancer Institute* 101, no. 19 (2009): 1348–1355.

HPV naive girls and women. In Southeast Asia and the Western Pacific region of Asia, although more than 20 countries have introduced HPV vaccination, only Bhutan, Maldives, Sri Lanka, Thailand, Federated States of Micronesia, Marshall Islands, Myanmar, Malaysia, South Korea, and Fiji have implemented HPV vaccination covering the entire countries.[13] Programs cover selected regions/provinces within India, Indonesia, and the Philippines. The challenges for HPV vaccination are similar to elsewhere: lack of awareness, the low standing of cervix cancer elimination in the political agenda, lack of advocacy for women, vaccine misinformation, vaccine hesitancy, anti-vaccine campaigns, perceived excess harms, vaccine costs and affordability, confusion on morality and sexual mores, and lack of strong recommendations from healthcare providers.

Given the vast potential for cervical cancer prevention and its social relevance, the WHO has called for implementation of three interventions with high coverage, namely, HPV vaccination, screening for early detection and treatment of lesions by 2030, and setting incidence-elimination threshold to less than 4/100,000 women. The WHO has proposed this three-pronged approach to be implemented before 2030. Almost all Asian countries need to invest substantially and plan judiciously to meet the implementation targets. Hence, data systems to monitor implementation coverage are critical.

---

[13] Laia Bruni, Anna Saura-Lazaro, Alexandra Montoliu, Maria Brotons, Laia Alemany, Mamadou Saliou Diallo, Oya Zeren Afsar, D. Scott LaMontagne, Liudmila Mosina, Marcela Contreras, Martha Velandia-Gonzalez, Roberta Pastore, Marta Gacic-Dobo, and Paul Bloem, "HPV Vaccination Introduction Worldwide and WHO and UNICEF Estimates of National HPV Immunization Coverage 2010–2019," *Preventive Medicine* 144 (2021): 106399,10.1016/j.ypmed.2020.106399; Rei Haruyama, Sumiyo Okawa, Hiroki Akaba, Hiromi Obara, and Noriko Fujita, "A Review of the Implementation Status of and National Plans on HPV Vaccination in 17 Middle-Income Countries of the WHO Western Pacific Region," *Vaccines (Basel)* 9, no. 11 (2021): doi.org/10.3390/vaccines9111355.

Cancer Screening in Asia

Cancer screening is mostly sporadic, without poor organization, coverage, and quality assurance in most Asian countries, with the exception of South Korea, Singapore, Thailand, Taiwan, and the Hong Kong special administrative region. In most countries, the primary screening method is based on cytology with screening activity, except for Bangladesh, India, and Indonesia, where visual inspection of the cervix with acetic acid (VIA) is mainly used as a primary screening method.[14] Thailand has switched over to HPV testing-based screening from cytology recently using COBAS 4800 platform. The high negative predictive value for cervical neoplasia even for a single baseline HPV test is impressive, and it has allowed screening intervals to be extended up to ten years. WHO recommends using HPV DNA detection rather than VIA or cytology as the primary test for screening, management, and treatment approaches, if infrastructure allows.

HPV screening has been recently piloted in Sri Lanka. Screening uptake rates are dismally low (~5 percent) in countries such as Bangladesh, India, and Indonesia, whereas they range between 30 and 60 percent in countries such as Japan, South Korea, Singapore, Taiwan, and Thailand. Cervical cancer incidence rates have substantially declined following screening programs in Singapore, South Korea, Hong Kong, and Taiwan. The linkage between screening and treatment needs to substantially improve in Asian countries with some screening activity. In the future, given the performance profile of different screening tests, the high accuracy, objectivity, reproducibility, and negative predictive value associated with HPV testing makes it the most preferred test to be considered for implementation in new and upcoming screening programs in Asian countries.

---

[14] Eiko Saitoh Aoki, Rutie Yin, Kemin Li, Neerja Bhatla, Seema Singhal, Dwiana Ocviyanti, Kumiko Saika, Mina Suh, Miseon Kim, and Wichai Termrungruanglert, "National Screening Programs for Cervical Cancer in Asian Countries," *Journal of Gynecological Oncology* 31, no. 3 (2020): e55, doi.org/10.3802/jgo.2020.31.e55; Bruni et al., "HPV Vaccination Introduction Worldwide."

Breast cancer screening programs in Asia are fewer than cervix cancer screening initiatives. Large scale mammography-based screening programs are on-going in Japan, Hong Kong, Singapore, South Korea, and Taiwan. Singapore was the first country in Asia to offer biennial mammography screening for 50 to 69 year-old women since 2002. In 2014, a formal evaluation indicated that the breast cancer detection rate in the Singapore program was 182.1 per 100,000 women screened, and the positive value was 1.7 percent; the interval cancer rate was 75.1 per 100,000 screen negatives and the sensitivity and specificity were 75.1 percent and 85.7 percent respectively.[15] The Korean National Cancer Screening Program (KNCSP) recommends biennial breast cancer screening through mammography for women aged 40 to 69 years. The KNCSP has been effective in reducing breast cancer mortality by 59 percent among Korean women aged 40 to 69 years.[16] The program has switched over to digital mammography screening from screen film mammography.

South Korea has an ongoing colorectal cancer (CRC) screening program based on annual fecal immunochemical testing (FIT) for adults aged 50 years and above and triage of FIT-positive persons using colonoscopy.[17] The results of Korea's national colorectal cancer screening program from 2006 to 2013, involving 20.6 million people, indicated a 6.4 percent FIT positivity rate and compliance rate of 46.6 percent for diagnostic investigations of FIT positive persons; side effects within three

[15] Kunsei Lee, Hyeongsu Kim, Jung Hyun Lee, Hyoseon Jeong, Soon Ae Shin, Taehwa Han, Young Lan Seo, Youngbum Yoo, Sang Eun Nam, Jong Heon Park, and Yoo Mi Park, "Retrospective Observation on Contribution and Limitations of Screening for Breast Cancer with Mammography in Korea: Detection Rate of Breast Cancer and Incidence Rate of Interval Cancer of the Breast," *BMC Women's Health* 16, no. 1 (2016): 72, doi.org/10.1186/s12905-016-0351-1.

[16] Eunji Choi, Jae Kwan Jun, Mina Suh, Kyu-Won Jung, Boyoung Park, Kyeongmin Lee, So-Youn Jung, Eun Sook Lee, and Kui Son Choi, "Effectiveness of the Korean National Cancer Screening Program in Reducing Breast Cancer Mortality," *NPJ Breast Cancer* 7, no. 1 (2021): 83, doi.org/10.1038/s41523-021-00295-9.

[17] John Hoon Rim, Taemi Youk, Jung Gu Kang, Byung Kyu Park, Heon Yung Gee, Jeong-Ho Kim, and Jongha Yoo, "Fecal Occult Blood Test Results of the National Colorectal Cancer Screening Program in South Korea (2006–2013)," *Scientific Reports* 7, no. 1 (2017): 2804, doi.org/10.1038/s41598-017-03134-9.

months after colonoscopy accounted for 0.17 percent of all procedures, with bleeding being the most common. In an observational cohort study, a biennial FIT screening program in Taiwan achieved a 62 percent reduction in CRC-related mortality.[18] Singapore launched colorectal cancer screening in 2004, and citizens as well as permanent residents aged 50 or more years were invited to screen for colorectal cancer annually using free FIT kits from the Community Health Assist Scheme annual FIT screening in primary care clinics under the Integrated Screening Program.

In Asia, Taiwan is the only country with an oral cancer screening program.[19] Around 4.6 million people with areca nut and tobacco habits have undergone biennial oral cancer screening in Taiwan. However, the program has yet to impact oral cancer incidence and mortality. A national stomach cancer screening program using upper gastrointestinal imaging or gastroscopy for people aged 40 years has also been on-going since 2002.

The Challenge of the COVID-19 Pandemic for Cancer Control in Asia

The COVID-19 pandemic has dramatically affected cancer healthcare, with substantial impact on health systems around the world and the whole Asia, with emphasis on managing the pandemic at the expense of other essential and elective health services.[20] This situation has put backwards all

---

[18] Han-Mo Chiu, Sam Li-Sheng Chen, Amy Ming-Fang Yen, Sherry Yueh-Hsia Chiu, Jean Ching-Yuan Fann, Yi-Chia Lee, Shin-Liang Pan, Ming-Shiang Wu, Chao-Sheng Liao, Hsiu-Hsi Chen, Shin-Lan Koong, and Shu-Ti Chiou, "Effectiveness of Fecal Immunochemical Testing in Reducing Colorectal Cancer Mortality from the One Million Taiwanese Screening Program," *Cancer* 121, no. 18 (2015): 3221–3229.

[19] Shu-Lin Chuang, William Wang-Yu Su, Sam Li-Sheng Chen, Amy Ming-Fang Yen, Cheng-Ping Wang, Jean Ching-Yuan Fann, Sherry Yueh- Hsia Chiu, Yi-Chia Lee, Han-Mo Chiu, Dun-Cheng Chang, Yann-Yuh Jou, Chien-Yuan Wu, Hsiu-Hsi Chen, Mu-Kuan Chen, and Shu-Ti Chiou, "Population-Based Screening Program for Reducing Oral Cancer Mortality in 2,334,299 Taiwanese Cigarette Smokers and/or Betel Quid Chewers," *Cancer* 123, no. 9 (2017): 1597–1609; J.-Y. Lin, "Information System of Nationwide Population-Based Cancer Screening in Taiwan," *Journal of Global Oncology* 4, no. Suppl. 2 (2018): doi.org/10.1200/jgo.18.84500.

[20] Mengyuan Dai, Dianbo Liu, Miao Liu, Fuxiang Zhou, Guiling Li, Zhen Chen, Zhian Zhang, Hua You, Meng Wu, Qichao Zheng, Yong Xiong, Huihua Xiong, Chun Wang,

cancer control efforts, and cancer patients are at great risk of complications and death. In Asia, the impact of COVID-19 on cancer service delivery—such as screening, diagnosis, treatment, follow-up, and end-of-life care—has been substantial. In many countries, the existing few cancer treatment facilities were designated and transitioned to COVID care centers, which had a telling effect on access to diagnosis, treatment, and follow-up care.

Conclusion

There is substantial variation across Asian countries in terms of national response to cancer control, efficiency of cancer healthcare services, and the availability and access to cancer early detection programs and the means of healthcare financing. On the one hand, universal healthcare is not available in most LMICs in Asia, leading to financial toxicity and high out of pocket healthcare expenditure wrecking household incomes and stability. On the other hand, high income countries such as Singapore and South Korea have done well compared to Asian LMICs. Political commitments, adequate budgetary allocation of resources, phased implementation of well-thought-out programs, improved infrastructures and human resources, universal healthcare available for all segments of society, efficient and socially conscious public-private partnerships, and development of efficient data systems are urgently needed to avoid the glaring inequity in cancer prevention and cancer care between countries in Asia.

Rengaswamy Sankaranarayanan, MD, MBBS, is Director of Preventive Oncology at Karkinos Healthcare Private Limited in Vidya Vihar, West

Changchun Chen, Fei Xiong, Yan Zhang, Yaqin Peng, Siping Ge, Bo Zhen, Tingting Yu, Ling Wang, Hua Wang, Yu Liu, Yeshan Chen, Junhua Mei, Xiaojia Gao, Zhuyan Li, Lijuan Gan, Can He, Zhen Li, Yuying Shi, Yuwen Qi, Jing Yang, Daniel G. Tenen, Li Chai, Lorelei A. Mucci, Mauricio Santillana, and Hongbing Cai, "Patients with Cancer Appear More Vulnerable to SARS-CoV-2: A Multicenter Study During the COVID-19 Outbreak," *Cancer Discovery* 10, no. 6 (2020): 783–791.

Mumbai, India. He earned a Bachelor of Medicine, Bachelor of Surgery, and is a trained clinical oncologist with over 40 years of experience in research, planning, implementation, and evaluation programs for cancer screening, control, and information systems at the population level, in health systems, and in hospital contexts. He was recently appointed at the Advisory Board of the India-U.K. Cancer Research Initiative and is working as a Special Advisor on Cancer Control for the World Health Organization International Agency for Research on Cancer (WHO-IARC) in Lyon, France.

Chapter 11: Major Cancer Problems and Prospects for Prevention: A European Perspective

Walter Ricciardi

Walter Ricciardi discusses challenges and strategies to address the cancer pandemic within the European context, by featuring initiatives across Europe—like the Mission on Cancer. While continuing to foster research efforts, these initiatives aim at supporting and strengthening national commitments that should promote, on the one hand, prevention, diagnosis, and treatment of cancer, and, on the other hand, the quality of life of cancer patients, survivors, and their families as well as caregivers.

Cancer is an umbrella term for more than 200 diseases. These have in common the uncontrolled growth and spread of abnormal body cells, affecting tissues and organs. Considering that Europe has a quarter of all cancer cases and less than ten percent of the world's population, it is evident that cancer is a huge threat for Europe's citizens and health systems. Each year, 2.6 million people in the twenty-seven European Union countries (EU-27) are diagnosed with cancer. This number is expected to increase rapidly because of aging populations, unhealthy lifestyles, and unfavorable environmental conditions. Almost three quarters of all cancers in the European Union (EU) occur in people aged sixty or above. Without strong action, the number of cancer cases in Europe will increase by twenty-five percent by 2035.

Although survival rates of several cancer types have improved over the last decades, cancer still kills 1.2 million people in the EU-27 each year. The probability of receiving a timely diagnosis of cancer and of surviving the disease differs substantially across Europe because of major inequities in access to cancer knowledge, prevention, diagnostics, treatments, and care. The chances of surviving cancer also depend highly on the type of cancer, as some cancers are still not well understood, including several childhood cancers.

The current COVID-19 pandemic puts high pressure on health systems' capacities and resources. This is a severe threat to cancer prevention, detection, and treatment. It may also impact funding for cancer research, innovation, and care, as countries may reset their priorities and reallocate resources. At the same time, the COVID-19 pandemic has also shown health systems' and society's resilience and potential to adapt rapidly to changing circumstances, as it has accelerated the development and acceptance of new technologies as well as built strong collaborations across sectors and borders.

Increasing survival proportions results in more Europeans living with and after cancer. There are more than twelve million cancer survivors in Europe. However, being cancer-free does not mean being free of the cancer experience. Many survivors experience side-effects from treatment, which may only become apparent years after completing treatment and may intertwine with other comorbidities as survivors get older. Physical and mental health problems significantly impact the survivors' quality of life, affecting their ability to play a full role in society and in the workforce. In addition, many survivors experience stigmatization. This is reflected in difficulties in getting a job or having a career and in obtaining health insurance or other financial products (e.g., life insurance for a mortgage). This situation generates a substantial burden for cancer survivors and their families but also for countries' health systems and society in general.

Given that the challenges that arise from cancer for European citizens and countries are vast, conquering cancer in Europe calls for multiple actions by many stakeholders, both at the national level and EU level. At EU level, citizens, cancer patients, survivors and their family members and caregivers may benefit from bundling of cancer knowledge, sharing of expertise, and exchange of data. The EU could offer large scale research on less prevalent cancers by providing a platform for sharing knowledge and data and for exchanging experiences from best practices and innovations within countries. Previous EU Research and Innovation Programmes and other actions have addressed various challenges in cancer research, prevention, and care. However, the increasing burden of cancer in Europe and the rapidly increasing costs of cancer for health systems and society require collaboration on an ambitious European scale, innovating and integrating fundamental, translational, clinical, and interventional research, underpinned by supportive policy and legislation, as well as a strong commitment from member states to break barriers across Europe.

As an integral part of the Horizon Europe Framework Programme for Research and Innovation (2021–2027),[1] a set of European Research and Innovation Missions aim to deliver solutions to some of the greatest challenges facing Europe. Cancer is one of these challenges. The Mission report produced explains how a mission-driven approach can save and improve the lives of millions of European citizens exposed to cancer and its risk factors.[2] It sets out the goal of the Mission on Cancer and makes recommendations on how to achieve this goal.

In designing the Mission on Cancer, the European Commission invited a Board of European experts—on cancer research, innovation, policy, healthcare provision and practice—to define an ambitious and measurable goal with a substantial impact on and relevance for society and European citizens. The Commission also asked the Board to propose a coherent set of actions to achieve this goal in a set timeframe. These actions will be implemented through Horizon Europe and other instruments of the European Union and its Member States and aligned with other initiatives at EU and Member State level.

In finalizing this Mission report, the Board was assisted by the Cancer Mission Assembly, inputs from a wide network of experts and organizations, including academic, private sector, and advocacy groups. In addition, the Board received input from the twenty-seven Member States, members of the European Parliament, and several Directorates-General of the European Commission, as well as a number of consultations and

---

[1] European Commission, "Horizon Europe," 2021, ec.europa.eu/info/research-and-innovation/funding/funding-opportunities/fundingprogrammes-and-open-calls/horizon-europe_en.
[2] European Commission, "Conquering Cancer, Mission Possible," September 2020, ec.europa.eu/info/publications/conquering-cancermission-possible_en.

engagement sessions with EU citizens, cancer patients, and survivors organized in their countries and native language or in online meetings with participants from across the entire EU.

This Mission report will be used as a basis for further engagement activities involving stakeholders and citizens and for defining a broad strategy for the first four years of the Horizon Europe Programme. Synergies will be developed with national cancer plans and other actions of Member States, with the actions of other Horizon Europe Missions and with research and investment programs, as well as with other EU policies and actions, in particular the Europe's Beating Cancer Plan.[3]

The Mission on Cancer will address the whole cancer control continuum; including risk factors; survivorship support; end-of-life care; rare and poorly understood cancers; cancers in children, adolescents/young adults, and the elderly; cancers in socially or economically vulnerable families and among people living in remote areas; and cancer across all member states. While the Mission provides directions and objectives for research and innovation, it will also generate evidence on factors that limit effective policy and support actions to conquer cancer. In this regard, the Mission's actions will be able to make an important contribution to the Europe's Beating Cancer Plan. At the same time, the Cancer Plan will provide opportunities to complement the Mission on Cancer.

The overall goal of the Mission on Cancer is: "By 2030, more than 3 million lives saved, living longer and better."[4] This goal is consistent with United Nations Sustainable Development Goal (SDG) 3: "Ensure healthy lives and promote well-being for all at all ages." The target of this SDG for non-communicable diseases for 2030 is "to reduce by one third premature

---

[3] European Commission, "Europe's Beating Cancer Plan: A New EU Approach to Prevention, Treatment and Care," February 3, 2021, ec.europa.eu/commission/presscorner/detail/en/ip_21_342.

[4] European Commission, "Conquering Cancer, Mission Possible."

mortality from non-communicable diseases through prevention and treatment and promote mental health and well-being."[5]

Given the high level of ambition, a comprehensive plan of bold actions supported by all member states and stakeholders—including patients, survivors, caregivers, and the wider public—is required to achieve the Mission's goal. Effective interventions are needed to improve: (1) prevention; (2) diagnostics and treatment of cancer; and (3) the quality of life of cancer patients, survivors, and their families and caregivers. Hence, these areas are considered the pillars of the Mission. Effective interventions in all these areas require a thorough understanding of cancers, with their causal factors and mechanisms, and their impact of the health of individuals and on healthcare systems; therefore, understanding is considered the basis for actions. Furthermore, effective policy measures are needed, and resources should be allocated to ensure that citizens and other stakeholders in all Member States have equitable access to high-quality prevention, diagnostics and treatment, care and support, including access to research funding and knowledge. Finally, as underscored in the report of Prof. Mariana Mazzucato, "Governing Missions in the European Union,"[6] the success of the mission-oriented process will lie in the set-up of novel flexible governing structures to correctly balance with an effective portfolio management that enables cross-sectoral and cross-institutional coordination.

Understand Cancer, Its Risk Factors, and Its Impact

Understanding is a key starting point for effective actions to save lives and improve the quality of life of persons with and after cancer, their families, and their caregivers. What we do not understand, we cannot address effectively. Understanding the biological processes in human cells is crucial

---

[5] The Global Goals for Sustainable Development, "Goal 3: Good Health and Well-Being," 2021, www.globalgoals.org/3-good-health-and-wellbeing. See also United Nations Department of Economic and Social Affairs, "The 17 Goals," 2021, sdgs.un.org/goals.

[6] Mariana Mazzucato, "Governing Missions in the European Union," 2019, ec.europa. eu/info/sites/default/files/research_and_innovation/contact/documents/ec_rtd_mazzucat o-report-issue2_072019.pdf.

for diagnosing cancer and developing effective treatments. Despite developments in cancer treatment, some cancers are still resistant to all available therapies, and some well-known targets are still untreatable with current drugs. A special focus is deemed necessary on anti-cancer medication innovation for childhood cancers, cancers in adolescents and young adults, and cancers in the elderly because these populations have distinct age-related biological and clinical characteristics.

Understanding the complexity of cancer and the role of factors and determinants (e.g., lifestyle, environment, workplace exposure, sex/gender, and age) is important for developing effective preventive measures. Some factors are known to play a role in the development of cancers, but their precise impact is not yet clear, whereas other causal factors remain to be discovered. Moreover, changing human behavior has proven to be a challenge. Therefore, what is needed is a greater understanding of how people perceive health threats and cancer risks, how they address them, how they behave, and how unhealthy behaviors can be reasonably changed. Furthermore, there is an urgent need to obtain a better understanding of the impact of cancer treatments on patients, both to optimize treatments and improve the patients' quality of life. Many people experience physical and mental health problems even years after their cancer diagnosis and initial treatment. Understanding how everyone reacts to treatment and how treatment affects the patients' and survivors' mental health is crucial for developing more effective care and for supporting patients and their caregivers.

Prevent What is Preventable

Despite improvements in cancer detection and treatment, there is a need for cancer prevention and health promotion to remain a very high priority. Lifestyle is a risk factor for many cancers and, although persistent, a modifiable factor. Around one third of deaths from cancer are due to the five leading behavioral and dietary risks: tobacco use, alcohol use, high body mass index, low fruit and vegetable intake, and lack of physical activity—as described in the European Code against Cancer.[7] Furthermore, cancer is the leading cause of work-related deaths. The International Labour Organization estimated that over 106,000 cancer deaths in Europe in 2016 were attributable to occupational causes.[8]

Early detection of cancer can improve cancer treatment outcomes and prevent or reduce the deterioration of health and well-being. Early detection can be achieved by screening, creating awareness of suspicious signals among the population, and screening patients at risk of cancer. Despite the Council Recommendation on cancer screening adopted unanimously by the Health Ministers of the EU in 2003,[9] in most Member States cancer screening is still not fulfilling the criteria set for population-based, organized programs. Prevention is particularly suited for creating synergies with other EU Research and Innovation Missions, as well as with the European Green Deal,[10] the Farm to Fork Strategy,[11] the European Health Data Space,[12] and the Europe's Beating Cancer Plan.[13]

---

[7] World Health Organization and International Agency for Research on Cancer, "European Code against Cancer: 12 Ways to Reduce Your Cancer Risk," 2021, cancer-code-europe.iarc.fr/index.php/en/.

[8] World Health Organization and International Labour Organization, *WHO/ILO Joint Estimates of the Work-Related Burden of Disease and Injury, 2000–2016: Global Monitoring Report* (Geneva: World Health Organization and International Labour Organization, 2021), www.ilo.org/wcmsp5/groups/public/---ed_dialogue/---lab_admin/documents/publication/wcms_819788.pdf.

[9] European Commission, "Report from the Commission to the Council, the European Parliament, the European Economic and Social Committee and the Committee of the Regions: Implementation of the Council Recommendation of 2 December 2003 on Cancer Screening (2003/878/Ec) /* Com/2008/0882 Final */," 2003, eur-lex.europa.eu/legal-content/EN/TXT/HTML/?uri=CELEX:52008DC0882&from=PL.

[10] European Commission, "A European Green Deal: Striving to Be the First Climate-Neutral Continent," 2021, ec.europa.eu/info/strategy/priorities-2019-2024/european-green-deal_en.

[11] European Commission, "Farm to Fork Strategy: For a Fair, Healthy and Environmentally-Friendly Food System," 2021, ec.europa.eu/food/horizontal-topics/farm-fork-strategy_en.

[12] European Commission, "European Health Data Space," 2021, ec.europa.eu/health/ehealth/dataspace_en.

[13] European Commission, "Europe's Beating Cancer Plan."

Optimize Diagnostics and Treatments

Many lives have been saved and the quality of life of patients and survivors has improved because of early diagnosis and better treatments. However, many cancers are still diagnosed at an advanced stage and are very aggressive or resistant to all therapies currently available.

An improved understanding of the etiology, development, and spread of poorly understood cancers could provide new biomarkers for diagnostics and new targets for therapies of all cancers. This approach would include highly lethal and rare cancers as well as cancers occurring in children, adolescents, young adults, and the elderly with distinct age-related biological and clinical characteristics for which currently no effective treatment is available.

The translation from development of breakthrough diagnostic technologies and identification of new targets for treatment into clinical trials is still too long. This process of translation requires further development of improved methodological validations and rapid implementation in cancer care. A mission-driven approach aims to translate research breakthroughs into improved diagnostics and effective treatments, and to support equitable and timely access to optimal cancer diagnosis and treatment for each patient in all Member States.

Support the Quality of Life

Increasing incidence and survival rates will result in many more EU citizens who, in the near future, will need to find ways to live a good life with or after cancer. Therefore, an important part of the Mission's goal is to achieve the best possible quality of life for everyone in the EU who is exposed to cancer in some way and in some phase of their lives.

Supporting the quality of life of people exposed to cancer requires a thorough understanding of their cancer-related problems. For patients and survivors, some issues may be (late) side-effects of cancer treatment, symptoms, comorbidities and functional disability (which will increase with age), mental and reproductive health problems. Many cancer survivors experience difficulties in returning to work because of persistent side-effects but also due to ignorance, stigma, and hesitation on the part of employers. Obtaining health insurance or other financial products may also be difficult or expensive. This difficulty may also increase for individuals with a known family history of certain (hereditary) cancers or polygenic risks. Special attention should be paid to survivors of childhood cancer as they are particularly vulnerable due to early life disruption. Two thirds of childhood cancer survivors experience adverse effects in adulthood. This situation negatively impacts their career opportunities, income, social relationships, and starting a family. It is important to support caregivers who care for cancer patients with psychosocial help as well as to offer practical and financial assistance when needed.

The Mission on Cancer aims to contribute to a better understanding of (late) treatment side-effects, symptoms, comorbidities, functional disabilities, and psychosocial needs, and to relieve symptoms, improve palliative care, and provide survivorship support. The Mission also aims at improving access to quality of life and survivorship support in all Member States. Besides research and innovation, this approach calls for policy and support actions, adjustments of legal frameworks, and close collaboration with EU citizens, cancer patients and survivors, as well as their caregivers. Fundamental for all actions is that each action be co-designed, co-implemented, and co-evaluated with those who should benefit from these interventions.

Ensure Equitable Access

One of the core values across the European Union is the shared commitment to universal access to high-quality care based on equity and solidarity. Unhindered access to prevention and care is often under pressure within health systems, particularly in the case of cancer, due to widely shared pressures on limited resources. This situation impacts all Mission's areas. Hence, such a challenge should be addressed in order to reach the Mission's goal.

According to recent European Commission reports, Europe is characterized by inequitable access to cancer prevention and timely, high-quality diagnostics and treatment. These inequities depend on geographic and socio-economic disparities between and within countries, which have a profound impact on cancer incidence and survival. With no assurance of equitable access to preventive measures, new achievements in the field of cancer research and innovation will not be distributed evenly within Europe and among its most vulnerable populations. In particular, equitable access implies access to education to improve citizens' (digital) health literacy, promote the overall cancer expertise (e.g., by training healthcare professionals), and foster research and innovation.

Improving access within Member States requires a better understanding of why some policy tools have not been implemented effectively and what could be done to address inequities in access to prevention, diagnostics, treatments, and quality of life for anyone exposed to cancer. In addition, empowering patients should make it possible for them to gain more control over their care and life and to address high value personal issues.

Major Cancer Problems and Prospects for Prevention: A European Perspective Hence, achieving equitable access calls for: (1) a strong commitment from Member States; (2) availability and optimal use of research and clinical data; (3) strong promotion of research and innovation, supported by establishing at least one Comprehensive Cancer Infrastructure (CCI) in each Member State; and (4) the EU-wide acknowledgment of the urgent need to transform the culture around cancer.

The COVID-19 Global Pandemic and Cancer

In 2020 and 2021, the COVID-19 crisis has negatively affected cancer care at an unprecedented speed. The aftermath of this crisis poses significant threats to prevention and treatment, as well as to research and innovation, which are critical to facilitate improvements. In this exceptional situation, the Mission on Cancer—together with other European efforts—offers an excellent opportunity to address these threats. The ambitious Mission on Cancer aims to improve cancer prevention, diagnostics, treatments, and quality of life of people exposed to cancer by relying on a new level of research and innovation. Such engagement will also provide an important stimulus to the whole European healthcare system and its economy and thereby contribute to societal recovery from the COVID-19 crisis. The Mission on Cancer is an essential and fundamental element in providing a coherent vision and detailed instruments for action to achieve the ambitious goals of the Europe's Beating Cancer Plan.

COVID-19 has demonstrated, beyond doubt, the critical importance of health for any society. The recent pandemic clearly shows that the absence of health leads to severe economic, political, and societal consequences for Europe. COVID-19 has also laid bare critical insufficiencies in healthcare system preparedness, adaptability, and resilience. While the COVID-19 pandemic is unprecedented in terms of incidence and mortality, it is foreseeable that—with determination, political will, and rapid scientific and technological advances—the world will be able to manage the pandemic. Unfortunately, this will not be the case with cancer, which will remain one of the major killers in Europe.

Conclusion

The Mission on Cancer will be a major driving force to apply the lessons learned from the current COVID-19 crisis to find solutions to the cancer challenge and beyond. We have seen an unprecedented willingness in technology adaptation, collaboration across sectors and borders—including extensive data sharing—genuine communication and alignment between healthcare and research, remarkably shortening the implementation of research findings and the ability to mobilize and allocate considerable funding resources at short notice.

The Mission on Cancer has been developed in an age of distrust in science and scientists, facts and evidence. Anti-science ideology is gaining ground and health research is being weaponized in politics, particularly by the far right. Citizens often do not see the benefit of research and question the benefits of research programs.

The missions under Horizon Europe recognize this context and have been developed with the aim of improving society and the lives of EU citizens and residents.[14] Moreover, the word "citizen" is key: just as the food and soil mission is not just for farmers[15] and the oceans mission is not just for fishermen,[16] the cancer mission is not just for cancer patients.

> Missions are one of the main novelties of Horizon Europe. By addressing important societal challenges, such as cancer and climate change, through ambitious but realistic research and innovation activities, they will make clear to citizens how the EU can make a real difference in their lives and in society as a whole. They boost the impact of EU-funded research and innovation by mobilising investment and EU wide efforts around measurable and time-bound goals around issues that affect citizens' daily lives.[17]

Much thought has been given to the involvement of citizens in the missions by their creator, Prof. Mariana Mazzucato. As she writes in the introduction to her report, "Governing Missions in the EU":

> Citizen movements have always been central to achieving social change—including labour movements which brought us one of the greatest social innovations of our time: the weekend! Today there is a growing green movement—including the youngest school children—bringing the climate emergency right to the top of public priorities. We must harness this drive for change across

---

[14] European Commission, "Horizon Europe."

[15] European Commission, "EU Mission: A Soil Deal for Europe," 2021, ec.europa.eu/info/research-and-innovation/funding/fundingopportunities/funding-programmes-and-open-calls/horizon-europe/missions-horizon-europe/soil-health-and-food_en.

[16] See European Commission, "EU Mission: Restore Our Ocean and Waters," 2021, ec.europa.eu/info/research-and-innovation/funding/funding-opportunities/funding-progra mmes-and-open-calls/horizon-europe/missions-horizon-europe/healthy-oceans-seas-coastal-and-inlandwaters_en.

[17] EuroCities, "Eurocities Secretary General among the Top Experts Selected to Define Horizon Europe Mission," July 31, 2019, eurocities.eu/latest/eurocities-secretary-general-among-the-top-experts-selected-to-define-horizon-europe-mission/.

different parts of our population to allow R&I [Research and Innovation] across Europe to tackle the greatest challenges of our time. And if we allow it to change how we 'do' on the ground, it will become the key source of our future competitiveness. The opportunity is too great to miss.[18]

Moreover, she continues:

Mission-oriented innovation cannot be top-down. It must inspire and harness the full creativity of citizens to tackle problems as urgent as climate change, rising inequality or the challenge to establish more caring societies. In order to inspire society at large, missions need to have widespread legitimacy and acceptance. This means, among other things, that mission setting must find its way to the centre of the political priority-making process and involve citizens in a serious way.

In this context, it is critical to develop a sound and transparent process to select missions, frame them, and to assess missions along the way so that they have the right checks and balances. This requires a strong level of public trust.

Ensuring public trust must start with acknowledging that research and innovation are not separate to society, only populated by academics and policy experts.[19]

The overall intention is that the missions should help develop and embed citizen engagement and consultation in European policy making, thus making the missions a key policy instrument to secure the future and success of the European project. The cancer mission is not just about cancer: it is also about democracy, and we assume our responsibility and obligation to consult citizens seriously and meaningfully.

---

[18] Mazzucato, "Governing Missions in the European Union," 3.
[19] Mazzucato, "Governing Missions in the European Union," 6.

Walter Ricciardi, MD, MPH, MSc, is President of the World Federation of Public Health Associations. He graduated in medicine and earned a doctorate in public health medicine from the University of Naples, Italy. He currently holds the title of Professor of Hygiene and Public Health at the Universita Cattolica del Sacro Cuore in Rome, where he is also Director of the Department of Public Health and Deputy Head of the Faculty of Medicine. He is the editor of the *European Journal of Public Health* and the *Oxford Handbook of Public Health Practice*, and founding editor of the *Italian Journal of Public Health*.

Chapter 12: The Rising Cancer Pandemic in Latin America: Major Cancer Problems and Prospects for Prevention

Michail K. Shafir

In Latin America and the Caribbean there are striking differences among nations regarding the stage of disease and time of diagnosis as well as the incidence and survival. These differences depend on ethnicity, race, and socioeconomic status. Hence, Michail Shafir examines the very different scenarios that can be encountered by pointing to challenges— worsened by the COVID-19 pandemic—in realizing prevention, monitoring the incidence of specific cancers (i.e., breast, gastric, and cervical), tracing the uneven presence of cancer registries, strengthening the healthcare systems, providing healthcare services, and addressing social and national inequities in access to healthcare.

Globally, cancer is a leading cause of death in 134 countries. An estimated 19.3 million new cancer cases are diagnosed across the world each year and this number is expected to rise to 24 million by 2035. Most of this increase will occur in low- and middle-income countries, which are the least capable of confronting the cancer pandemic or affording costly therapies, often due to important lack of infrastructures.

Cancer is the leading cause of death in the Americas. In 2008, cancer accounted for 1.2 million deaths, 45 percent of which occurred in Latin America and the Caribbean. The projected number of cancer deaths in Latin America and the Caribbean would rise from 1.2 million to 2.1 million from 2008 to 2035. The International Agency for Research on Cancer (IARC) predicted that the cancer burden will increase by 55 percent by 2040, affecting 6.23 millions of people, if no further action is taken to prevent and control it.[1] However, in 2019 the Pan American Health Organization (PAHO) provided some encouraging signs by showing a decrease in mortality for cancers in twelve Latin American countries: Argentina 17 percent; Colombia 8.2 percent; Chile 12 percent; Brazil 18.8 percent; Peru 20.6 percent; El Salvador 6.5 percent; Costa Rica 7 percent; Paraguay 7.7 percent; Honduras 9.8 percent; Panama 17.3 percent; Nicaragua 4 percent; and Mexico 15.2 percent.[2]

About a third of all cancer cases could be prevented by avoiding key risk factors. These include tobacco use, harmful consumption of alcohol, unhealthy diet, and physical inactivity.[3] Vaccinations and screening programs are effective interventions to reduce the burden of specific types of cancers. Many cancers have a high chance of cure if detected early and treated adequately.[4]

In Latin America and the Caribbean there are striking differences regarding the stage of disease and time of diagnosis as well as the incidence and survival depending on ethnicity, race, and socioeconomic status. Moreover, the number of cancer programs and treatment centers is not necessarily suited to the size of the country. The largest countries are Brazil

---

[1] World Health Organization and International Agency for Research in Cancer, "Latin America and the Caribbean: Source: Globocan 2020," March 2020, gco.iarc.fr/today/data/factsheets/populations/904-latin-america-and-the-caribbean-fact-sheets.pdf. See also World Health Organization and International Agency for Research in Cancer, "Global Cancer Observatory (GCO)," 2021, gco.iarc.fr.

[2] World Health Organization and Pan American Health Organization (PAHO), "Cancer," 2021, www.paho.org/en/topics/cancer.

[3] World Health Organization and Pan American Health Organization (PAHO), "Annual Report of the Director 2019: Advancing the Sustainable Health Agenda for the Americas 2018–2030. Executive Summary," 2019, iris.paho.org/bitstream/handle/10665.2/51608/Annualreport2019_eng.pdf?sequence=1&isAllowed=y.

[4] Kathrin Strasser-Weippl, Yanin Chavarri-Guerra, Cynthia Villarreal-Garza, Brittany L. Bychkovsky, Marcio Debiasi, Pedro E. R. Liedke, Enrique Soto-Perez-de-Celis, Don Dizon, Eduardo Cazap, Gilberto de Lima Lopes Jr., Diego Touya, João Soares Nunes, Jessica St. Louis, Caroline Vail, Alexandra Bukowski, Pier Ramos-Elias, Karla Unger-Saldana, Denise Froes Brandao, Mayra E. Ferreyra, Silvana Luciani, Angelica Nogueira-Rodrigues, Aknar Freire de Carvalho Calabrich, Marcela G. Del Carmen, Jose Alejandro Rauh-Hain, Kathleen Schmeler, Raul Sala, and Paul E. Goss, "Progress and Remaining Challenges for Cancer Control in Latin America and the Caribbean," *Lancet Oncology* 16, no. 14 (2015): 1405–1438.

with a population of 213 million, Colombia (51 million), Argentina (45 million), Peru (33 million), and Venezuela (28 million). However, all these countries have scattered cancer programs, concentrated in very large cities, and only the wealthier populations have easier access to cancer care. Venezuela has a disjointed cancer care program due to an unstable political and economic climate. At the same time, a smaller country, Uruguay, with a population of 3.5 million, has a very organized national cancer program, and it offers universal cancer care.

Latin American countries participate in the CanScreen program of the International Agency for Research on Cancer (IARC), launched in 2019.[5]

Other data help us to characterize the current Latin American context regarding cancer.

> The most frequently diagnosed types of cancer among men are: prostate (21.7%), lung (9.5%), colorectal (8%), bladder (4.6%) and stomach (2.9%). Among women, the types of cancer with the highest incidence are: breast (25.2%), lung (8.5%), colorectal (8.2%), thyroid (5.4 %) and cervical (3.9%).[6]

Moreover,

> The lifetime risk of being diagnosed with cancer ranges from 26% (1 in 4 persons) in Uruguay to 11% (1 in 10 persons) in Guyana. The corresponding cancer mortality risk ranges from 14% (1 in 7 persons) in Uruguay to 7% (1 in 15 persons) in Mexico. There are

---

[5] World Health Organization and International Agency for Research in Cancer, "Canscreen 5," 2019, canscreen5.iarc.fr. See also Vijay Shankar Balakrishnan, "COVID-19: Cancer Care at Stake in Low- & Middle-Income Countries," *Oncology Times* 43, no. 8 (2021): 33, doi.org/10.1097/01.COT.0000749948.96214.8e.

[6] World Health Organization and Pan American Health Organization (PAHO), "World Cancer Day 2020: I Am and I Will," 2021, www3.paho.org/hq/index.php?option=com_content&view=article&id=15687:world-cancer-day-2020-i-am-and-iwill&Itemid=39809&lang=en. See also World Health Organization and International Agency for Research in Cancer, "Latin America and the Caribbean: Source: Globocan 2020."

marked variations in the incidence and mortality rates of specific cancers across countries: for example, cervical cancer varies sixfold for incidence, from 39 per 100,000 in Bolivia to 7 in Guadeloupe, and a striking 15-fold for mortality, from 19 in Jamaica to 1 in Martinique. While the highest prostate cancer incidence rates are seen in the Caribbean, with 189 per 100,000 in Guadeloupe, the lowest are estimated in Honduras (25). In Bolivia, the most common cause of cancer death is gallbladder cancer.[7]

COVID-19 Pandemic and Cancer in Latin America

The Covid 19 pandemic has complicated access to care of cancer patients. In April 2021, the PAHO's survey revealed that in Latin America cancer screening and treatment were disrupted in 52 percent of countries.[8] However, this information depends on tumor registries, which in many countries are neither accurate nor complete.[9] For example, according to Leandro Colli, MD, PhD, and Medical Oncologist at University of Sao Paulo in Brazil, the northwest of the country was affected by COVID-19 harder than the south since the public health system is imbalanced across the country and is severely challenged in poorer regions. He added that the government is not being transparent with the health data, and this lack of transparency worsens the nation's ability to address the complexity of the health situation.[10] Moreover, since the start of the COVID-19 pandemic, the average number of cancer diagnoses has plummeted considerably in all Brazilian regions, resulting in approximately 1,500 undiagnosed cancer cases per month.[11]

---

[7] The Cancer Atlas, "Latin America & the Caribbean," 2021. See also World Health Organization and Pan American Health Organization (PAHO), "Annual Report of the Director 2019."

[8] World Health Organization and Pan American Health Organization (PAHO), "World Cancer Day 2020."

[9] Strasser-Weippl et al., "Progress and Remaining Challenges for Cancer Control in Latin America and the Caribbean."

[10] Personal Interview.

[11] Balakrishnan, "COVID-19: Cancer Care at Stake in Low- & Middle-Income Countries."

As the COVID-19 pandemic continues, it becomes even more critical to ensure continuity of cancer care. PAHO issued a guidance aimed at reorienting cancer services, prioritizing those people with cancer amenable to treatment, avoiding any cumulative delays in treatment, and preventing an increase in avoidable deaths from cancer. In particular, in order to strengthen cancer programs in Latin America post-COVID-19, PAHO recommended to:

- create national cancer plans with adequate financing, human resources, management, and sufficient monitoring;
- improve screening programs and cancer registries, including creating these registries where they are not available yet or improving their accuracy, when the data gathered are inaccurate or insufficient, by training cancer registrars and sharpening quality indicators;
- strengthen screening and early detection of cervical cancer in women, by striving to eliminate the occurrence of this cancer, which is preventable but very lethal;
- insure sufficient human resources and sufficient infrastructures, including education, to foster the capabilities of all health providers;
- invest in more accurate and widespread pathology services, efficacy, and affordability of cancer drugs, as well as diagnostic and therapeutic technologies;
- develop capabilities for palliative care.[12]

In addition, PAHO presented an overall plan for establishing:

- a national control of cancer for each country in Latin America and the Caribbean;
- primary prevention strategies by developing programs to eliminate tobacco use, limit consumption of excessive alcohol, decrease the consumption of red meat in diets, as well as smoked meat and fish and increase the intake of fruits and vegetables, increase physical activity, promote vaccination programs against papilloma virus and hepatitis B;
- screening and early detection for cervical cancer, breast cancer, and colorectal cancer;

---

[12] World Health Organization and Pan American Health Organization (PAHO), "Cancer."

- greater opportunities to diagnose and treat by offering anatomopathology services, surgery facilities, radiation therapy, and chemotherapy, including programs for pediatric oncology;
- palliative care services and access to opioids for pain control in advanced painful cancers.[13]

For PAHO, implementing these plans and achieving these goals depend on national, institutional commitments, but the involvement of communities is needed to strengthen the overall quality of care available to each citizen.

"Best Buys": Techniques for Cancer Prevention and Early Detection

In addressing the complexity of cancer prevention and early detection in Latin America, a survey of the existing literature stresses the following successful practices:

- cervical cancer tests (Papanicolaou, HPV, and iodine) should be performed in all women starting at age 30;[14]
- HPV vaccination should be made available for girls and boys starting at early adolescence. In women, this vaccination will decrease the incidence of cervical cancer by 90 percent when vaccinated against HPV by age 15. In boys, when vaccinated before the age of 15, it will reduce penile cancer by 90 percent;
- mammograms and sonograms should be performed starting at age 40-50 to reduce the incidence of breast cancer; • tests aimed at detecting occult blood in stool should be performed beginning at age 50 to address the risk of colorectal cancer. Further investigations require rigid sigmoidoscopy and colonoscopy;
- digital rectal exam should be performed beginning at age 50 to monitor the prostate.

---

[13] World Health Organization and Pan American Health Organization (PAHO), "Annual Report of the Director 2019."

[14] HPV means Human Papilloma Virus.

What Is the Cancer Reality in Latin America?

In the Latin American continent, there is a marked inequality in cancer care and access to diagnostic and treatment centers, due to poor education and high incidence of poverty. Specific issues deserve particular attention.

Cancer Registries in Latin America

In 2011, only 21 percent of countries in Latin America had a population-based cancer registry, though in only 7 percent the quality of the information gathered was high. As a result, accurate estimations of cancer burden and risks faced by different countries are not possible. The 2013 Lancet Oncology Commission on cancer control in Latin America and the Caribbean showed the shortage of local scientific evidence and economic data regarding cancer prevention and control.[15] Moreover, the authors reported that cancer control programs faced inadequate structural funding, inequitable distribution of resources and services, and insufficient care for many populations based on socio-economic, geographical, and ethnic factors. Accurate, updated, and comparable data are essential to measure effectiveness of health programs. Because of the absence of a real priority assigned to cancer control, the dearth of development of cancer registries is unsurprising. Thus, because of insufficient effective cancer control programs, what concerns cancer registration can be thought of as the tip of the iceberg.[16] More positively, in the past few years cancer registries were added in Argentina, Brazil, Chile and Colombia.[17]

Well-functioning registries provide accurate data regarding incidence, prevalence, mortality, and information efforts to reduce the cancer burden

---

[15] Paul E. Goss et al., "Planning Cancer Control in Latin America and the Caribbean," *Lancet Oncology* 14, no. 5 (2013): 391–436.

[16] Silvina Arrossi, "Cancer Registration and Information Systems in Latin America," *Lancet Oncology* 16, no. 14 (2015): 1400–1401.

[17] Marion Pineros, M. Graciela Abriata, Les Mery, and Freddie Bray, "Cancer Registration for Cancer Control in Latin America: A Status and Progress Report," *Pan American Journal of Public Health (Revista Panamericana de Salud Publica)* 41 (2017): e2, doi.org/10.26633/RPSP.2017.2.

on individuals and on the whole society. Moreover, registries should also provide data regarding the proportion of the population surviving a cancer, the years of life lost due to cancer death, and the years of life with disability following the initial diagnosis by detailing the type and stage of cancer.[18] Finally, in Latin America, the mortality of pediatric cancers is among the highest in the world.[19]

Breast Cancer in Latin America

The incidence of breast cancer in Latin America is increasing yearly, disproportionately when compared to Europe and the United States. The number of cases is unevenly distributed in different countries in Latin America and even within regions of the same country. Women in larger cities have better access to care than those in smaller towns or rural areas. Several studies—conducted in 2006, 2010 and 2013—concluded that breast cancer is the most frequent cancer in the continent and kills more women than any other cancer. The economic burden and inequalities in access to care, particularly in lower socioeconomic strata, result in late diagnoses and unequal therapeutic outcomes. For instance, in the United States 60 percent of breast cancers are diagnosed at earlier stages. Conversely, in Brazil and Mexico only 20 percent and 10 percent respectively are diagnosed at an early stage. The cancer mortality-to-incidence ratio for Latin America is 0.59, compared to 0.43 for the European Union, and 0.35 for the United States.[20]

---

[18] Pineros, Abriata, Mery, and Bray, "Cancer Registration for Cancer Control in Latin America: A Status and Progress Report."

[19] Scott C. Howard, Raul C. Ribeiro, and Ching-Hon Pui, "Strategies to Improve Outcomes of Children with Cancer in Low-Income Countries," *European Journal of Cancer* 41, no. 11 (2005): 1584–1587.

[20] The mortality-to-incidence ratio is generally used as a high-level comparative measure to identify inequities in cancer outcomes, and it "can serve as an insightful indicator of cancer management outcomes for individual nations." See Eunji Choi, Sangeun Lee, Bui Cam Nhung, Mina Suh, Boyoung Park, Jae Kwan Jun, and Kui Son Choi, "Cancer Mortality-to-Incidence Ratio as an Indicator of Cancer Management Outcomes in Organization for Economic Cooperation and Development Countries," *Epidemiology and Health* 39 (2017): e2017006, doi.org/10.4178/epih.e2017006.

In the case of breast cancer, these differences are mainly related to the lack of national regulations and guidelines requiring screening mammography. Because of insufficient political commitment, what results is the low rate of mammographic screening particularly among the poorer and more rural women, affecting early detection and causing a lack of adequate epidemiologic data. Moreover, the possibility of testing hormone receptors and molecular markers is not available to all patients. In an important number of cases, instead of more focused surgical procedures, mastectomy appeared to be the operation of choice, usually performed by gynecologists or general surgeons. Some countries in Latin America are making more progress, mostly because of implementing universal care, improving cancer registries, and promoting public health education, particularly in Argentina, Uruguay, and Costa Rica.[21]

Gastric Cancer in Latin America

Gastric cancer is a highly lethal disease. In Central and South America, stomach cancer mortality rates are among the highest in the world. Examining forty-eight population-based registries in thirteen countries and data regarding nation-wide cancer deaths obtained from the mortality database of the World Health Organization in eighteen countries reveals that the highest incidence of this cancer is in Chile, Costa Rica, Colombia, Ecuador, Brazil, and Peru. Males in Chile and females in Guatemala are affected with some of the highest mortality rates in the world. Between 1997 and 2008, the incidence rates declined by 4 percent annually in Brazil, Chile, and Costa Rica. Between 1997 and 2008, the mortality declined 4 percent annually in Chile and Costa Rica. Cancers of the cardia region are less frequent than non-cardia cancers.[22] These differences in cancer types and incidence may be related to differences in prevalence of Helicobacter

---

[21] See Eduardo Cazap, "Breast Cancer in Latin America: A Map of the Disease in the Region," *American Society of Clinical Oncology Educational Book* 38 (2018): 451–456.

[22] The gastric cardia is the area of mucosa located distal to the anatomic gastroesophageal junction.

Pylori and other risk factors such as diet.[23] A high incidence and mortality is noted in high altitude Andean countries, such as Chile and Colombia, related to smoke-cured preserved meat and fish, and to reuse cooking oil (which is high in carcinogens such as nitrosamines) added to a high prevalence of Helicobacter Pylori.[24]

Cervical Cancer in Latin America

In Latin America and the Caribbean there is a very high incidence of women diagnosed with cervical cancer, and a large percentage of them die prematurely. This cancer, however, could be prevented. Early diagnosis would prevent the occurrence of advanced cases and significantly decrease mortality. Despite prevention and screening efforts, cervical cancer remains one of the leading causes of cancer mortality in Latin America, with incidence percentages two to four times higher than in high income countries and with even higher rates in women who do not live in urban settings or are less educated and suffer because of poverty or low income.

Most cervical cancers (i.e., 70 percent in Latin America) are caused by the Human Papillomavirus, mainly subtypes 16 and 18, which are covered by the available HPV vaccines. In order to prevent cervical, penile, and oral cancers, these vaccinations should be administered to preadolescent girls and boys, before their first sexual encounter. Through the auspices of the Pan-American Health Organization, the HPV vaccines are available in most Latin American countries at deeply discounted prices. Initially,

---

[23] See Maria Del Pilar Diaz, Gloria Icaza, Loreto Nunez, and Sonia A. Pou, "Gastric Cancer Mortality Trends in the Southern Cone: Disentangling Age, Period and Cohort Patterns in Argentina and Chile," *Scientific Reports* 10, no. 1 (2020): 1526, doi.org/10.1038/s41598-020-58539-w.

[24] See Monica S. Sierra, Patricia Cueva, Luis Eduardo Bravo, and David Forman, "Stomach Cancer Burden in Central and South America," *Cancer Epidemiology* 44, Suppl. 1 (2016): S62–S73; Javier Torres, Pelayo Correa, Catterina Ferreccio, Gustavo Hernandez-Suarez, Rolando Herrero, Maria Cavazza-Porro, Ricardo Dominguez, and Douglas Morgan, "Gastric Cancer Incidence and Mortality Is Associated with Altitude in the Mountainous Regions of Pacific Latin America," *Cancer Causes Control* 24, no. 2 (2013): 249–256; Michail Shafir, "Gastric Cancer Prevention Proposal for Pilot Study" (Master of Public Health, Icahn School of Medicine at Mount Sinai, 2016).

Argentina, Mexico, Panama, and Peru started a national vaccination program in 2011. The counterpoint is that a few countries—e.g., Bolivia, Nicaragua, Venezuela, and Honduras—have been unable to implement a national vaccination program due to limited infrastructure and support staff, as well as insufficient political will. Even in countries with a national vaccination program, only about 50 percent of adolescents received both doses. There have also been religious organizations that did not approve of the vaccinations, alleging that they would lead to promiscuity.

Screening is a complicated issue. In urban settings, relatively well-to-do women have access to cytology studies with Papanicolau smears as well as HPV DNA determination. Among poor and rural women, cytology has been unreliable due to lack of supportive facilities. Hence, for this population a simple screening by staining the cervix with Lugol iodine and/or white vinegar could lead to requiring cryotherapy of any suspicious lesions. This simple screening method is available and practiced, and many Latin American countries have adopted it. However, paradoxically, not even this simple method is available in the public sector in Brazil, Chile, Cuba, Dominican Republic, Ecuador, Honduras, Panama, Paraguay, Peru, and Uruguay. These countries should be encouraged to implement these programs for rural, indigenous, and poor women.

In conclusion, HPV vaccination programs should be encouraged, introduced in the nations where they are not yet available, and administered by relying on health personnel working in schools. In other words, the HPV vaccine should be administered in ways similar to the other vaccination programs already in place, like those for avoiding measles and diphtheria.[25]

Focusing on Healthcare Systems in Latin American Countries

In most Latin American countries, there is a marked inequality in income

---

[25] See Brittany L. Bychkovsky, Felicia M. Knaul, and Gilberto de Lima Lopes Jr., "Cervical Cancer in Latin America," *ASCO Connection*, July 26, 2017, connection.asco.org/blogs/cervical-cancer-latin-america.

and access to care. Public hospitals are often inadequate and poorly staffed, and cancer care is often insufficient and inefficient. Private hospitals deliver adequate care, but only a small percentage of cancer patients can afford care in these private facilities.

Bolivia has a health law that covers all maternal-child care until the child is 5 years old. Health care is free in public hospitals for all adults after the age of 50, but neither health issues that depend on roadside accidents are covered, nor diseases between the ages of 5 to 50. In Santa Cruz, the wealthiest city in Bolivia, the Cancer Institute is private. Most patients cannot afford to be treated there, although non-governmental organizations provide financial support. On the high Bolivian Andes mountains, cancers are caused by environmental pollution. Silver miners are exposed to the toxic arsenic and mercury, and they develop skin, lung, and bladder cancers. In the Amazonian northeast of the country, leather factories discharge cadmium and manganese into the nearby rivers. Consequently, in the neighboring population there is a high incidence of esophageal and gastric cancers.

Paraguay has a public Cancer Institute that provides free cancer care. However, it has limited resources and is in a rural area, two hours away from the capital city. Some private hospitals provide a very limited free cancer care. A recent law was passed by Congress to develop a national comprehensive cancer program.

Uruguay has the most developed social program, and it has a satisfactory cancer registry. In many instances cancer care is offered at low cost or free.

In 1936, Chile established free public hospitals for indigent patients, a first in Latin America. These hospitals were also teaching hospitals and trained medical students and residents. In particular, the National Cancer Institute was affiliated with a free university hospital. Another Cancer Institute is private but provides free cancer care to indigents, including surgery, radiation, and chemotherapy. After the 1973 military coup by Army General Augusto Pinochet (1915–2006), public hospitals were no longer financed, and health care was mostly provided by a proliferation of private hospitals. Several decades later, in 2005, after the end of the

Pinochet dictatorship, a social health program, called AUGE, was developed to provide free medications for noncommunicable diseases, including cancer drugs, and an attempt was made to revitalize public hospitals.[26]

As indicated earlier, the lack of adequate national cancer registries is negatively affecting cancer care. Death certificate data are often unreliable because the needed health information is incomplete. A few examples are needed. In Chile there are three provincial cancer registries: one in Antofagasta in the north, and Bio Bio and Valdivia in the continental south. There is no centralized national cancer registry. In Cuba, all medical care is free for the entire population. However, there are scarce data on cancer statistics. In Venezuela, the statistical data on cancer were missed for several years, and the quality of delivery of cancer care is unknown.

Conclusion

Latin America sees an increasing incidence of many cancers. Many of these cancers are preventable, particularly those that are caused by tobacco use, pesticides, alcohol abuse, Helicobacter Pylori, and HPV—in case of cervical, penile, and oropharyngeal cancers. Public health environmental issues should be urgently addressed. Education regarding HPV vaccines in adolescents should be promoted, leading to vaccination campaigns that could prevent cervical, penile, and oropharyngeal cancers. While these educational and vaccinal efforts appear to be feasible in public schools, they might still be more complex in religious schools because of misconception regarding the relation between this vaccine and sexual

---

[26] "AUGE is a universal health plan which provides explicit healthcare guarantees (garantías explicitas de salud, GES) with regard to coverage for 80 health problems which have been established by law. All Chilean men and women, whether they are in the public healthcare system ... or have a private health insurance plan ... are guaranteed coverage for these health problems. These guarantees constitute a right which must be granted whenever any Chilean is diagnosed with one of these pathologies and meets the requirements set for each one." Government of Chile, "10 Years of Auge: Achievements, Guarantees and How the Health Plan Works," 2015, www.gob.cl/en/news/10-years-of-augeachievements-guarantees-and-how-the-health-plan-works/.

behaviors. Campaigns offering regularly free tests, which could detect breast cancer and cervical cancer at early developing stages, are essential to improve early diagnosis and consequently improve mortality rates. Finally, to establish national cancer registries appears to be of fundamental importance for promoting cancer prevention and treatment programs.

Michail K. Shafir, MD, MPH, FACS, is Clinical Professor of Surgery and Oncological Sciences at the Ruttenberg Cancer Center at the Icahn School of Medicine at Mount Sinai and attending surgeon at the Mount Sinai Hospital, New York. Former President of the New York Cancer Society and member of the Executive Council of the New York Surgical Society, he is also a member of major surgical and cancer societies, such as the American College of Surgeons and the Society of Surgical Oncology, as well as a core member of the Surgery Committee of the Cancer and Leukemia Group B (CALGB), a major national cooperative group for clinical trials in cancer.

Part 5
Surviving Cancer

Chapter 13: Ruminations from a Patient to Future Provider: Cancer as a Lifelong Journey

Bridgette Merriman

A Boston College alumna, Bridgette Merriman, now medical student, describes her journey with cancer in early childhood— from the early symptoms to the diagnosis, and then to chemotherapy. Cancer is a lifelong journey. It continues to impact one's life, even being a survivor. In her case, it can ultimately lead to acquire the needed training and dedicate herself to caring for people, even children, struggling with cancer.

"Is This Normal?"

Life in fifth grade was great. I participated in my first competitive sports leagues, had a blast playing in the neighborhood, and absolutely loved learning in school. What could be better? But that fall, I began to notice some nondescript symptoms.

It was tough to catch my breath at swim practice. *You are still adjusting to this new breathing pattern* I told myself. My doctor suggested an inhaler for exercise-induced asthma. I later developed a cough. The deep, vibratory, kind. *But who doesn't have one of those?* I also found a large lymph node on my neck. "Mom, is this normal?" I stared at myself in the bathroom mirror, seeing the uneven bulge where my neck met my shoulders. A provider believed the large lump I originally found, and more palpable masses, to be backed up glands. Given my chronic cough, the time of year, and the fact that they were 'squishy,' she said to keep an eye on them and come back in a few weeks if they persist. *The lumps were solid as marbles.*

At the same time, I had been losing a few pounds. But I was a "robust" child, and we attributed my changing body composition to swimming. These things seemed *normal.*

By February 2009, the little symptoms that we attributed to this or that were enough to make the diagnosis, but we weren't seeing it. Things culminated to a point that was impossible to ignore. I was absolutely exhausted at my championship swim meet—I barely made it through my 30-second race. *What is happening? My times are going in the wrong direction.*

> "It looks like you're gasping for air," my dad joked. *It felt like I was!*
>
> "Is she eating?" my coaches asked my parents. *I was!* Yet my bathing suit that had once fit like a glove was baggy in places it should not have been.

More strange occurrences followed on our family vacation to Florida. While the rest of my family developed a warm sun-kissed glow, I seemed to be paler than when we arrived. And that cough? It continued nonstop. I even slept in my own area, propped up with pillows, a cup next to me into which I spit the phlegm, but there was no relief. "Just get it out!," my parents called out at night. *I am, but I can't stop.*

"Must Be Mono"

Back from vacation, we decided to return to the doctors' office before school resumed. We were relieved to secure an appointment with our pediatrician. *He will know what's going on.* While only a month had passed since I was last seen, much had changed. I lost another ten pounds, and the lymph nodes had grown in both size and number. My doctor had a strange presence about him; moving between my chart and me, examining my lymph nodes, even taking a measuring tape out to assess their size. *I was right, they don't move.*

As he was writing lab and imaging orders, my mom noticed him write *STAT* across the sheet. She broke the silence. "Man, it must be mono or pneumonia, right?"

> My doctor just looked at us, "Mmm... we will run some tests and see. I will call you tonight." *It's Friday afternoon, how "stat" must it be?*

Another oddity at the x-ray appointment; the technician kept going back and forth in front of my changing area, bringing different folks with her to review my image, before letting my mom and me go. "She must be new," we muttered to ourselves. If only we knew what that poor woman saw.

Then the Phone Call Came

I heard the telephone ring around 9:00 p.m. My mom cried, ran down the stairs, and shouted for my dad. Just that afternoon, he was at our neighbors' house explaining all that had transpired. They are both providers at our local hospital and were putting two and two together as my dad spoke to them. "Go home, be with your family, call us when they call you." *They knew.*

My parents told me to pack a bag because we were going to the hospital. When I asked if we would be there long, they just said to bring a book. *I guess that means yes? I never had to go to the hospital for me, what was going on?*

The hospital was a whirlwind. Walking past folks sitting in the waiting room and lining the halls, hearing the beeps of machines and moans of pain and concern, I felt so out of place. We checked in at the pediatric desk and were practically swarmed upon arrival. Within minutes, I was ushered into a room, IV placed, whisked to do another x-ray, and this time, I experienced a new test, a CT scan. *These will become your new normal.*

Moments from this night are seared into my memory with such detail that, as I close my eyes writing this, I'm transported back.

> *My reflection in the ceiling mirror stared back at me as I was wheeled down the hall; I am wearing my favorite Red Sox shirt, jeans, and gaudy pink glasses I thought were stylish. The nurse held my arm as contrast went in. I felt it spread through my body. I*

panicked—it felt as though I wet my pants, but it was only the heat of the dye.

Everyone around me was acting as if I was incredibly sick, but I felt fine. *What was going on?* Later, I sat on the emergency room bed, and a man ushered my parents into the hallway. They returned visibly upset; it was the first time I'd seen my dad cry. The man walked to my bedside and stood eye-to-eye with me. Though I did not understand what was happening, at that moment, the one thing I did understand was that this person was here for *me*. He introduced himself as my oncologist and then said the words that no one should ever have to hear.

"Bridgette," he said, "you have cancer. It's Hodgkin's Lymphoma. But it's curable." I was relieved; hearing "curable" wiped away the fear that had risen inside of me. I think that moment determined how the rest of my journey would play out. From the very beginning, my oncologist, I, and by nature everyone else in my life focused on the silver linings; *curable* was always center stage. The scary terms of *stage four, high-risk, metastasized*, were afterthoughts, so much so that it took years before I fully grasped the gravity of my situation.

He briefly explained the "game plan" to me: biopsy the next morning, PET scan after, inpatient stay until chemotherapy began. My oncologist then asked what questions I had. I had been nodding along. Though these words did not make complete sense to me, I knew that I was sick, and there was a plan to make me better. What more did I need to know? I asked the only thing that was on my mind. "Will my parents be okay?"

I never thought about death. I never thought about the potential bad outcomes. Maybe it was childhood innocence, maybe it was optimism, maybe it was faith. Who knows what it was, but what I did know, is that everything would be okay.

Entering the Twilight Zone

I kept track of my journey through CaringBridge, an online blog forum, describing everything in detail to friends and family that subscribed to my page. I envisioned myself as the spunky, witty, teenage protagonists in the books that I obsessed over, creating her viral blog posts practically daily. I loved it! I wrote about my procedures, described how the local anesthetic felt, explained what needle sizes were. I even included pictures of some devices and equipment! I guess the future doctor in me was blossoming.

Later, I received the bad news. For the semi-permanent IV, I couldn't get the one that is surgically put in. I needed the one that goes in halfway up my arm, and a tube travels up my arm, around my shoulder, and across my collar bone. Oh, and that tube is inside one of my veins-not arteries, veins. I was so scared because this is done while you are awake, and even though there is numbing cream, there are still four needles going into you, and that makes me queasy. When the lady who would be doing it to me came in, the numbing cream on my arm already worked its magic. Before she started anything else, we had to wait for my nurse, Kristin, to get the relaxing medicine. When it went into my IV (it was on my hand), it burned!!!! It felt like my hand and as the medicine traveled up my arm, the rest of my arm was on fire! Then, Shery, the lady doing my big IV started to work. First, she gave me a shot of numbing medicine to numb under my skin. For 10 seconds, I got that same burning sensation, only she gave it to me fast, so the fire burned even stronger than before. While she fed the wire into my vein, she would squeeze every once in a while, and what I felt was almost a crunch. That also hurt. Finally, Shery was done putting in my IV after 4 numbing fire shots. That was one of the bad things that happened.

After the wrapping was put on to keep the wire in place, I started bleeding. A lot. The shirt that I had on was all red on the sleeve. To prevent more bleeding, Kristin (my nurse) put gauze on my arm. Later, my arm started to turn purple, and I was afraid because that is a sign that the IV wasn't put in right. That means it would have to be taken out and put back in again! The nurses came to make sure that I definitely needed it put in again. One thought the gauze was put on too tight, and asked me to take it off. It turned out the gauze was put on too tight. My arm turned back to normal soon. That gave me a scare, and that is one of the reasons why my day was horrible.

I also got the IV that was on my hand, and making it swell, out. Kristin let me take it out because of all the tape around it, and the part inside me was like a piece of floss. Soft and stringy. That part of my day was like hallelujah.[1]

Chemo came, and my hair went. As it started to fall, I got a shorter cut. *Makes the transition more palatable,* people told me. I was excited for a new 'do.

"Make it look like Alice from *Twilight*" and I showed my hairdresser movie scenes for inspiration. While showering a few days later, my hair fell out in such big clumps that it grossed me out more than made me sad. I knew it was time to shave it.

So I did. And my cousin gave the sweetest act of kindness I've ever received; he shaved his head with me. We are best friends to this day.

"What Does It Feel Like?"

What does it *feel* like to have cancer? To go through chemotherapy and radiation? I have always struggled to describe these experiences to others because they are feelings that are incredibly niche and unique to each patient. As with many things in healthcare and beyond, cancer is more of a "one size fits one" than a "one size fits all." Yet, ironically, uttering a single word such as "neupogen," can elicit the same moans, bitter laughter, and sensation descriptions, from almost every patient. At the same time, I am a firm believer that, sometimes, our brains prevent us from fully understanding and internalizing the experiences of others, in order to protect and shield ourselves from that trauma. So even if there *was* a perfect way to describe what cancer feels like, is it fair of me to invite those who

---

[1] Bridgette Merriman, "Journal," *CaringBridge*, February 23, 2009, www.caringbridge.org/visit/bridgettemerriman/journal.

have not gone through it themselves to share those feelings? Is it even possible? I did not think so, until I got my COVID vaccine.

The night following my vaccine I could not stop crying, and it was not just because of the physical pain I felt. I anticipated the soreness and exhaustion that usually comes with vaccines, so I could not understand why I was literally brought to my knees from the sensation that flooded my body. Then it hit me: the *only* other time in my life I had *that* specific feeling was during chemo.

The deep bone aches in my back, hips, and femurs, pulsed through my skeleton. The ebb and flow of my bone marrow working hard and preparing my immune system was the same pain I felt during chemo. It was the same pain that woke me in the middle of the night in 2009, when the neupogen shots finally kicked in, signaling my marrow springing back to life. It was the same pain that came from my rapidly dividing cells, collateral damage from the chemo. I recognize how lucky and blessed I am for my treatment experience. I did not have many of the side effects that people warned me about, that I prepared myself to experience, never threw up, had a cold sore, or lost my appetite. Just intense fatigue and hair loss. My gratitude and appreciation for my body's response to chemotherapy grows each year as I learn more about what the chemotherapy medicines were *actually* doing to my body. As I witness friends and family members navigate their own cancer journeys, I am pained to see them go through things that I *should* have experienced. Survivor's guilt shows itself in insidious ways.

I now understand how horrible chemotherapy is. I didn't when I was sick. Maybe ignorance was bliss. Chemotherapy is *poison*. It is toxic ammunition. We dump it into an incredibly sick person; a person betrayed by their own body, being eaten by a monster growing inside of them, over which they have no control. We fill a person with poison, hoping their body is strong enough to withstand it and for the poison to win before the cancer does. I realize that my experience only scratches the surface of what cancer and its treatment can do to a person and their loved ones.

Life Beyond Me

My cancer journey was also my first introduction to global health and health equity. One infusion day, I met a doctor from Ethiopia who was visiting my oncologist. I learned that they are members of an organization whose aim is to establish sustainable pediatric and adolescent oncology care systems in low-resource countries. They explained to me that children in other countries also get cancer, but many elements beyond the molecular biology of cancer contribute to the child's ability to beat their disease. Factors such as distance from a care center, access to specialists and patient-to-provider ratios, affordable treatment and care, all impact a child's ability to survive. I thought to myself, *How is it that, just by luck of the draw, I was born with this hospital right in my city? We are all children with similar illnesses, yet such different healthcare opportunities determine our ability to survive and thrive?*

I have continued to keep health equity and accessibility as a passion since then. Advocacy for justice in all realms of life underlies the service, organizations, and movements to which I dedicate my time. I do not feel compelled in this pursuit, as if I am indebted to something. Rather, it is a desire to make a difference and promote positive change that fills me with a sense of purpose and meaning. Some groups holding a special place in my heart include my local hospital and a camp for children and families affected by cancer and other life challenges. I have worked with these organizations since 2009 and will continue for many years to come. During college, I was devoted to Dance Marathon and raising support for Boston Children's Hospital and its patients. Today, I lead student service and advocacy groups whose missions aim to serve adolescent parents and their children, folks obtaining gynecologic procedures, and oncology patients. Advocating for equity and justice is an integral part of my being and will continue as such in my education, future career, and personal life.

My New Normal

By July of 2009, I was in remission. Focus shifted from curing me, to making sure I stayed healthy. The complexities of follow-up care quickly became routine: CT scans, chest x-rays, blood work, echocardiograms, EKGs, screenings for secondary cancers, ultrasounds, genetic screening, and the list continues.

While this was done to protect my physical health, I learned that there are complexities to survivorship; cancer is more than getting sick and getting better. What about the fears that instantly consume my thoughts when I feel a lump or a bump? When I got mono and immediately assumed the worst? Survivor's guilt I feel when I learn about someone's death, why did I survive? Do I have to do something spectacular to make my life "count"? Can I have a family? What if I get cancer again, and this time it wins?

Cancer is a *life* event. I explored the ways in which cancer continues to impact young adult survivors for my thesis throughout my senior year of college. Some folks hold being a survivor at the very core of their identity, and others keep it in the past. Some remember their treatment experience, and others were just babies at the time of their illness. But no matter the age at diagnosis, specific cancer, treatment length, or how often one thinks about their cancer journey, the same underlying questions and fears unite us all.

These uncertainties do not necessarily develop over years; sometimes they are implanted the moment a child receives their diagnosis. These uncertainties are constant reminders that being *different* from other people can be isolating, both during treatment and for years to come. I was fortunate to learn about Camp Good Days and Special Times, a camp where I'd be surrounded by kids like me, kids with cancer. My parents signed me up that very day. That summer, I rode the bus in eager anticipation; I had preconceived ideas based on what my friends told me about their camps, but I would soon learn that Camp Good Days is different. Counselors dressed in fun costumes greeted the bus, hugging each of us as we stepped off. The week was filled with activities beyond my wildest dreams: archery, scuba diving, magic shows, and hot air balloons! But best of all, for the first time in months, I was normal. No more wearing a bandana or an itchy wig to cover my bald head, no more explaining the "funky tube" in my arm, no more sad looks from adults. I was just Bridgette.

My favorite weeks of the year are the ones I spend there, once as a camper, now as a counselor. I love connecting with my campers and watching them come out of their shell, seeing their smiles as they are finally able to participate in "normal kid" activities. But they, too, share the same "survivor fears." Several years ago, a camper asked me why, if all campers had cancer, does it seem that none of the counselors had cancer? Her unspoken question stung my heart: *is there life after being a pediatric cancer patient?*

Being a survivor is not necessarily tattooed across our foreheads, and it is scary not knowing what happens next. The intensity of care dedicated to "beating the cancer" sometimes seems to outweigh "life after cancer." Her face lit up once I showed her a picture of my first year at camp, when I was bald. Another camper's confusion shifted into the biggest smile when I told her that we share the same oncologist, and another friend and I joke that we are "cancer buddies." I find myself repeating this saying often, but its repetition does not make it any less true; while I am not happy that other people experience some of these hardships, it is comforting to know that I am not the only one.

Just as much as there is hope and courage at Camp Good Days, there is also some sadness. I say goodbye to campers every year. Sometimes, it is a goodbye forever. The opening ceremony is one of my favorite traditions at camp; campers and counselors take time to reflect on our past, those who supported us, those who are with us, and those who can no longer join us. There are many names that I write on my remembrance rock, and the list grows each year.

I have known in my heart for as long as I have wanted to pursue medicine that I was going to be a pediatric oncologist. Although I am fascinated with each specialty in medicine, nothing fills me with the same awe and gratitude as pediatric oncology. I cannot wait to follow my oncologist's footsteps, being just as patient centered and family focused as he is, for my future patients, for children like my campers, for kids like me.

"Am I Lucky?"

Am I fortunate that I had cancer? In a weird way, yes. My experience has directed my vision and understanding of not only medicine, but what it means to embrace the fragility of human connection. My life is an extension of my cancer journey: career goals, service, and advocacy work. I work hard to become a pediatric oncologist, always seeking opportunities to learn and grow. I have a genuine and deep-rooted desire to give back; it's my purpose. I began to learn about equity and justice because of my cancer, and today, advocacy and justice consume my thoughts just as much, and maybe even a little bit more, than studying.

For what seemed like forever, my dream of becoming a doctor was in the far-off distance. Now, all of a sudden, it's becoming a reality. The email that made me cry of happiness even more than my first medical school acceptance, was the one I got from my doctor, signed "your colleague." I still tear up reading it.

I am currently a second-year medical student, and every day I love medicine more, love my patients more, and am more excited to be their provider. I am where I'm meant to be, I cannot imagine any other life circumstance that would have brought me here.

My peers from Boston College may remember our school's invitation to ask ourselves these questions, and answer them honestly: *what brings you joy, what are you good at, and what does the world need you to do?* My life journey helps me to answer those questions with confidence. From patient to future provider, my cancer journey helped develop who I am and who I want to be. I can't wait until the day I'm a doctor, helping kids battle their diseases. I believe that challenges aren't meant to break people but rather help them recognize their passions and shape their future. For better or for worse, in sickness and in health, till death do us part, cancer is part of me.

> So bye bye!! Oh, this most likely will be my last CaringBridge update. If it is, I hope that you have enjoyed it as much as I have. Thank you and I love you all.

One more thing, I will attach new pictures later tonight so you can see some of the fun I had this summer and my new hair-do. I LOVE the way my hair grew back. It is soft and curly and really blonde.

- Bridgette :)[2]

––

Bridgette Merriman is a second-year medical student at Boston University School of Medicine, pursuing her dream career of becoming a pediatric oncologist. At medical school, she leads several student organizations, including the Student Oncology Society; conducts research on the impact of COVID-19 on pregnant and parenting adolescents; and assists providers in the Teen and Tot clinic, caring for adolescent parents and their children.

––––––––––––––

[2] Merriman, "Journal," September 26, 2009, www.caringbridge.org/visit/bridgettemerriman/journal.

Chapter 14: Climbing Together

Woody Hubbell

Woody Hubbell suffered from cancer during his college studies. He stresses the outstanding care he received and the remarkable support and accompaniment that he enjoyed from healthcare professionals, friends, and family members. Care is more that a diagnostic prowess, a high-tech diagnosis, an up-to-date pharmacological arsenal, and a targeted therapy. Care is also shaped by competent and dedicated caregivers, loving family members, and supportive friends.

December 14, 2017. I remember it like it was yesterday. It is very cliche to say this, but it really does not feel that long ago. I was studying for my accounting final in Walsh Hall at Boston College when one of my roommates walked in. "Hey Woody, the RD [Resident Director] wants you to report to health services as soon as possible." "Weird," I thought, "I wonder what this could be." I had gone into health services two weeks earlier and had been diagnosed with strep throat. I was taking antibiotics for it, but when those ran out, I immediately felt sick again. Once again, I visited health services, and the doctor did not know what was going on, so he conducted a blood test and told me he would get back to me in two-three days. Well, now it was two days later, and I was getting my results.

As I walked to health services, I thought to myself "I have no idea what this could be, but whatever it is, maybe it could get me out of finals." I walked in the building and was immediately placed in a room. Shortly after the doctor came in to speak with me. I will never forget what he said, "The white blood cell count of a normal person is about 10,000, your white cell count is 300,000. Looking at your platelets, the number for a normal person is 150,000 to 450,000. Yours is 9,000, low enough to the point where if you got a bloody nose right now, I do not know if I would be able to stop it."

Wow. I began feeling pretty uncomfortable as you could imagine (especially since earlier that week I had a bloody nose that lasted about three hours). He told me these numbers were similar to that of a leukemia patient. I felt like I had been hit by a truck for about four seconds. After that, I decided I was going to beat this thing. The doctor asked me if I had any friends who would be willing to go to Brigham and Women's Hospital (BWH) with me to get further testing done. "Great, this guy thinks I have cancer and no friends who want to go to the hospital with me either," I thought. Luckily, my roommate Peter was available and made the trip with me.

The next few days consisted of a lot of medical tests, tons of phone calls, and one final diagnosis, Acute Lymphoblastic Leukemia. At this point, I had accepted that I had blood cancer, but I had hoped it was Hodgkin's lymphoma because that is the type of cancer Eric Berry of the Kansas City Chiefs had. Since we are both superior athletes, I figured it would be cool to have the same kind of cancer.

When I was first diagnosed, I was abruptly removed from my life as a college student and placed into cancer patient world. It was also ten days before Christmas. I was scared but thankfully not lonely. I was allowed as many visitors as could fit in the room. The sounds of my friend's voices watching football calmed me and lulled me to sleep. My family came to Boston and spent the entire week celebrating Christmas in my hospital room. We all consider it our favorite Christmas because everyone was together, just living in the moment and appreciating all that life had given us. I spent the next month in the hospital. My friends and mom were by my side the entire time. Being able to have the physical presence and connection with my family and friends aided me in my emotional journey with cancer treatment and possibly in turn with my physical recovery. I feel for the new patients diagnosed during the COVID global pandemic. I understand the unique problems COVID-19 poses. Hopefully conversations started regarding future health risks and how to keep the patients' emotional health foremost in their treatment plans.

I began a month of inpatient treatment with my doctor, Marlise R. Luskin, at BWH followed by a three-month clinical trial of inotuzumab. I had many visits from friends and family, as well as professors and a man who would become a great friend, Fr. Tony Penna. Tony works as the BC Men's Hockey chaplain and also teaches a theology class at BC, which I took last year (no Father Tony, I do not hold a grudge against you for only giving me an A-).

I took a medical leave of absence from BC and went back home to Minnesota for the following few months. Living at home was tough during this time because there was so much going on at BC that I missed. I missed my friends going on spring break, missed Marathon Monday, and missed ESPN's College Gameday at BC against Clemson. That left me with a bittersweet feeling since I had followed the team incredibly closely, had multiple friends on the team, and my one college football dream was to go to Gameday at BC (other than when the BC football coach Jeff Hafley takes us to the Playoff). I had also missed my girlfriend, Carlisle, run the New York City marathon in my honor, as she had raised over $9,000 for the American Cancer Society. Watching so much life happen while I was at home was exciting and a bit saddening. I could not help but feel a little left behind. My friends lifted my spirits by passing a #WoodyStrong banner around to different college campuses, letting me know that they stood with me. All in all, it was tough being away, but my friends, family, and the BC community made me feel that I was loved.

It was not all bad. I got to watch my brother's senior high school football season as they made it to the state championship. I would talk in the stands with my uncles, dad, and brothers about how the players on the field should be acting more like Tim Riggins and then come home for a great meal prepared by my mom. I worked with a great team at the University of Minnesota as well. I am grateful that Boston and Minnesota are the two places I received care since there are not many spots in the world to find better healthcare.

I came back to BC a year later, finishing up my sophomore year having missed just two semesters. I was incredibly nervous, but the semester began feeling somewhat regular. Early on in my first semester back, I went to mass on upper campus with my girlfriend. It was being presided by Fr. Tony, and I was excited to say hello. He gave me a wave at the beginning and looked incredibly happy to see me there. He celebrated a great mass, and at the end, he gave me a quick shoutout, saying I had been through a lot, and asked everyone to give me a warm welcome back. People started clapping as I gave a little wave and felt very much back into the swing of things at BC. Carlisle and I walked back to my room after mass, and I really did not say much. Once we got to my room she asked if I was feeling ok since I was acting quiet and had an odd look on my face. I immediately burst into tears. How on Earth did I get so lucky to be surrounded by so many great people? What did I do to deserve this? That simple gesture was all I needed to realize that the people in my life are special, and I was absolutely not in this alone. God is great, God is effing great.

During that semester, another time I felt lucky to be back was when I was hanging out at 282 Foster Street, where some buddies of mine lived. I was nervous to be living alone and wondered if I could handle the transition back into school after a year off. People were just moving back for the semester, and my friend Hugh had just arrived. I had gotten to know him a good bit early during our sophomore year, but I did not know him incredibly well. When he walked in, he was surprised to see me. He said, "Woody it is great to have you back man, just know you are always welcome here." Since then, I have become much closer with Hugh, but at the time, I thought how genuine that was. It really hit me how much people care. I have never told him how much that simple "you are always welcome here" meant to me in my transition back. It was that much more comforting since about half of my friends had gone abroad in my first semester back. Thinking back on it, it is wild how much of a difference those five words made and helped put my mind at ease.

After that, I had convinced myself "I can do this, no problem." I mainly hung out at the BC Rose Garden and at Foster Street and had an awesome time that semester. I got to visit friends in Madrid, I got back into club baseball, helping the team to its first ever world series bid, and I made a bunch of new friends in Chestnut Hill. The next year was just as fun, if not more. All my friends abroad came back acting like they were changed people, and it was their senior year so that was exciting as well.

My treatment at Dana Farber and the University of Minnesota continued, but all went well. I lived as a faux senior for that year, as all my friends were set to graduate, but I had another year. I was unsure what this year would look like, but I was also excited. I was able to meet an idol of mine, Mark Herzlich, who is a former BC football great linebacker who was diagnosed with cancer while in school like me. I briefly told him my story and how he was an inspiration to me and got a photo with him. Overall, the year was awesome even with it being cut short due to COVID. At the end of the year, Billy, a buddy of mine through baseball, asked me to live with him and his friends for my real senior year. I had never met any of them, but once again, I was luckier than ever because they have become great friends of mine as well.

It is hard to discuss going to the hospital on a frequent basis and leave out the outbreak of COVID-19. The pandemic threw a wrench into the system of providing care around the world and hit patients especially hard. With so many new precautions taken and strict new protocols, most hospitals would only allow the patient to come in for treatment. Before the pandemic, I would typically go to the hospital with my girlfriend or my mom. It was nice having company in the hospital because they were great at making me comfortable. As one could guess, going to chemotherapy appointments with loved ones makes it almost feel easy. However, with the new protocols due to COVID-19, I was making trips to the hospital alone. Even with this change, I consider myself lucky for a few reasons. I was able to build up a familiar relationship with my nurses and doctor by this point. Since I had already been receiving treatment for two and a half years, I had a great relationship with my medical team and was able to catch up with them when I would make solo trips to the hospital. I am lucky to have a team I was able to be comfortable around because this made my appointments during COVID-19 much easier to get through. I know that not everyone else can say that.

Balancing treatment, school, and social life is definitely weird, but I made it work. I would go to appointments on a monthly basis with my girlfriend, on some occasions getting sick and making her act as my nurse (my mom had this duty when I lived at home). I was able to go to football tailgates and keep up with schoolwork. I have become the go-to to talk about spinal taps and bone marrow biopsies with my grandma, Punkin, who has also begun receiving them. I have three brothers and two sisters, and there is a good bit of friendly sarcasm in my family, so talking about my cancer has not been a problem there.

Some people would ask me more timidly regarding my health. Since I was diagnosed at 19 while in college, my friends were along for the journey. There were some moments of loneliness, mostly because I was removed from normal life. My friends did not make cancer a lonely process for me. I am now 23 and working. A friend of mine who is my age was recently diagnosed with lymphoma. I went to lunch with him, and we talked about what cancer and treatment is like. I am happy he was comfortable talking to me and thankful I could offer him support. A cancer diagnosis is scary, but you do not need to be lonely. Sharing on my cancer is a great opportunity to open up conversation, and I am honored to being a part of it.

Woody Hubbell graduated from Boston College in 2021, majoring in finance and entrepreneurship with a minor in history. In 2017, he was diagnosed with acute lymphoblastic leukemia and began a three-year treatment process at Boston's Dana Farber Cancer Institute. Today, he lives in Minneapolis and works at the investment bank and financial services company Piper Sandler, within their healthcare group.

Chapter 15: A Cancer Diagnosis: Raw Emotion, Front and Center—How Your Life Changes in a Second

Laura Campbell

A Boston College staff member, Laura Campbell, vividly describes how cancer disrupted her life and, in very similar ways, affects the lives of any worker. It makes a great difference if the employer's healthcare plan and the working environment support patients in their ordeals and in the process of recovery. Hence, while her personal narrative teaches us about her individual experience, at the same time her story further highlights the ethical urgency of critically examining workplaces and healthcare systems, with the services that they provide, by paying attention to those who are left out from what could benefit their personal health and the health of the whole society.

My name is Laura Campbell, and I work in Catering at Boston College. I was diagnosed with breast cancer in November 2017. A cancer diagnosis is paralyzing. The words are suspended in air. When the doctor confirms, "Yes, it is breast cancer," you are stunned, and when the mental processing begins, you start to panic. Am I going to die? Will I need chemotherapy? Will I lose my hair? What about my family, my husband, and daughter? Why me? All these private thoughts take seconds until you gather yourself, take a deep breath, pull up your bootstraps, and ask your doctor what's next. For my breast cancer, Ductal Carcinoma in Situ, or DCIS—a contained cancer in the breast ducts—my cancer cells started to break free from the "in situ" part, thus requiring lymph node removal during my lumpectomy surgery to see if any of the escaped cells made their trek elsewhere in my body. Thankfully, they did not. The cancer was contained. It was removed with clean margins and only required twenty-one radiation treatments commencing one month after surgery. I am also taking the drug Anastrozole for five years as my cancer was estrogen positive.

I am blessed to be here to tell my story. Early detection is paramount. It saved my life. I am grateful for the excellent care of my medical team at the Beth Israel Hospital in Boston and Needham. They provided me with medical expertise, compassion, and encouragement when I needed it most, and still do to this day. I am also extremely grateful to have the health insurance that Boston College offers its employees. My financial worries were nonexistent as cancer is very, very expensive.

I am a three-year Breast Cancer Survivor. I still have my fears and anxieties as my yearly mammogram approaches. The weeks leading up to that day are challenging. Some days I am inconsolable, I go to ground, I cry, I scream, and I can get nasty to those closest to me. I wish I did not behave this way, but I do.

However, without the love and support of those closest to me—my husband Rick in particular—I do not think my outcome would have been as positive. He was and continues to be my rock.

Even before you hear these fateful words, "Yes, it is cancer," you endure the words "maybe it is cancer." It is like a journey that starts with the dreaded call from the hospital telling you, "We need you to come back for more imaging, we need to do an ultrasound, we need to do a needle biopsy, we need to do a breast MRI, now we need to do a guided MRI biopsy...." Well, you know the rest. It is a mentally challenging and paralyzing waiting game. If only there was a way to move this process along more smoothly and humanely. You constantly hold your breath and wait. As the singer Tom Petty (1950–2017) sang, "The waiting is the hardest part."[1]

Lastly, what I learned from this experience is that life is fleeting. We must live in this moment, for this moment is all we have. So, to all of you who are reading these words: take that trip, use the fine china, go for that walk, do not hold a grudge, call that friend, always be kind, make plans, do not wait until you retire, do it now. A close friend of mine, also a breast cancer survivor, once said to me, "Laura, we are all five minutes away."

---

[1] Tom Petty and the Heartbreakers, "The Waiting," 1981, https://www.youtube.com/watch?v=uMyCa35_mOg.

How true a statement for us all. I wish you all good health. Thank you for this opportunity to speak and allowing me to share my story.

⁂

Since 2008, **Laura Campbell** is lead waitstaff at Boston College Heights Catering. She has been married to Rick for 33 years, and her daughter Emma graduated from Boston College in 2020. She lives in Salem, NH, and is a breast cancer survivor.

Chapter 16: Another Reason to Bring Cancer into the Realm of Global Public Health: The Insularity of Cancer Patients and How Global Public Health Might Get Them Better Connected

James F. Keenan, SJ

As a cancer survivor and a Boston College faculty member, James Keenan, SJ, stresses how urgent it is to consider cancer a global health emergency and how this approach implies a necessary and beneficial change of perspective. In fact, cancer is usually experienced as a personal ordeal, centered on who is affected. As he indicates, shared accompaniment and advocacy—as in the case of women's grassroots organizations of breast cancer survivors—further exemplify how new forms of collective support, social action, and lived solidarity contribute to change the patterns of cancers' stories by giving voice and agency to the patients and survivors who are voiceless and disempowered.

In October 2006, my dermatologist discovered an anomaly on my lower back that turned out to be a thin melanoma. It was subsequently removed, and the border were checked. I was told that my borders were clear, that my stage 1 melanoma was caught early, and that I was very fortunate. I was assured that survival rates were very high and that only 3 percent ever advanced to higher stages.

On August 4, 2008, I discovered in my groin a swollen lymph node. On August 26th a three-inch tumor was removed and biopsied. On August 28th, I was informed that I was at a stage III, possible Stage IV melanoma.

In a lay person's terms, I had not had a recurrence. Rather my original melanoma had migrated before it was removed. Though the borders were clear, I was not, in fact, melanoma free. Instead, the sentinel node had functioned well and collected these cells over the nearly two years since it was discovered. But now I had to find out through a lymph node dissection that was scheduled for September 26 whether the cells were solely contained in the sentinel node or whether other nodes or other organs had become infected.

During the month of waiting, because of a variety of reported aches and pains, I had two scans for brain tumors, one for a pulmonary embolism, and another for a deep vein thrombosis. All were negative.

I was a white male, professional, living in Boston, being treated at Mass General Hospital (MGH). My oncologist was chair of melanoma at MGH, and my surgeon was incredibly regarded and informative. I could not have had better physicians. Still, even in this very privileged situation, I had a fifty percent chance of survival over the next five years, *if* the sentinel node had done its work and the cancer had not spread. My odds were much worse if the cancer had migrated elsewhere.

After my surgery when my lymph nodes in my left leg were removed and biopsied, I learned that no other cancer cells were discovered elsewhere, including my hip and pelvis. I would now begin a twelve-month treatment at MGH of interferon. For the first month, I would have daily infusions, and after that, I would inject myself three times a week with the drug that caused, as physicians told me, "flu-like symptoms."

I have to say that every time I had an infusion or later every time that I injected myself, those three words seemed to minimize or even ridicule the actual impact of each injection. During the year, I had two extended hospitalizations occasioned by significant life-threatening bouts of cellulitis. In December 2009, I concluded my interferon treatment, and ten years later my oncologist informed me that we no longer needed to meet. Though a few weeks later, another stage one melanoma appeared on my arm and was removed, it seems that I have now "beaten" my original cancer.

Cancer as a Global Public Health Issue

When I learned that this conference was treating cancer as a global public health issue, I was surprised. I say this not only as a cancer survivor but also as one who accompanied my niece who fought three years against a leukemia, to which she succumbed in 1999 at the age of 19. I did not see the connection between cancer and global public health. Moreover, as an ethicist, I have taught a fairly popular course, "HIV/AIDS and Ethics," here at Boston College since I arrived twenty years ago. The course is fundamentally an introduction to Global Public Health through the lens of HIV.

I had thought that the overriding concern of Global Public Health was the risk of communicable infection. The rise of global public health awareness universally paralleled the emergence and on-going threat of HIV/AIDS.1 In fact, in 2014, the Journal *Global Public Health* focused on the synergy between HIV/AIDS and Global Public Health.[1] In 2015, The World Health Organization narrated from 2000 to 2015 how the organization only began to implement a global public health strategy in response to HIV/AIDS in Africa in 2000 and then outlined all the different ways that such a strategy reframed the international response to local outbreaks of the virus.[2] HIV/AIDS taught the human community that we needed Global Public Health to get out the same message about matters of prevention. We could only subdue the virus if we cooperated globally. Indeed, prevention strategies for HIV/AIDS are critical. Thus, as a Catholic ethicist, I worked for some time arguing for a rationale that Catholics and their health care and educational institutions could support both condom use and needle exchange programs precisely as prophylactic strategies against the spread of HIV/AIDS.[3]

---

[1] Nora J. Kenworthy and Richard Parker, "HIV Scale-up and the Politics of Global Health. Introduction," *Global Public Health* 9, nos. 1-2 (2014): 1–6, doi.org/10.1080/17441692. 2014.880727; Christopher J. Colvin, "Evidence and AIDS Activism: HIV Scale-up and the Contemporary Politics of Knowledge in Global Public Health," *Global Public Health* 9, nos. 1–2 (2014): 57–72.

[2] World Health Organization, "Global Health Sector Response to HIV, 2000–2015: Focus on Innovations in Africa," 2015, apps.who.int/iris/bitstream/handle/10665/198065/9789241 509824_eng.pdf?sequence=1&isAllowed=y.

[3] James F. Keenan, ed., assisted by Jon D. Fuller, Lisa Sowle Cahill, and Kevin T. Kelly, *Catholic Ethicists on HIV/AIDS Prevention* (New York: Continuum, 2000); James F. Keenan, ed., assisted by Jon D. Fuller, Lisa Sowle Cahill, and Kevin T. Kelly, *Eticistas Católicos e Prevenção da AIDS* (Sao Paulo: Edicoes Loyola, 2006). See also James F. Keenan, "Prophylactics,

Furthermore, early on, in 2007, the connection between tuberculosis (TB) and HIV generated the need for a combined global public health policy in light of the emergent one on HIV. The *New England Journal of Medicine* specifically addressed the issue of tuberculosis as a global public health concern, seeing the issue of contagion and morbidity as mutually relevant.[4]

Toleration, and Cooperation: Contemporary Problems and Traditional Principles," *International Philosophical Quarterly* 29, no. 2 (1989): 205–220; James F. Keenan, "Applying the Seventeenth-Century Casuistry of Accommodation to HIV Prevention," *Theological Studies* 60, no. 3 (1999): 492–512; James F. Keenan, "Catholics Fighting the Spread of HIV: Exposing and Encountering the Same Problems in the Virgin Islands as around the World," *Catholic Islander* 14 (1999): 13; James F. Keenan and Jon D. Fuller, "Condoms, Catholics and HIV/AIDS Prevention," *The Furrow* 52 (2001): 459–467; James F. Keenan and Jon D. Fuller, "Tolerant Signals: The Vatican's New Insights on Condoms for H.I.V. Prevention," *America* 183 (2000): 6–7; James F. Keenan and Jon D. Fuller, "Church Politics and HIV Prevention: Why Is the Condom Question So Significant and So Neuralgic?," in *Between Poetry and Politics: Essays in Honour of Enda McDonagh*, ed. Linda Hogan and Barbara FitzGerald (Dublin: Columba Press, 2003), 158–181, reprinted in James F. Keenan and Jon D. Fuller, "Church Politics and HIV Prevention: Why Is the Condom Question So Significant and So Neuralgic?," in *30 Años de VIH-SIDA: Balance y Nuevas Perspectivas de Prevención*, ed. F. J. de la Torre Diaz, *Cátedra de Bioética* (Madrid: Universidad Pontificia Comillas, 2013), 207–228; James F. Keenan and Jon D. Fuller, "The Language of Human Rights and Social Justice in the Face of HIV/AIDS," *Budhi: A Journal of Ideas and Culture* 8, nos. 1–2 (2004): 211–233; James F. Keenan and Jon D. Fuller, "Educating in a Time of HIV/AIDS: Learning from the Legacies of Human Rights, the Common Good, and the Works of Mercy," in *Opening Up: Speaking out in the Church*, ed. J. Filochowski and P. Stanford (London: Darton, Longman and Todd, 2005), 95–113; James F. Keenan, "Four of the Tasks for Theological Ethics in a Time of HIV/AIDS," in *Concilium: AIDS*, ed. R. Ammicht-Quinn and H. Haker (London: SCM Press, 2007), 64–74; James F. Keenan and Enda McDonagh, "Instability, Structural Violence and Vulnerability: A Christian Response to the HIV Pandemic," in *Progressio* (London: Progressio, 2009): 1–10; James F. Keenan, "HIV/AIDS: The Expanding Ethical Challenge," in *Beauty, Truth and Love: Essays in Honour of Enda McDonagh*, ed. Eugene Duffy and Patrick Hannon (Dublin: Columba Press, 2009), 126–148, reprinted in James F. Keenan, "HIV/AIDS: The Expanding Ethical Challenge," in *30 Años de VIH-SIDA: Balance y Nuevas Perspectivas de Prevención*, ed. F. J. de la Torre Diaz, *Cátedra de Bioética* (Madrid: Universidad Pontificia Comillas, 2013), 51–70.

[4] Mario C. Raviglione and Ian M. Smith, "XDR Tuberculosis—Implications for Global Public Health," *New England Journal of Medicine* 356, no. 7 (2007): 656–659.

In both these instances the status of those infected or at risk to infection became a significant issue for HIV/AIDS and tuberculosis, not least because there was not a cure for either. While one is a virus and the other an illness communicated by droplets of bacteria, the two came together precisely by the risk of communication among vulnerable populations. As if to mark the expanding interests of global public health, *The Lancet* in a 2008 essay entitled, "Global Public Health: A Scorecard," opened with these words: "Global health is attracting an unprecedented level of interest."[5]

Of course, the more recent outbreak of Ebola in 2014 again brought together through global public health the issues of risk, communicability, and social vulnerability of that highly infectious virus.[6] And after that, the value and relevance of global public health increased again as Ebola entered into the narratives.[7]

Then came COVID-19.

I was in fact teaching my course on HIV/AIDS when COVID broke out. Students studying one pandemic were encountering first-hand a new one. The global public health issues came to the fore; the students quickly sought out the emerging congruencies between the two pandemics, including their modes of transmission, incubation, vulnerability, and those most at risk.

Not surprisingly the precarity that COVID prompts in the world dovetails the lessons learned from HIV. Global Public Health has evidently emerged today as having greater contemporary social relevance with

---

[5] Robert Beaglehole and Ruth Bonita, "Global Public Health: A Scorecard," *Lancet* 372, no. 9654 (2008): 1988–1996, at 1988.

[6] Paul Farmer, *Fevers, Feuds, and Diamonds: Ebola and the Ravages of History* (New York: Farrar, Straus and Giroux, 2021); James F. Keenan, "Paul Farmer Went to Africa to Fight Ebola. He Found a People Devastated by War and Racism," *America*, March 12, 2021, www.americamagazine.org/arts-culture/2021/03/12/paul-farmer-book-review-ebola-africa-health-240206.

[7] Shamimul Hasan, Syed Ansar Ahmad, Rahnuma Masood, and Shazina Saeed, "Ebola Virus: A Global Public Health Menace: A Narrative Review," *Journal of Family Medicine and Primary Care* 8, no. 7 (2019): 2189–2201.

COVID-19, but again it emerges significantly because of its impact as a highly communicable illness.

It was in 2009 that the medical community with public health officials began recognizing the relevant interdependency between two communicable illnesses with a third non-communicable, but infectious one. The linking of HIV/AIDS and tuberculosis with malaria helped us to see how the social, economic, and political context of human vulnerability needed to be coordinated. Bringing malaria more clearly under the tent of global public health helped us to see that we should think beyond the risk of infection from one human being to another as the gateway to public health.[8]

Still, malaria's infectiousness is what brought it into the purview of global public health. From the 1950s, the social sources that bred the risk of malaria came to the attention of early global health workers.[9] Similarly, infectiousness becomes the group heading for other global health concerns like dengue fever that are in the air in these years.

In 2020, global health concerns focus on the infectiousness of different epidemics, as was noted in a recent article in the *AMA Journal of Ethics* where Abraar Karan, in "Responding to Global Public Health Crises," implicitly presumes that global public health epidemics are rooted in infectiousness as he notes: "Epidemic outbreaks such as Ebola, dengue, Zika, measles, and influenza have all made international headlines within the last few years."[10]

Bringing Cancer into Global Public Health

[8] Marco Vitoria, Reuben Granich, Charles F. Gilks, Christian Gunneberg, Mehran Hosseini, Wilson Were, Mario Raviglione, and Kevin M. De Cock, "The Global Fight against HIV/AIDS, Tuberculosis, and Malaria: Current Status and Future Perspectives," *American Journal of Clinical Pathology* 131, no. 6 (2009): 844–848.

[9] Ambrose O. Talisuna, Peter Bloland, and Umberto D'Alessandro, "History, Dynamics, and Public Health Importance of Malaria Parasite Resistance," *Clinical Microbiol Review* 17, no. 1 (2004): 235–254.

[10] Abraar Karan, "Responding to Global Public Health Crises," *AMA Journal of Ethics* 22, no. 1 (2020): E3–4, at E3, doi.org/10.1001/amajethics.2020.3.

Bringing cancer into the Global Public Heath tent is a significant act. As a matter of fact, in 2011 cancer came into sight with global public health officials when, after recognizing AIDS defining cancers like Kaposi sarcoma (KS) and aggressive non-Hodgkin lymphoma (NHL) as well as cervical cancer (CC), they made connections between HIV/AIDS and cancer in Africa.[11]

Since then, cancer has been emerging as a global public health concern. Still, when one Googles "When did Cancer become a Global Public Health pandemic," the first item proffered is the Global Cancer Center of the American Cancer Society,[12] and the second item is the announcement of the Boston College conference that generated these papers.[13]

There are many reasons to bring cancer under the tent of Global Public Health. Above all the global numbers are daunting. As one of the world's leading killers, there were in 2018 more than 18 million new cases and 9.5 million deaths. In 2040, there are predictions of 29.5 million new cases and 16.4 million deaths.[14] Second, global public health would heighten attention to the enormous disparity regarding treatment resources available around the world. Third, universal preventative educational strategies could bring behavioral changes, from routine and periodic check-ups to greater awareness of environmental impact on cancer rates.

Inasmuch as I was invited to contribute to this conference and collection precisely because of my own personal history of cancer, I would like to add a fourth reason by arguing how much the life of the cancer patient could improve if cancer care and treatment learned lessons from

[11] Sam M. Mbulaiteye, Kishor Bhatia, Clement Adebamowo, and Annie J. Sasco, "HIV and Cancer in Africa: Mutual Collaboration between HIV and Cancer Programs May Provide Timely Research and Public Health Data," *Infectious Agents and Cancer* 6, no. 1 (2011), 10.1186/1750-9378-6-16.

[12] American Cancer Society, "Our Global Cancer Control Work," 2021, www.cancer.org/health-care-professionals/our-global-health-work.html.

[13] Ed Hayward, "Conference to Address Rise in Global Cancer," *BC News,* September 2021, www.bc.edu/bc-web/bcnews/science-tech-andhealth/biology-and-genetics/global-cancer-pandemic-conference.html.

[14] National Cancer Institute, "Cancer Statistics," September 25, 2020, www.cancer.gov/about-cancer/understanding/statistics#.

global public health. Under the umbrella of public health, regardless of the illness, the patient is pre-eminently considered under a social context. The strategies for a person at risk to COVID, HIV, Ebola, TB, or malaria are well rehearsed. If those at risk of infection become infected, automatically others in their circle are affected. There is a constitutive social impact to whatever developments happen in the course of a patient's diagnosis, quarantine, care, or treatment. At every phase of their being under the umbra of whatever social health threat there is they are socially considered, understood, or treated.

Significantly, the social contextualization of the patient does not mean that issues of the patient's own personal autonomy are overlooked. Though the patient is seen in a social context, the decision-making capabilities of the patient are not necessarily compromised. Without a doubt, the gay community kept the at-risk or HIV-infected person as autonomously in charge of decision-making as one could be, but they were also part of a community of people. As Anthony Pinching and Kenneth Boyd noted twenty years ago, "This infection is so intensely private in its transmission, the disease so isolating and so personally devastating in its impact, it readily distinguishes the reality of what people are and do, from the rhetoric of what others may feel they should be and do. AIDS has forced us to recognize that respecting individual rights is a critical safeguard for the health of the community, as well as for the person."[15]

Moreover, their own personal decisions in a social context eventually became matters of the public agenda through advocacy. Reflecting on the first 20 years of AIDS in the *New England Journal of Medicine*, New York's Kent A. Sepkowitz commented,

> In the 1970s, Washington-based, organized advocacy groups that focused on particular diseases were few; now at least 150 organizations exist.... Activism by patients with AIDS has

---

[15] Anthony J. Pinching, Roger Higgs, and Kenneth M. Boyd, "The Impact of AIDS on Medical Ethics," *Journal of Medical Ethics* 26, no. 1 (2000): 3–8, at 3. See also Keenan, "Developments in Bioethics from the Perspective of HIV/AIDS."

influenced advocates for patients with other diseases, including breast cancer, Parkinson's disease, Alzheimer's disease, and juvenile diabetes. Using creative approaches rather than following the established rules of lobbying, AIDS activists created a new model. ... Today, patients are routinely consulted regarding the design of studies, and community-based research is conducted across the country.[16]

With the notable exception of breast cancer, however, other cancer patients are still very much operating in a private, personal, fairly insular context. Admittedly, I did think of the social significance, not of my cancer, but of my treatment in one way. I knew how privileged I was with my insurance and access to Boston-area facilities. I often thought that others should have access to the treatment that I had. When someone "catches" any of the more socially connected illnesses, we think, yes, it could happen to anyone. Not so with cancer. Perhaps because it is not infectious, there is a certain distancing with cancer. Ask almost any cancer victim or survivor (other than breast cancer), they will acknowledge an awkward silence or an experiential distance between others and the cancer carrier. Unlike other illnesses, cancer is not something you catch, it is not something that merits the estimation, anyone could get it. Rather, if you get cancer, you are the unlucky one. The cancer survivor is a particular individual; not a class. And your passage to treatment is much more personal, tailor-made (and private) than those with the illnesses mentioned above. Google cancer treatment and immediately you find the options or individualized treatment plans that you can make. It is remarkable the marketing of cancer as an autonomous, take-charge affair.

Indeed, one of the ways that I survived was becoming familiar with my cancer. I do not mean melanoma; I mean, my melanoma. It was mine, and I was personally going to subdue it. Many people accompanied me in my

---

[16] Kent A. Sepkowitz, "AIDS—the First 20 Years," *New England Journal of Medicine* 344, no. 23 (2001): 1764–1772, at 1770. On breast cancer, see Elizabeth Williams's chapter in this volume.

fight, but not fellow cancer patients. I was a lone patient. I never met others with melanoma except during my first month of treatment when I received daily infusions in a common space. But, after that first month, I never spoke again with another person who had melanoma. Nor did I meet one. At no time did any caregiver, professional or otherwise, refer to the experience of another cancer patient. I was in a category of one.

I did not hide my cancer, but no one really engaged it either, not at least the way I have encountered the phenomenon that other patients do who have HIV, COVID, TB, or malaria. In my fourteen months of treatment and in my subsequent nine years of treatment, I never met or was introduced to another cancer patient, nor was I offered anything to read that reflected at all the experiences of another cancer patient.

My relations were always singularly with my caregivers. Though I injected myself with interferon for eleven months three times a week knowing each time that I was inducing "flu-like symptoms," I never met another person who had to manage their health in a similar way, who could share what they may have learned to make the affair more doable. In fact, I never met another person who took interferon, even though I am sure my doctors read plenty of accounts of their patients who discussed at length the experience of taking interferon. It was helpful for my doctors, but not for me?

I have no idea of what other cancer survivors did when they got cellulitis.

I learned that I had to protect myself from sun, but I never met others who developed their own strategies for sun protection.

Like other cancer victims and survivors, I could underline the singularity of my experience by highlighting how insular my own cancer-care was. I am not complaining about the care I received from MGH. How could I? My team of caregivers was remarkable. But my treatment was never socialized as other patients of other illnesses were. The only people I shared my experiences with were those who did not have similar experiences. And, therein, even the act of sharing became even more an insular occasion.

Placing cancer under global health makes the phenomenon of fighting cancer much less a personal struggle and much more a social one. Not only does it bring the caregivers and research under the tent of global public health, but it brings the more isolated patient there too, a place where the patient could learn from others about strategies of understanding, accepting, and surviving. In this way, other cancer patients could have the experience that women with breast cancer have of meeting, learning from, and standing with others in similar situations, grappling with life and death matters. Now, more than fifteen years after I was first diagnosed with cancer, I realize that socializing cancer and providing social encounters to cancer victims could provide a support as well as other benefits that I never had. Again, the lessons from HIV and breast cancer are notable.

Five years ago, I was diagnosed with prostate cancer, and though I am in only a regular, but vigilant, monitoring stage, having undergone three biopsies and three scans, I have never met another such cancer patient as part of my treatment. Informally, I now have learned to ask men my age, do they have it and how do they manage it, but my caregivers have never suggested that my treatment should be other than my singular engagement with them, the caregivers. Bringing cancer under the tent of global public health will offer the cancer caregiver and researcher the benefit of shared, collective, and reported experiences. Hopefully, the same opportunities will be shared with their patients. [17]

At Boston College, **James F. Keenan**, SJ, is Vice Provost for Global Engagement, Canisius Professor in the Theology Department, and Director of Jesuit Institute, and held the Gasson Chair and then the Founders Professorship in Theology. He authored and edited over a dozen books and hundreds of articles and book chapters, and founded and directed the Moral Traditions Series of volumes in theological ethics

----

[17] want to thank my research assistant Aidan O'Neill for his very helpful work in preparing and editing this essay.

published by Georgetown University Press. Globally, he was the founder and co-chair of the network Catholic Theological Ethics in the World Church.

Conclusions:
Looking
at the
Future

Chapter 17: A Global Strategy for Eliminating Cervical Cancer: Challenges and Opportunities

Silvia de Sanjosé

Striving to be focused and concrete, Silvia de Sanjosé offers a specific example to inform present and future commitments in the ongoing cancer pandemic by articulating a global strategy for eliminating cervical cancer. Cervical cancer, which is preventable, is a global public health problem. It is the fourth most common cancer, with over 600,000 new cases diagnosed every year and it is the fourth leading cause of cancer death in women worldwide. Most of these cancer cases occur in low-resource settings where women are not screened regularly. While highlighting these ongoing challenges, the author stresses the existing opportunities for prevention, screening, and vaccination.

Cervical caner is a largely preventable disease but remains the fourth most common cancer, with over 600,000 new cases diagnosed every year.[1] Further, it is the fourth leading cause of cancer death in women worldwide.[2] Most of these cases occur in low-resource settings where women are not screened with practical approaches regularly. In recognition of cervical cancer as a public health problem, the World Health Organization (WHO) has set ambitious targets to scale-up effective prevention strategies as part of the Global Strategy, including 90 percent coverage of human papillomavirus (HPV) vaccination for adolescent girls,

---

[1] International Agency for Research on Cancer, "GLOBOCAN 2020: New Global Cancer Data," *Union for International Cancer Control*, December 17, 2020, www.uic.org/news/globocan-2020-new-global-cancer-data.

[2] Jacques Ferlay, Morten Ervik, Frédérick Lam, Murielle Colombet, Les Mery, Marion Piñeros, Ariana Znaor, Isabelle Soerjomataram, and Freddie Bray, "Global Cancer Observatory: Cancer Today," *International Agency for Research on Cancer*, 2020, goi.iarc.fr/today.

70 percent of women screened twice in their lifetime with high-performance tests by ages 35 and 45, and treatment for 90 percent of precancerous lesions.[3] The strategy is based on the current knowledge of the natural history of cervical cancer and the existing prevention tools.

After years of studying the link between cervical cancer and a sexually transmitted infection, some viral types of the HPV family were recognized to play a vital role in the carcinogenic process. HPV is unequivocally linked to almost all cervical cancer cases (95 percent of cases) and a large proportion of anal cancer cases (88 percent of cases attributable to HPV).[4] HPV is also causally associated with a varying percentage of cancers of the vulva, vagina, penis, and a subset of head and neck cancers (HNCs), particularly tonsillar cancer.[5] Within the spectrum of HPV oncogenic types, HPV 16 is the most prevalent in all HPV-related cancer sites. HPV 16 is the most frequently detected at the population level, and it is by far the predominant type causing invasive cervical cancer worldwide (~60 percent), followed by HPV 18 (~15 percent). Moreover, HPV 16 is also involved in a more significant proportion in other body sites like anal mucosa or head and neck tumors, particularly the oropharynx.[6] HPV 16 is considered one of the essential human carcinogens.

---

[3] See World Health Organization, *Global Strategy to Accelerate the Elimination of Cervical Cancer as a Public Health Problem* (Geneva: World Health Organization, 2020).

[4] Mark Schiffman, John Doorbar, Nicolas Wentzensen, Silvia de Sanjosé, Carole Fakhry, Bradley J. Monk, Margaret A. Stanley, and Silvia Franceschi, "Carcinogenic Human Papillomavirus Infection," *Nature Reviews Disease Primers* 2 (2016): 16086, doi.org/10.1038/nrdp.2016.86.

[5] Catherine de Martel, Damien Georges, Freddie Bray, Jacques Ferlay, and Gary M. Clifford, "Global Burden of Cancer Attributable to Infections in 2018: A Worldwide Incidence Analysis," *Lancet Global Health* 8, no. 2 (2020): e180–e190.

[6] Silvia de Sanjose, Beatriz Serrano, Sara Tous, Maria Alejo, Belen Lloveras, Beatriz Quiros, Omar Clavero, August Vidal, Carla Ferrandiz-Pulido, Miquel Angel Pavon, Dana Holzinger, Gordana Halec, Massimo Tommasino, Wim Quint, Michael Pawlita, Nubia Munoz, Francesc Xavier Bosch, Laia Alemany, and RIS HPV TT VVAP Head Neck study groups, "Burden of Human Papillomavirus (HPV)-Related Cancers Attributable to HPVs 6/11/16/18/31/33/45/52 and 58," *JNCI Cancer Spectrum* 2, no. 4 (2018): doi.org/10.1093/jncics/pky045.

HPV infection is generally acquired through sexual contact, and the majority of the infections will resolve spontaneously with an adequate immune response. However, when the infection remains for an extended period, which can mean years in immunocompetent subjects, there is a disruption of the normal cell cycle inducing an abortive infection. It is this situation that increases the woman's probability of developing a pre-neoplastic lesions or invasive cancer.

Screening

The long latency between disease and cancer has made effective cervical cancer screening possible. In high resource settings, cervical cytological— i.e., Papanicolaou ('Pap') test—screening programs have substantially reduced mortality and incidence where it has been possible to organize and maintain them. The cytological exam of cervical cells through the microscope allows identifying the virus's harm to the human cells. The identification of these anomalies has been the subject of multiple classifications. The most recent one is the Bethesda system, where anomalies are classified as cervical intraepithelial neoplasia (CIN) grades I, II, and III. Precancer is now considered CIN2, CIN3, or CIN3. Morphological change identification suffers from observation error, particularly the lower grade lesions <CIN3. To run a high-profile screening using cytology assessment, very high levels of quality control are needed to reduce diagnosis inaccuracies. Furthermore, cervical cytology has proven challenging to expand in lower resource settings making secondary prevention a hard-to-reach outcome.[7]

Vaccination

---

[7] Schiffman, Doorbar, Wentzensen, de Sanjose, Fakhry, Monk, Stanley, and Franceschi, "Carcinogenic Human Papillomavirus Infection"; Guglielmo Ronco, Joakim Dillner, K. Miriam Elfstrom, Sara Tunesi, Peter J. F. Snijders, Marc Arbyn, Henry Kitchener, Nereo Segnan, Clare Gilham, Paolo Giorgi-Rossi, Johannes Berkhof, Julian Peto, Chris J. L. M. Meijer, and International HPV screening working group, "Efficacy of HPV-Based Screening for Prevention of Invasive Cervical Cancer: Follow-up of Four European Randomised Controlled Trials," *Lancet* 383, no. 9916 (2014): 524–532.

In 2006, after years of intense research, two prophylactic vaccines became available. A bivalent vaccine (BV), covering HPV 16 and HPV 18, and the quadrivalent vaccine (QV), covering two low-risk types, HPV 6 and HPV 11, associated with benign HPV genital warts and the two most oncogenic types, HPV 16 and HPV 18. Later, the QV was expanded to add five more types (NV) that included, in addition, the HPV 31, 33, 45, 52, and 56.[8] Recently, a new BV has also been commercialized, and a couple more are in the pipeline.

The high efficacy of these vaccines against infections, pre-neoplastic lesions, and cancer has been paramount. In girls around ages 9 to 15, using these vaccines before sexual exposure is probably the most cost-effective measure to reduce the incidence and mortality of HPV-related cancers. Vaccination of boys is also recommended, although the impact at the population levels is half of that expected when vaccinating girls.

As of December 2019, although 122 countries have implemented HPV vaccination programs in their national programs, supply, funding, and policy constrain the introduction in vaccination programs of the HPV vaccine in low and middle-income countries (LMIC). To date, only 6 percent of adolescent girls worldwide have received HPV vaccination, most of whom reside in high-income countries, and still 245 million girls were not yet eligible for vaccination in 2021. While seventy out of eighty-six high-income countries had introduced the HPV vaccines in 2019, only twenty out of eighty-one of the low, and lower-income countries had done so.[9]

---

[8] Mario Poljak, "Prophylactic Human Papillomavirus Vaccination and Primary Prevention of Cervical Cancer: Issues and Challenges," *Clinical Microbiology and Infection* 18, Suppl. 5 (2012): 64–69; Vivien D. Tsu, D. Scott LaMontagne, Phionah Atuhebwe, Paul N. Bloem, and Cathy Ndiaye, "National Implementation of HPV Vaccination Programs in Low-Resource Countries: Lessons, Challenges, and Future Prospects," *Preventive Medicine* 144 (2021): doi.org/10.1016/j.ypmed.2020.106335; Silvia de Sanjose, Maria Brotons, D. Scott LaMontagne, and Laia Bruni, "Human Papillomavirus Vaccine Disease Impact Beyond Expectations," *Current Opinion in Virology* 39 (2019): 16–22.

[9] Laia Bruni, Anna Saura-Lazaro, Alexandra Montoliu, Maria Brotons, Laia Alemany, Mamadou Saliou Diallo, Oya Zeren Afsar, D. Scott LaMontagne, Liudmila Mosina, Marcela Contreras, Martha Velandia-Gonzalez, Roberta Pastore, Marta Gacic-Dobo, and Paul Bloem,

Global Challenges

Screening and treatment programs remain essential for secondary prevention of cervical cancer for the millions of adult women who are not eligible for orwill not be reached by HPV vaccination in the coming decades.[10] If worldwide we manage to vaccinate 90 percent of the target girls, the addition of twice-lifetime HPV testing could considerably accelerate cervical cancer reduction and move faster towards the elimination goal.[11] However, implementing adequate screening strategies for the existing resources to adopting high coverage of a robust screening approach, like a molecular test to detect HPV, involves many challenges, particularly in resource-limited settings. Ideally, countries with unsuccessful screening approaches should move from cytology or visual inspection with acetic acid (VIA) to objective and reliable tests like HPV testing with validated assays. Testing for HPV by measuring the viral DNA or RNA has been expanded in many countries, particularly in high-resource settings.[12] The possibility of having low-cost HPV tests that involve minimal laboratory needs is becoming a reality. However, an

---

"HPV Vaccination Introduction Worldwide and WHO and UNICEF Estimates of National HPV Immunization Coverage 2010–2019," *Preventive Medicine* 144 (2021): doi.org/10.1016/j.ypmed.2020.106399. See also personal communication from Scott LaMontagne (PATH, Center for Vaccine Innovation and Access: Policy, Access and Introduction functional area, University of Washington, Seattle, WA) and Laia Bruni at the Institut Catala d'Oncologia (ICO).

[10] Silvia de Sanjosé and Francesca Holme, "What Is Needed Now for Successful Scale-up of Screening?," *Papillomavirus Research* 7 (2019): 173–175.

[11] Karen Canfell, Jane J. Kim, Marc Brisson, Adam Keane, Kate T. Simms, Michael Caruana, Emily A. Burger, Dave Martin, Diep T. N. Nguyen, Elodie Benard, Stephen Sy, Catherine Regan, Melanie Drolet, Guillaume Gingras, Jean-Francois Laprise, Julie Torode, Megan A. Smith, Elena Fidarova, Dario Trapani, Freddie Bray, Andre Ilbawi, Nathalie Broutet, and Raymond Hutubessy, "Mortality Impact of Achieving WHO Cervical Cancer Elimination Targets: A Comparative Modelling Analysis in 78 Low-Income and Lower-Middle-Income Countries," *Lancet* 395, no. 10224 (2020): 591–603.

[12] World Health Organization, *WHO Guideline for Screening and Treatment of Cervical Pre-Cancer Lesions for Cervical Cancer Prevention*, 2nd ed. (Geneva: World Health Organization, 2021).

urgent need to generate the capacity of producing the required volume of tests remains a challenge.

Prevention

Three essential elements are critical for secondary prevention of cervical cancer: self-sampling, HPV testing, and rapid treatment for those eligible. Self-sampling is key to increasing screening coverage by avoiding a gynecological exam through speculum examination. The sampling of women's vaginal cells, combined with molecular testing of oncogenic HPV types, results in a high accuracy approach to detect precancerous lesions.[13] The inclusion of a second sequential screening test, commonly referred to as a "triage test," is an additional option to increase the specificity of a screening approach and identify women at the highest risk of developing cervical cancer who require follow-up.

WHO guidelines for screening and treating cervical precancerous lesions were updated in 2021.[14] The recommendation for women in the general population is HPV testing between ages 30 and 49, with repeat screening every 5–10 years (for a minimum of twice-per lifetime screening), implemented with either an HPV test-and-treat approach or an HPV test-triage-treat approach.

In case of women living with HIV (WLHIV), the WHO recommendation is an HPV test-triage-treat approach starting at age 25 and with repeat screening every 3–5 years. Unfortunately, we still need to improve screening management among WLHIV. WLHIV have a high

---

[13] Marc Arbyn, Sara B. Smith, Sarah Temin, Farhana Sultana, Philip Castle, and Collaboration on Self-Sampling and HPV Testing, "Detecting Cervical Precancer and Reaching Underscreened Women by Using HPV Testing on Self Samples: Updated Meta-Analyses," *BMJ* 363 (2018): doi.org/10.1136/bmj.k4823; David Hawkes, Marco H. T. Keung, Yanping Huang, Tracey L. McDermott, Joanne Romano, Marion Saville, and Julia M. L. Brotherton, "Self-Collection for Cervical Screening Programs: From Research to Reality," *Cancers (Basel)* 12, no. 4 (2020): doi.org/10.3390/cancers12041053; Ashwini Kamath Mulki and Mellissa Withers, "Human Papilloma Virus Self-Sampling Performance in Low-and Middle-Income Countries," *BMC Women's Health* 21, no. 1 (2021): doi.org/10.1186/s12905-020-01158-4.
[14] World Health Organization, *WHO Guideline for Screening and Treatment of Cervical Pre-Cancer Lesions for Cervical Cancer Prevention.*

prevalence of HPV and are more likely to experience a persistent infection that progresses to cervical precancer. Due to the low specificity of HPV tests to rule out precancer, a second test among high-risk human papillomavirus-positive women (HR-HPV) is, therefore, necessary to determine who needs to be treated. However, an optimal strategy remains to be identified. Settings using HPV as primary screening use cervical cytology as a second test, or in LMIC, the commonest triage is VIA. VIA is a largely provider-dependent test with highly variable accuracy.

Furthermore, WLHIV have a high level of recurrences, as high as 30 percent.[15] Although managing HIV infection with antiretrovirals is essential for a good immune response, the fact that WLHIV that are regular users of antiretroviral therapy (ARV) maintain high levels of detectable HPV infections suggests an immune impairment not fully restored amid viral treatment. Most guidelines recommend initiating ARV as soon as HIV is diagnosed to sustain, as much as possible, a sound immune system.

Our team is working on a combined screening strategy for LMIC among women aged 30–49 years old. The age restriction targets precancerous lesions that will be easily managed with no surgery-based treatments. The proposed primary screening test is a self-sampling approach for oncogenic HPV DNA testing with genotype identification. HPV-negative women have a low-level risk of having a precancer or cancer and therefore can go back to screening in five or ten years.

For those women with a positive test, the risk of precancer is classified by the oncogenicity of the HPV type detected. HPV-positive women undergo a gynecological visit. An image is taken and ranked through a well-

---

[15] Michael H. Chung, Hugo De Vuyst, Sharon A. Greene, Nelly R. Mugo, Troy D. Querec, Evans Nyongesa-Malava, Anthony Cagle, Samah R. Sakr, Stanley Luchters, Marleen Temmerman, Elizabeth R. Unger, and Christine J. McGrath, "Human Papillomavirus Persistence and Association with Recurrent Cervical Intraepithelial Neoplasia after Cryotherapy vs Loop Electrosurgical Excision Procedure among HIVPositive Women: A Secondary Analysis of a Randomized Clinical Trial," *JAMA Oncology* 7, no. 10 (2021): 1514–1520.

validated artificial intelligence (AI) algorithm.[16] Combining the HPV genotype and the image evaluation provides an excellent stratification of the women's risk. This stratification will direct the management of the patient. Either treat her, follow up with her, or send her home. There are indications that this strategy can be helpful irrespective of HIV status, can be low cost, and can be performed by trained health workers. Combined with ablative approaches, managing can be completed in one single visit for most patients when lesions are visible and not too large. Referral for surgical methods would then be restricted to fewer women.

Conclusion

We need to increase vaccination coverage among girls, hoping that a one-dose vaccine will provide good enough efficacy against cervical cancer. Self-sampling using an HPV test may be the only path to reach every woman at least twice in their lifetime. However, it remains necessary to have availability of HPV tests at an affordable cost. Visual inspection of the cervix with acetic acid is being downgraded as a correct approach to screening. However, the complement with automated technology using AI approaches may increase the performance considerably, although we are still under a period of active research.

Furthermore, all the presented strategies consider minimizing crowded spaces and unnecessary physical exams when the world is being impacted by the COVID pandemic.[17] Managing precancerous lesions with thermal ablation has improved the accomplishment of treatment compared to the

---

[16] Kanan T. Desai, Brian Befano, Zhiyun Xue, Helen Kelly, Nicole G. Campos, Didem Egemen, Julia C. Gage, Ana-Cecilia Rodriguez, Vikrant Sahasrabuddhe, David Levitz, Paul Pearlman, Jose Jeronimo, Sameer Antani, Mark Schiffman, and Silvia de Sanjose, "The Development of 'Automated Visual Evaluation' for Cervical Cancer Screening: The Promise and Challenges in Adapting Deep-Learning for Clinical Testing," *International Journal of Cancer* (2021): doi.org/10.1002/ijc.33879.

[17] Nicolas Wentzensen, Megan A. Clarke, and Rebecca B. Perkins, "Impact of COVID-19 on Cervical Cancer Screening: Challenges and Opportunities to Improving Resilience and Reduce Disparities," *Preventive Medicine* 151 (2021): doi.org/10.1016/j.ypmed.2021.106 596.

use of cryotherapy at an equal efficacy. Finally, we need to explore more accurate approaches to screen and manage WLHIV, considering this population's high rates of treatment failures.

Silvia de Sanjosé, M.D., Ph.D., works with the Division of Cancer Epidemiology and Genetics of the National Cancer Institute, National Institutes of Health, in Rockville, MD, and ISGlobal (Institute of Global Health) in Barcelona, Spain. She has over thirty years of expertise in epidemiology of human papilloma virus (HPV) and related cancers. She served as the President of the International Papilloma Virus Society (2015–2018) and has been Co-Chair of the Cape Town, Sydney, and Barcelona (virtual) conferences of the inactivated poliovirus vaccines (IPVs). She is an affiliated professor at the Department of Epidemiology of the University of Washington in Seattle.

Chapter 18: Cancer in the Context of Global Inequities and Disparities in COVID Times: An Ethical Reflection

Andrea Vicini, SJ

The ethical reflection on cancer stresses that addressing the global cancer pandemic is hampered by the existing inequities and disparities in providing healthcare, to citizens across the planet, which are further exacerbated by the global pandemic caused by COVID-19. Thinking about the future requires us to consider the social, cultural, and religious contexts where inequities limit efforts aimed at preventing, diagnosing, and providing care. Ethically, a multilayered approach that strives to promote research, prevention, and therapies, and that engages individuals, institutions, and populations in collaborative efforts is promising and generates realistic hopes.

Cancer is ubiquitous. Just as cancer cells keep growing, unbound, the presence of cancer in people's lives and in society keeps spreading. Moreover, context matters. In the peripheries of our world, anything that relates to cancer is colored with the specificity of each context. The presence or absence of healthcare institutions, or the limited healthcare resources available within them, have negative consequences on addressing cancer at any stage, from prevention, to diagnosis, to therapy, and to following up on cancer survivors.

For the bioethical tradition, differences in the healthcare systems, as well as in the services that hospitals, clinics, and healthcare professionals can offer, reveal the injustices that people experience. These injustices demand attentive analysis and bold interventions to address and remove the systemic and structural inequities that limit or inhibit access to healthcare.

A critical assessment of our social inequities is necessary by challenging what the late physician and anthropologist Paul Farmer (1959-2022) has rightly called the "pathologies of power."[1] Whether one considers poor neighborhoods in our cities and the disarray of healthcare in rural contexts in the Global North or whether one focuses on the status of healthcare systems and instructions the Global South, indignation and outrage should inform our ethical response. Justice is urgently needed because the presumption is that health is a human right. Humankind should strive to pursue health for everyone, everywhere.

To focus on inequities in health means to consider how social injustices affect people's health and shape how we provide care or how we avoid caring for the health needs of people and of the whole environment. In the U.S. and elsewhere, racial discrimination is one of these tragic social factors that exclude, marginalize, and worsen the health of people and of the whole society.

Scholars attentive to ethical dynamics in society continue to raise our awareness and provoke our response and action. Prof. Elizabeth Williams has been outspoken in allowing us to hear the pleas of Black women suffering from breast cancer, plagued by the too many social factors that make them struggle in poverty.[2] Aana Vigen too has highlighted how, in the U.S., gender and race inequities burden women.[3]

In the Global South, the control and domination of colonial powers has inhibited human, social, cultural, political, and economic developments and has deprived nations of their rich human and natural resources. The *pushing out* of healthcare professionals trained in the Global South, because of the limited opportunities for their professional flourishing, and the *pull effect* of rich nations attracting trained healthcare

---

[1] Paul Farmer, *Pathologies of Power: Health, Human Rights, and the New War on the Poor*, California Series in the Public Anthropology (Berkley: University of California Press, 2005).

[2] Elizabeth A. Williams, *Black Women and Breast Cancer: A Cultural Theology*, Anthropology of Well-Being Individual, Community, Society (Lanham, MD: Lexington Books, 2019). See also prof. Elizabeth Williams's chapter in this volume.

[3] Aana Marie Vigen, *Women, Ethics, and Inequality in U.S. Healthcare: "To Count among the Living,"* Black Religion, Womanist Thought, Social Justice (New York: Palgrave Macmillan, 2006); Aana Marie Vigen, *Women, Ethics, and Inequality in U.S. Healthcare: "To Count among the Living,"* 2nd ed., Black Religion, Womanist Thought, Social Justice (New York: Palgrave Macmillan, 2011).

workers to hospital wards in the Global North, exemplify how, in our global economy, the colonial histories continue what has been called the "brain drain."[4] Colonization, with its economic exploitation and social dependence, takes new, pervasive forms that keep affecting the quality of care that can be provided in the world's peripheries.

The global COVID pandemic has opened the eyes of the whole humanity to the urgency of promoting health globally. What affects one person has the potential of affecting everyone. As Pope Francis tirelessly reminds us, everyone and everything is interconnected.[5] Moreover, in the Global North, the COVID pandemic highlighted our vulnerabilities. As citizens of developed countries, we thought that our technologically developed healthcare could protect us from incoming pandemics. Instead, we discovered our fragility and lack of preparedness, and the inequities that shape our neighborhoods and working places.[6] Minorities paid the higher price in human suffering with repercussions on the overall quality of prevention, diagnosis, and therapy of other health conditions, including cancer. Among the citizens, particularly those belonging to minorities, one will continue to see the consequences of the changes and restrictions on offering basic health services that were required and implemented during the global pandemic. The COVID global vaccination process continues, but it shows inequities in access to vaccines between rich and poor countries and in setting up the vaccination campaigns.

A strong commitment to promote healing in the global, multiple contexts where people live is urgently needed. We all long for healing. Hopefully, we all aim at promoting healing in inclusive ways, without excluding anyone and with a preferential option for those in greater need, who are more vulnerable, and for the poor in our midst.

---

[4] As an example, see Ruth Groenhout, "The 'Brain Drain' Problem: Migrating Medical Professionals and Global Health Care," *International Journal of Feminist Approaches to Bioethics* 5, no. 1 (2012): 1–24.

[5] See *Laudato Si'*, nos. 117 and 138 and *Fratelli Tutti*, nos. 96, 138, 259.

[6] Cristian Timmermann, "Pandemic Preparedness and Cooperative Justice," *Developing World Bioethics* 21, no. 4 (2021): 201–210.

For over two millennia, the Christian tradition understood healing very broadly. Healing concerns concrete persons, peoples, societies, and cultures. It is holistic. It aims at global flourishing. It reaches out to the depth of our heart, memory, and imagination. It touches our bodies and all our relationships. It includes the social, cultural, religious, and political living environment. Finally, healing concerns the planet too.

Today, we should continue this long healing tradition, maybe in new ways. In the past, historic events and economic challenges transformed healthcare and its presence locally and globally. Contemporary events continue to challenge and change this commitment: from the global pandemic caused by the COVID-19 virus to the global epidemic of AIDS—the acquired immunodeficiency syndrome caused by the human immunodeficiency virus (HIV)—as well as tuberculosis and malaria, to more localized epidemics like those caused by the Ebola virus in some countries within the African continent.[7] These challenging health crises urge us to renew our commitment to the healing of people and societies by promoting justice in practices, institutions, and social dynamics. These crises, however, do not modify the ultimate goal that we pursue, that is, to promote healthy living conditions on our planet for all human beings and to offer up-to-date high-quality care to all citizens, particularly those most in need. We do not have a cure for many cancers, but we can already promote healing in multiple ways. We could call it a more just "relational and social healing."

Concretely, in our global context marked by shocking inequalities and unacceptable inequities, the access to new therapies and techniques should not become a further occasion for discrimination. The Roman Catholic insistence on the preferential option for the poor—whoever they are and wherever they live—is prophetic and longs to be implemented.[8]

---

[7] On AIDS, see Jacquineau Azetsop, ed., *HIV and AIDS in Africa: Christian Reflection, Public Health, Social Transformation* (Maryknoll, NY: Orbis Books, 2016). On Ebola, see Paul Farmer, *Fevers, Feuds, and Diamonds: Ebola and the Ravages of History* (New York: Farrar, Straus and Giroux, 2020).

[8] Alexandre A. Martins, "Ethics and Equity in Global Health: The Preferential Option for the Poor," in *Ethical Challenges in Global Public Health: Climate Change, Pollution, and the*

Moreover, increasingly, in many instances, a diagnosis of cancer is not a death sentence anymore—if diagnosis is prompt and therapies are available. To be affected by cancer is an ordeal, but, with competent and caring help, we can go through it. In many cases, we might heal and survive cancer.

However, other human and ethical challenges surface and burden us. We need to learn how to live with the consequences of successful therapies because sometimes they change our bodies in ways that are quite unpleasant. We need to learn how to deal with the latent anxiety of being a survivor and risking recurrence. In other words, the importance of outstanding cancer research and efficacious therapies should be integrated with a constant attention given to the lived experiences of people, accompanying them in their struggles and ordeals, and joining them in striving for greater social and global justice. Hence, we should consider research, prevention, therapy, and then people's narratives.

Research and Its Applications

Research helps us to understand the complexity of cancers, from their causes to their development. These studies should also contribute to appreciate how people are affected and how we should care for those suffering from cancer. Moreover, civil society should intervene to prevent cancers by addressing the social, cultural, and political factors that influence the occurrence and presence of cancers in today's world and in people's lives. In very specific ways, the chemicals used in homes and

---

Health of the Poor, ed. P. J. Landrigan and A. Vicini, SJ (Eugene, OR: Pickwick Publications, 2021), 96–105; Alexandre A. Martins, "*Laudato Si'*: Integral Ecology and Preferential Option for the Poor," *Journal of Religious Ethics* 46, no. 3 (2018): 410–424; Alexandre A. Martins, *The Cry of the Poor: Liberation Ethics and Justice in Health Care* (Lanham, MD: Lexington Books, 2020), 59–75. See also Stephen J. Pope, "Proper and Improper Partiality and the Preferential Option for the Poor," *Theological Studies* 54, no. 2 (1993): 242–271; Stephen J. Pope, "Christian Love for the Poor: Almsgiving and the 'Preferential Option,'" *Horizons* 21, no. 2 (1994): 288–312; Joseph Curran, "Mercy and Justice in the Face of Suffering: The Preferential Option for the Poor," in *Hope & Solidarity: Jon Sobrino's Challenge to Christian Theology*, ed. S. J. Pope (Maryknoll, NY: Orbis Books, 2008), 201–214.

working places, what people eat, drink, and breathe, where they live and how they work, all these contextual factors intervene in humanity's quality of life and health. While not every environment is potentially cancerogenic, we see what needs to be done to make healthier each social context by limiting and avoiding what affects human health and the health of the whole planet. Scientific research should study everything that can help us to acquire a deeper knowledge of diseases—even geography and history—aiming at helping sick people by offering to them diagnostic tools, accessible effective therapies, and eventually a safe environment. Bioethicists want this to happen and work to make it happen.

Cancer research should also be conducted in ethical ways, avoiding any double standard that differentiates between patients in the Global North and patients in the Global South. Large cohorts of patients might be more easily gathered in the Global South, but the ethical standards required might not be enforced—whether one thinks of accurate and accessible informed consent or studies requiring placebos but with patients unaware they are taking a placebo when comparable efficacious therapies could be given to them.[9] Moreover, the burden of research that weighs heavily on people in the Global South should translate in concrete benefits for their individual health (e.g., in terms of having access to prevention, diagnostic tools, and therapies) and healthy social environments. It is ethically unacceptable that double standards or exploitation in research practices occur by advocating that these populations do not have access to high quality healthcare services and the little that is offered to them matters. These abuses in research, and in cancer research, should not be tolerated.[10]

---

[9] Vijayaprasad Gopichandran and Varalakshmi Elango, "Data Ethics in Epidemiology: Autonomy, Privacy, Confidentiality and Justice," in *Ethics in Public Health Practice in India*, ed. A. Mishra and K. Subbiah (New York: Springer Berlin Heidelberg, 2018), 121–138.

[10] For two classic examples, see Marcia Angell, "Ethical Imperialism? Ethics in International Collaborative Clinical Research," *New England Journal of Medicine* 319, no. 16 (1988): 1081–1083; Marcia Angell, "The Ethics of Clinical Research in the Third World," *New England Journal of Medicine* 337, no. 12 (1997): 847–849.

Prevention

Testing for possible predispositions to develop cancer is available, as in the case of the BRCA 1 and 2 suppressor genes.[11] Knowing that we have a BRCA mutation means that, in the future, we are at much greater risk of developing breast and possibly ovarian cancer. Being tested for BRCA when our family history shows the presence of breast and ovarian cancers could inform us about our personal or familial predisposition to develop these cancers. Hence, we might want to get tested to identify our predisposition to be affected by these cancers. In these situations, the perception of risk dominates our imagination, emotions, and consciousness. We worry.

Moreover, testing might transform us and, in general, change the notion of patient. Even when we are healthy, testing investigates our predisposition to get cancer. In case of positive results, which confirm we carry a genetic mutation that predisposes us to be affected by cancer, we become patients well before any symptom. Hence, as a form of prevention, cancer testing requires careful assessment and competent accompanying in the decision-making process and in dealing with the testing outcomes.

The possibility to be tested allows us to identify our predisposition, and it can tell us something about our parents and siblings. However, we might not have a therapy able to cure us. People can be tested well before the insurgence of any symptoms. Even so, some want to avoid getting tested. Despite being part of a family marked heavily by hereditary breast and ovarian cancer, Amy Boesky decided not to get tested for the BRCA genes.[12] She has taken other measures to address her increased risk of developing breast and ovarian cancer, including the surgical removal of her ovaries and breasts. For her, the test was not the needed answer to her health concerns. Amy Boesky is not alone in turning elsewhere for the answers that she wants. Since the BRCA tests were introduced in 1996,

---

[11] The acronym BRCA means "BReast CAncer gene."
[12] Amy Boesky, *What We Have: A Memoir* (New York: Gotham Books, 2010).

surprisingly we have not seen long waiting lines outside the clinics, with women at risk waiting to be tested.[13]

From the point of view of theological bioethics, testing can be a helpful resource that empowers us by promoting the knowledge of our own selves even when therapies are not possible. In this case, access is needed: testing should be made available to all citizens. At the same time, testing might be perceived as invasive and giving us unwilled information. Hence, the possibility of not knowing should be protected.

Discernment allows us to reflect on, and decide, what is reasonably and realistically the best option. Bioethicists wonder, however, whether, ultimately, we lack in providing moral guidance. Moral critical reasoning should integrate personal stories, experiences, and situations to identify what is right. Competent, discrete, and respectful accompaniment should help us in our discernment and decision making.

Testing might also transform healthcare by emphasizing medicalization. Promoting health could appear to depend heavily on test results instead of being also influenced by how and where we live, by what we breathe, drink, and eat, and by our lifestyle. A more inclusive and holistic approach to personal and social health is appropriate and fruitful.

Therapies

New drugs and therapeutic strategies to treat cancer are needed. This simple and evident statement is quite challenging in healthcare contexts in the Global South, where diagnostic resources might be limited and where it might not be possible to provide the necessary therapies to all patients. In the global context, to think about cancer therapies presents systemic and structural ethical challenges. As Daniel Daly stressed, we should examine whether our structures are vicious or virtuous and, accordingly,

---

[13] As examples, see Victor R. Grann, Priya Patel, Anubha Bharthuar, Judith S. Jacobson, Ellen Warner, Kristin Anderson, Eiran Warner, Wei-Yann Tsai, Kimberly A. Hill, Alfred I. Neugut, and Dawn Hershman, "Breast Cancer-Related Preferences among Women with and without BRCA Mutations," *Breast Cancer Research and Treatment* 119, no. 1 (2010): 177–184; Steven A. Narod, "Should All Women with Breast Cancer Be Tested for BRCA Mutations at the Time of Diagnosis?," *Journal of Clinical Oncology* 30, no. 1 (2012): 2–3.

we should identify transformative strategies that could help in fostering virtuous dynamics, structures, and systems. [14]

Hence, we should avoid any reductive approach that betrays the complexity of providing cancer treatments. When we discover that we are affected by a cancer, we should be able to identify the type of cancer, its source, stage, and aggressivity, and have access to targeted therapeutic approaches. The hardship of demanding therapies should lead us toward an improved quality of life and, if it is possible, a restored health.

Surviving Cancer: Narratives and Support

People affected by cancer ask us to be present, competent, and compassionate. They want us to listen to their stories and struggles. They hope they will be understood, supported, and helped. Bioethicists hear their call and aim at promoting their well-being. In this interaction, which is shaped by personal narratives, three aspects should be stressed: the growth in awareness, the ability to address tensions, and the importance of participation and change.

Awareness

Cancers affect a very large number of persons and families around the world. For many others, testing will uncover their predispositions to get sick. Are we aware of the daily struggles of these people? This awareness is our responsibility, and it should shape our actions in today's society.

As bioethicists, becoming more aware does not depend only on us, on our own abilities, commitments, and strengths. We are not alone in this. First, cancer patients and cancer survivors can become our teachers by making us more aware of what they are enduring. Bioethicists should join them in strengthening our collective awareness of the ethical issues related to cancer.

Second, many people and organizations help us in raising our awareness about what prevention requires and what treatments demand. They are

---

[14] Daniel J. Daly, *The Structures of Virtue and Vice* (Washington, DC: Georgetown University Press, 2021).

breaking the silence and the shame around cancer. They want us to take more control of our health, how we live and work, as well as our living conditions on Earth.

Tensions

Awareness might lead us to change, often with tensions. In interacting with patients, we might deal with contrasting healthcare models: alternative or traditional forms of healthcare vs. today's Western approaches. The Mayan medicine, for example, interprets diseases and their causes by relating everything to the "heart." Moreover, for the Mayan people in Central America, the single, the family, the whole creation, and even the divine are part of a whole. A disease indicates a broken harmony within the self and with the cosmos. The traditional cures aim at recreating harmony. One could also discuss African traditional healing approaches[15] as well as Asian contributions.16 Western medicine, on the contrary, is high tech. It relies on tests, screenings, drugs, and invasive procedures. We are quite far from these more harmonic worldviews. Hence, tensions can occur between diverse worldviews and visions of healthcare.

Globally, in our pluralist, multicultural, and multireligious world, we all struggle with vulnerability, fragility, and sickness. We all long for healing and need efficacious treatments. But we address these needs differently because of our diverse visions of our body, society, and cosmos. Within this diversity, extra efforts are required to achieve a profound and respectful understanding and a constructive dialogue.

The highly specialized medical technology deployed to treat cancer implies extra tensions too. We need to decide about whether or not to test, to know about one's predisposition to get cancer, and to choose to pursue aggressive therapies or set limits to experimental techniques; and to

---

[15] Stan Chu Ilo, ed., *Wealth, Health, and Hope in African Christian Religion: The Search for Abundant Life* (Lanham, MD: Lexington Books, 2018). See also Rose Mary Amenga-Etego, "The Practice of Traditional Medicine and Bioethical Challenges," in *Bioethics in Africa: Theories and Praxis*, ed. Y. A. Frimpong-Mansoh and C. A. Atuire (Wilmington, DE: Vernon Press, 2019), 113–130.

become aware that we might have reached the point where we should let go and stop therapy after therapy.[16]

How do we deal with these tensions? First, we need to clarify our goals and pursue them with concrete choices adapted to our own context and our worldview. Second, we need to define our way of proceeding (e.g., to be informed about testing and therapies to discuss them in helpful ways). Third, after we have decided how to proceed, we should be able to confirm what we plan to choose or revise it by relying on the help of healthcare professionals, friends, family, support groups, and communities.

Finally, to address tensions within society and in our web of relationships, dialogue is a precious virtue that needs to be nurtured and strengthened. It can help us to address disagreements and differences.

Participation and Change

How do we foster awareness and ability to address tensions? In studying bioethical issues, Lisa Sowle Cahill focuses on participation, justice, and change as essentially human and intrinsically Christian and Catholic needed approaches.[17] Associations supporting cancer patients exist in many countries. They exemplify and embody care as well as medical, legal, ethical, and relational accompaniment. They are instances of efficient, efficacious, and caring participation. They should be strengthened and multiply. They highlight the transformative power of human creativity, care, and compassion.

Conclusion

Whether in research or healthcare practice, cancer is challenging and evendaunting. It could become an opportunity to continue changing how we think about health, bioethics, and social and ecclesial life, and how we

---

[16] Atul Gawande, "Letting Go: What Should Medicine Do When It Can't Save You?," *The New Yorker*, July 26, 2010, www.newyorker.com/magazine/2010/08/02/letting-go-2; Atul Gawande, *Being Mortal: Medicine and What Matters in the End* (New York: Metropolitan Books, Henry Holt & Company, 2014), 149–190.

[17] Lisa Sowle Cahill, *Theological Bioethics: Participation, Justice, and Change* (Washington, DC: Georgetown University Press, 2005).

believe and think theologically,[18] and how we live as citizens of the world. Cancer slows down and often halts our lives, and our ingenious, generous, loving, and virtuous commitment to promote health.

A cancer diagnosis tells us that cancer is not outside us but within us, and it becomes part of who we are. As Mayan indigenous people would say, cancer is around us but also in our "hearts." While we strive to improve prevention, diagnoses, and therapies, if we listen to the Mayan people, they invite us to connect also with our "heart," with our deepest self. It is not only outside, in our world and environment, but it is also inside, in our "heart" that we will find what might threaten us and what could contribute to making us sick. At the same time, it is not only with what is outside our bodies but also what is in our "hearts" that we will promote healing. In other words, what threatens us and what heals us are both in our own contexts and within us—in either case, within our reach.

Whatever will help us to be our true self—as individuals and as a society—will also lead us to deal with the challenges of being sick, suffering from cancer, and hopefully recovering from it. Hence, we might want to pay attention to our external context—to healthcare institutions and systems, to social structures and political arrangements—and, at the same time, to our "hearts." Many don't, and many others do not know how to do it. They turn to us for help and guidance. Together, we can help one another to be healed as much as possible, as individuals and as a society, both in the present and in the future.

––

At Boston College, **Andrea Vicini**, SJ, is Chairperson, Michael P. WalshProfessor of Bioethics, and Professor of Theological Ethics in the Theology Department and an affiliate member of the Ecclesiastical Faculty at the School of Theology and Ministry. MD and pediatrician (University

––––––––––––––––––––––––––––––

[18] Jake Bouma and Erik Ullestad, ed., *Cancer & Theology* (Des Moines, IA: Elbow, 2013); Leonard M. Hummel and Gayle E. Woloschak, *Chance, Necessity, Love: An Evolutionary Theology of Cancer* (Eugene, OR: Cascade Books, 2017).

of Bologna), he is an alumnus of Boston College (STL and PhD) and holds an STD from the Pontifical Faculty of Theology of Southern Italy (Naples). He taught in Italy, Albania, Mexico, Chad, and France. He is co-chair of the international network Catholic Theological Ethics in the World Church. His research and publications include theological bioethics, sustainability, global public health, new biotechnologies, and fundamental theological ethics.